THE I CHING ON LOVE

'Affection as the essential principle
of relatedness is of the greatest importance
in all relationships in the world.'

From Hexagram 54: *Quei Mei/The Marrying Maiden*

THE I CHING ON LOVE

A REINTERPRETATION OF THE I CHING
FOR PERSONAL RELATIONSHIPS
IN LOVE AND MARRIAGE

Guy Damian-Knight

BLANDFORD PRESS
POOLE · DORSET

First published in the UK 1984 by Blandford Press,
Link House, West Street, Poole, Dorset, BH15 1LL.

Distributed in the United States by
Sterling Publishing Co., Inc.,
2 Park Avenue, New York, N.Y. 10016.

ISBN 0 7137 1482 4 (cased)
ISBN 0 7137 1516 2 (paper)

British Library Cataloguing in Publication Data

Damian-Knight, Guy
  I Ching on love.
  1. I Ching   2. Astrology
  I. Title
  181'.11   B127.12

Typeset in 10/12 pt Photina by August Filmsetting, Haydock, St Helens

Printed in U.K. by Biddles Ltd, Guildford

CONTENTS

PREFACE

The I Ching On Love offers a new interpretation of the great Chinese book of wisdom, the *I Ching*. It has been my intention, not only to make this important work more accessible to the modern reader but also to keep faith with the spirit of the *I Ching* as I understand it.

While the *I Ching* concerns itself with human life and experience in all its complexity, I have limited myself in *The I Ching On Love* to only one aspect of our lives.

This book will be relevant to all those who are interested in improving their relationships with others in love, marriage and friendship.

Guy Damian-Knight
London

ACKNOWLEDGEMENTS

Grateful acknowledgement is made to the Richard Wilhelm/Cary F Baynes translation of the *I Ching* (Routledge & Kegan Paul) which has been of inestimable value and inspiration in the writing of *The I Ching On Love*. I would also like to make special mention of the various writings of C G Jung on the *I Ching* and also his *Modern Man In Search of a Soul* which helped me focus the present work on love.

In addition I would like to thank Anthony Hudson for his kindly support in so many ways during the writing of this work without whose original conception this interpretation would never have appeared. I have made endless demands upon his time and he gave it willingly, cheerfully and without complaining. This is in the spirit of the work.

Many thanks to David Perkins for his beyond-the-call-of-duty timely help in the final preparations, for typing, telling jokes, for being supportive and keeping the pace of work going. But then what are friends for?

For the loan of his smart electric typewriter, and laughter at the other end of the phone – day and night – Miles Hellon, thank you.

During the summer I took refuge at the home of Bill and Margaret Torrington, whose kindness, hospitality, tolerance, cups of tea, beautiful sea view over the back garden, and odd dram of whiskey did my spirits the world of good and enabled me to go on working.

Clearly it is impossible for me to acknowledge everybody who has helped – even unknowingly – by way of inspiration support and good will not only in the preparation of this work but over the years during which experience has provided many insights.

However, I would like to thank John Fuller for his many suggestions on the textual layout of the work and – in his busy life – taking the time to discuss the design of the cover format of *The I Ching On Love*, and for taking a special interest in the general presentation of the book. It is particularly auspicious that his first consultation of the *I Ching* while working on the design of this book drew up Hexagram 48, *The Well*. This hexagram describes the *I Ching* itself and the part it plays in the world.

Upon the original inception of *The I Ching On Love* it seemed appropriate to consult the *I Ching* for its judgment on the idea. Anthony and I asked whether or not such a book *could* be written; whether *The I Ching On Love* should be written; and whether or not any significant *value* might be attached to such a prospect. We received our answer in the hexagram, *Hexagram 1, The Creative*, without moving lines. This was, together with *The Well*, the most auspicious omen we could possibly receive for such a work.

Most of all I wish to offer my love and thanks to my wife, Debra, for designing the format, for typing the whole manuscript for the publisher, for editing the work, correcting English, spelling, syntax and for a thousand and one suggestions to help make improvements, and for her untiring patience and sheer hard work.

Needless to say, I alone remain responsible for any errors and ambiguities which somehow have managed to persist despite every effort to eradicate them.

Love and thanks

For Grace Callista
with love

INTRODUCTION

What is The I Ching?

The *I Ching* – or The Chinese Book of Changes – is principally a work of guidance. It was specially created by the ancient sages as an Oracle to be personally consulted by anyone seeking help and enlightenment on any conceivable subject. The wisdom of the *I Ching* has come down to us over a period of more than three thousand years (it is older than Christianity) and is the basis of two separate Chinese philosophies known as Confucianism and Taoism. It has been a source of spiritual, political and practical help to millions of people since it was first created.

It is said that no single person has ever been able to understand the *I Ching* completely. The reason for this is simply that the range and scope of its wisdom is so great that it contains the essence of every conceivable situation in the world. The *I Ching* is unique in its wisdom and relevance to all societies throughout all time.

How to Consult this Book

The *I Ching* was originally consulted by means of counting yarrow stalks from one hand to the other. However, for convenience, the modern practice is to use three coins, and this is the method adopted for *The I Ching On Love*.

The *I Ching* contains 64 hexagrams, each consisting of two trigrams. A hexagram is an arrangement of six lines, one placed on top of the other. Lines can be broken or unbroken, moving or unmoving. For example, Hexagram 1, *The Creative*, is represented like this:

(Six *yang* lines)

All the lines in this hexagram are unbroken and unmoving.
In Hexagram 2, *The Receptive*, all six lines are broken:

(Six *yin* lines)

Each of the four possible lines – *Yang, moving yang, yin, moving yin –*
used to make up any hexagram is given a number value. In order to
make up your hexagram, you will need to throw three coins at a time,
once for each line. Using the table below, you will be able to draw the
correct line for each throw of the coins. Each coin landing heads up is
a *yang*, and is given the value of 3. Each coin landing tails up is a *yin*,
and is given the value of 2. When you throw your three coins at the
same time to make one line, you will always, when adding the values
together, obtain a total of either 6, 7, 8 or 9. To make things simple,
the table below gives the values of all the possible lines.

Values of the lines

———O———	9	(3 Heads or 3 *yang*)
——— ———	8	(2 Heads and 1 Tail or 2 *yang* and 1 *yin*)
—————————	7	(2 Tails and 1 Head or 2 *yin* and 1 *yang*)
———X———	6	(3 Tails or 3 *yin*)

Values of 6 and 9 always indicate *moving lines* which change to their
opposites (see below).

11

Obtaining Your Hexagram

First take three coins in your cupped hands and shake them. Then throw them down in front of you on to a table or on to the floor. Repeat this process six times, writing down the lines as you go. The first throw always makes the bottom line. Draw the lines in two sets of three (*trigrams*).

Examples

Figure 1

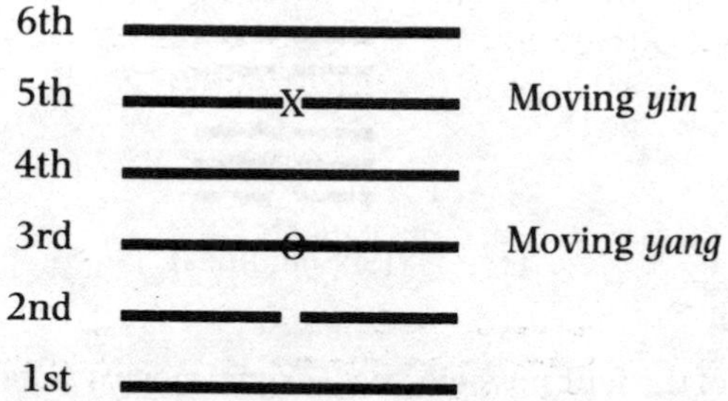

6th   ———————————

5th   ————X————   Moving *yin*

4th   ———————————

3rd   ————O————   Moving *yang*

2nd   ———— ————

1st   ———————————

Hexagram 30: Fires of the Heart

Figure 2

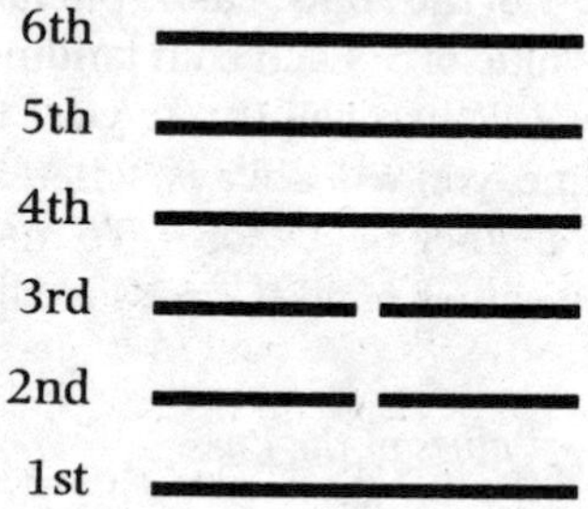

6th   ———————————

5th   ———————————

4th   ———————————

3rd   ———— ————

2nd   ———— ————

1st   ———————————

Hexagram 25: Innocence

In *Figure 1* above, the first line (*yang*) is unmoving, as are the second, fourth and sixth lines. Lines three and five, however, are moving. Line three was arrived at by throwing three heads (three *yang*), which give a total value of nine. The circle in the line indicates that the line moves or changes into its opposite, ———— ————, (see *Figure 2*). Line five was arrived at by throwing three tails (three *yin*), which give a total of six. The cross in the line indicates that it is moving or

12

changing into its opposite, ▬▬▬▬▬, (see *Figure 2*). All the other lines are unmoving. In *Figure 2*, you will see that lines one, two, four and six have been transferred over unchanged. *Figure 2*, Hexagram 25, is the new hexagram derived from *Figure 1*, Hexagram 30.

Having drawn your hexagram (and the second hexagram, if there are any moving lines), turn to the *hexagram chart* at the back of this book. You will see the *lower trigrams* (eight in all) running down the left-hand side of the page, and the *upper trigrams* running horizontally across the top of the chart. Find the two trigrams which together form your hexagram (see *Figure 3*). From the chart you will see that the hexagrams are numbered from 1 to 64; look up the number of your hexagram and find it in the text, or in the index of hexagrams.

Example

Figure 3

Hexagram 1 *The Creative* is made up of the following trigrams

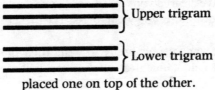

} Upper trigram

} Lower trigram

placed one on top of the other.

You will see that each hexagram answers eight questions. Each question concerns a different aspect of human relationships. They have been specially chosen for this book to cover the most important questions people ask about love and marriage. One of the questions may be precisely the one you want to ask, in which case, you should read the advice given in answer to that question.

However, as so often happens in love and marriage the situation may be more complex, when it would be more appropriate to read most or all of the advice given, if it is relevant to your situation. In this way, you will be able to build up a more complete picture.

The Lines

Each hexagram provides answers to the eight questions. Below these answers there is a section with the heading *The Lines*. The lines are numbered from one to six. Each line and the passage beneath relates to the lines of the hexagram you have drawn. If you look at the example given in *Figure 1*, you will see that this hexagram has two moving lines in the third and fifth places. If you drew this hexagram, you would read only the interpretations for the third and fifth lines. Lines which are not moving in your hexagram are not relevant to your case. Read only the moving lines.

Do not forget, however, that where there are moving lines in the hexagram you have drawn, a new hexagram is derived. Look up the new hexagram and read the passages under your questions, but ignore the lines completely.

Preparations

Before consulting the Oracle, you should assume the correct attitude. Sit in a comfortable chair or on the floor and remain quiet for a few moments, even closing your eyes and taking a few deep breaths in order to relax.

When you have cleared your mind and you feel relaxed, focus upon the question or questions you wish to ask. Try to picture the situation to yourself.

At this point, some people prefer to write their question down on paper in order to aid concentration, but you will soon find the way that suits you best.

It is not important for you to keep your question in mind while you are actually throwing the coins. In fact, you will find it more helpful if you try to think about nothing at all, by making an effort not even to talk to yourself.

Throw the three coins, first cupping them in both hands and write down each line as you go along until you have thrown all six lines.

Now read the hexagram to yourself without breaking your concentration. You will discover that you will automatically associate your thoughts and feelings with the guidance offered.

It is the great art of the *I Ching* to speak to your inmost heart and you will find that – gradually – your self-awareness will grow in a way impossible to describe.

The Questions

There are countless problems arising between people in love and marriage and no foolproof way of covering every area of interest. The method adopted in *The I Ching On Love* is to ask certain questions in a way which embraces many possible situations. It will be possible for the modern reader to relate his or her situation to one or more of the questions, each one of which has been specially chosen to touch upon the most crucial issues of the heart.

For example, behind all the machinations and self-justifications, illusions and fabrications we devise for ourselves when thinking about our feelings for others, may be questions as simple as 'Does this person love me?' or 'What is my heart's desire?.' For this reason the eight questions on love and marriage in this book are posed in the simplest and most basic way, while the varied 'answers' of the Oracle deal with the details.

It is always valuable when experiencing problems to ask questions. While the asking of questions does not presume the existence of answers, the value of asking lies in the fact that the mind is more able to focus on the problem. Herein lies the *possibility* of an answer.

If you isolate a question in your mind, you will find the effect will be to dispel confusion. If your mind is clear, you will be more receptive to the guidance offered by *The I Ching On Love*.

HEXAGRAM 1

The Creative (Talent)

This is the hexagram of strength, light, clarity, force, feeling, love, purpose and supreme creative energy. If you have drawn this oracle, you are in tune with the will of the universe. The driving force which impels you to carry off your deeds in love and action comes from the source itself. You have special gifts of insight and spiritual enlightenment and feel empowered to give to others your wisdom, perception and clarity of understanding in matters relating to the human condition. You have the force and the power to reach people, to touch them in their inmost hearts. Your natural condition is to be inspired, and you have the power to inspire others, to move them along spiritual paths, to open their eyes, to gently wake them from sleep and confusion.

You are a leader who recognises the potential for growth not only in terms of individual awareness, but also in terms of cultural and social awareness.

You have a natural facility for understanding the very nature of the way things work, and because the force described by this hexagram derives its power from the forces of love in the universe, you also have the power to sustain your effort in the work of enlightening and helping others. Within the scope of the oracle, there is the possibility for supreme achievement, but only in this kind of work. There is no room for the superficial, the superfluous, the unnecessary, the mediocre.

This is the oracle of the wise person who knows that his or her life must

17

give expression to the laws of the universe. In The Book of Changes, *there is no hexagram which represents more strongly the supreme power for constant and persevering self-renewal, leadership, and the creative expression of love in action. These are not passing qualities in your nature, they are fundamental to it. You intuitively apprehend the forces of good and evil operating in the world, and the necessary interplay between the negative and positive forces which create the tensions of dynamic activity.*

You display an untiring energy and devotion which springs from the heart, and you have the all-important ability to devote yourself to specific creative actions. The effect you have on others is sublimely positive. You are able to make your presence and influence known in the world in a most beneficial and inspiring way. You are relentless in your naturally-born desire to rise to the heights of awareness and love. You sense the power of the universe moving through you, and this lends a nobility of heart to your every endeavour.

1 Is This Person a Compatible Partner?

The short, but certain answer to this question is yes. There are no specific comments which one can make on the subject of compatibility, as in this case the hexagram should be taken as a whole. Therefore you are advised to consider the above and extract from it those elements which you feel particularly apply to your situation. It can be said, however, that the answer to the question on compatibility is in general terms highly favourable.

Within the relationship you are the person who assumes the responsibility for guiding and shaping. The initiative for creative action tends to come from you, and your partner is highly receptive to you. Without a receptive partner such as yours, your creative impetus would lose some of its power. You should be aware that your partner's role is essential to the full flowering of the relationship, and that he or she stands in relationship to you as *yin* does to *yang*. Your partner has the qualities which you lack and *vice versa*.

2 Does My Partner Love Me?

Because of your nature, you attract a special kind of love and a special kind of admiration from those who feel the benefit of your influence. It is your talent to reflect and guide by way of that love to still higher realms of enlightenment.

18

3 Do We Have a Future Together?

It is highly likely that you intuit the nature of time itself in an unusually evolved way. If you are not already conscious of some of its secrets, then you sublimely act upon a knowledge of them without full consciousness of doing so. End and beginning, birth and life and death, past, present and future, space and thought, etch out a pattern and define in their own way a cosmology, providing you with undreamt-of insights into the meaning of freedom. Herein lie the seeds of your creativity. Deep within the lattice-work of life itself, burns the flame of illumination. In whatever language you choose to express it, the force that lies at the source of that flame impels you forward through your work to bring unlimited light to the world.

4 What is the Most Important Attitude to Adopt at this Time?

You must always be ready to give of your time and your energy and your inspiration. Your talents can have no better use than to be put to the service of others through creative work and direct contacts with people who seek enlightenment.

You must not be impatient. You must remain in tune with the deeper harmony you feel underlies everyday existence. You must always be ready to make the best use of your clarity of understanding, and you must never allow yourself to forget that it is only the expression of love which will give force and importance to your work. You must constantly be a source of positive energy for others who are less aware than yourself.

5 Why Has Our Relationship Broken Down?

This is not an oracle of failure. The six unbroken lines indicating creative power imply no weakness. There is only one aspect of your nature which could have caused you to alienate yourself from your partner, and that is a tendency to live in an ivory tower of seclusion, losing contact with those elements in your nature which justify your life and your work.

You are a person of great will and great strength, and if these are not matched in your partner, then the responsibility for any division between you is entirely yours.

6 Will We Get Back Together?

Yours is the power of influence, of inspiration, of energy and of untiring devotion to love and creativity. You therefore have the moral and spiritual advantage in making the first moves towards a reconciliation. You should avail yourself of this. Failure to do so can only be seen as an ingrowing conceit which will threaten to consume your creative power. You must therefore reach out for those from whom you have become estranged. You must take the initiative, you must direct your gentle wisdom and understanding, and you must take the responsibility for reforging the links which have been broken. By tuning your mind to such a purpose, you will certainly succeed, even in unwholesome circumstances where others might fail.

7 What Can I Do to Put Things Right?

The principal and overriding activity in life should be to use one's energies to create order out of chaos. This requires creative insights, the wisdom to see the potential for good in people, the intuition to focus energies in the right place through the adherence to guiding principles in life, and the ability to respond with energy and vigour, with exact and appropriate effectiveness.

You seek throughout your life to cultivate and apply your inner perceptions and to express them in the higher art forms. Through what you have learned in your life, you are sometimes able to transcend existing orders and structures and to create new orders and structures of greater intricacy and greater complexity, which still have the power to illuminate an even greater simplicity. You have the remarkable facility to see simple answers to elaborate problems, answers which, seen in retrospect, seem to have been glaringly obvious for a very long time. You have the power and the ability to see, translate and communicate these answers. These are the ways in which you transform chaos into order, and these are the talents by which you would resolve any problems, should they occur.

8 What Do I Most Want from Life?

To enlighten others through the creative enlightenment of yourself. This hexagram's number is one. The act of creating the resolution of duality through a third, higher self, brings about unity.

THE LINES

One

You are a patient person of great inner worth. Your time is not yet come, but you are undeterred by superficial thoughts and are tranquil, honest and expectant. You need have no fear: for your time will come. Do not waste your energy worrying or fretting. Rely upon your spiritual strength to give you the wisdom to know when your energy is sufficient for you to move forward.

Two

Your qualities are positive, your energy is sufficient, you are talented, and you have a natural, beneficial influence over others which is untainted by any thoughts of personal recognition, gain or approval. You are already recognised by those who share your sense of destiny. You have yet to take your place, but it is inevitable that you will do so.

Three

The world is taking on a definitive shape and order. The work is successful and is received widely and favourably. Transition to the heights is taking place at this very moment and your mind is troubled, you cannot find rest easily. Do not allow yourself in such a vulnerable position to be toppled by the magnificence of such a transition. Do not let the power and the influence which has come to you distract your creative energy and power. Do not be lured into the obvious snares and traps which arise from thoughts of past mistakes and illusions, frustrations and resentments. Do not allow your creative energy to be sapped by entertaining unseemly thoughts. Instead, remain tuned to a clear destiny enfolded within your work.

Four

You have reached the fork in the road. You may express your creative power in an explicitly public fashion, or you may express your power in an explicitly private fashion. The oracle gives no preference to either path, and no indication as to which you should choose. It merely states that whichever path you choose will be the right one for you. Both paths reach the heights and both paths plumb the depths. Whichever path you choose, you must remain true to yourself in every undertaking.

Five

Here the line is superfluous to such a one as you. It merely acknowledges your position in relation to mankind as being one of the greatest and most important and vital influences in the world. All who follow your counsel will receive great benefit in their lives.

Six

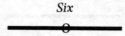

This line offers you a stringent warning. You must curb your unruly and unattainable ambitions and you must reflect seriously on the value of your life in relation to the world, to mankind in general and to the people who look to you for assistance and advice.

Everything is going wrong because of your misplaced sense of self-importance, and you have allowed your ego to run away with you. Such circumstances precede a sharp decline followed by a fall. In such a position you can expect no help. What is required is a fundamental change of heart.

If you have received six moving lines in Hexagram 1, *The Creative*, your situation is changing into that of Hexagram 2, *The Receptive*.

The power of the two hexagrams together is greater than that of either of the two hexagrams alone. Here are combined the strength arising from clarity of mind with the strength arising from purity of heart. Where decision is combined with action, your powers of achievement are heightened. This is the moment when the forces of *yin* and *yang* are in perfect harmony and in motion.

HEXAGRAM 2

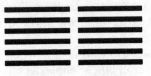

The Receptive

The person signified in the last hexagram, The Creative, finds a perfect complement in the person signified in this hexagram, The Receptive. The quality of leadership depicted in the first hexagram transforms into a fertile, receptive dimension in action. Compliant conformity takes the place of inspired initiative, which has the effect of giving meaning to a living force. As a complement to the creative power, a receptive person gives lustre and warmth, adding a dimension of reality to life. This is the hexagram of the earth as mother and of the mother as earth.

1 Is This Person a Compatible Partner?

You are not of an independent disposition, but shine best in the role of helping and completing the inspired initiatives of your partner. The type of person signified in the hexagram may not necessarily be female, although the qualities implied are those of tenderness, gentleness, compliance, but is a person rich in the ability to adapt existing resources of energy to workable wholes and forms.

You have the power to give beauty to an idea, form to a shape, colour to an image, harmony to music. Your ability is the ability to nurture, to make things grow. Yours is the ability to enrich and to fulfil, to assist and make real ideas, feelings and thoughts. In a sense, it is through people like you that the positive forces can translate into the works of nature on earth.

The context of meaning is most keenly felt when you are doing things in co-operation with others, especially your partner, but there are times when you need to withdraw into yourself in order to resolve important issues.

This is the only instance in your nature when you work without the guidance and assistance of other people. At all other times, you are a person of co-operation, with an extraordinary and highly meritorious capacity for hard work. As a partner, you are devoted and you are highly cherished.

2 Does My Partner Love Me?

Without reservation, the answer is yes. In a very profound way, you are both necessary to each other's fulfilment both as people and in the work that you do together, no matter what it may be. Emotionally you are positively interdependent.

Your relationship will have matured when you have both ceased to impose your will upon each other, but still retain access to those special feelings without fear of reproach.

3 Do We Have a Future Together?

The future together will be an increasingly fulfilling experience, with both of you able to realise your individual best potential, both of you wishing for the best to come out in each other, both complementing each other as *yin* and *yang*. The future has all the potential of being fruitful and joyful.

4 What is the Most Important Attitude to Adopt at This Time?

The attitudes you must avoid are those associated with stubbornness, narrow-mindedness and unwillingness to be moved. Anything which can be described as an unreceptive state of mind must be avoided. Attitudes to adopt are those correspondingly opposite to these negative traits.

These can be summed up by a willingness to be intuitively receptive and responsive to any positive, kindly influences which may be offered to you.

5 Why Has Our Relationship Broken Down?

As a person symbolised *The Receptive*, you stand in a special relationship to your partner, who will represent the creative and complementary force to your own nature. Because you are a naturally yielding person, and are soft rather than hard, giving rather than receiving, feeling rather than thinking, intuiting rather than reasoning, any upsets in the relationship will be caused by your adopting an inappropriate stance towards your partner.

Perhaps you have been overly aggressive or impulsive to your partner, or indeed, have tried to adopt the position of leadership in the relationship where this is unfitting. All of this is likely to have an inhibiting effect on your partner and will inspire resentment and mistrust. By acting in such a 'pushy' or imposing way, you display the most unattractive side of your nature and this will erode the relationship you have.

This is a great pity, as in most respects you are very well suited to one another.

6 Will We Get Back Together?

Since you and your partner are by nature complementary to each other, and naturally suited, a reconciliation is certainly possible. If the division between you has arisen for the reasons given in the last answer, then you will find that if you revert to your natural way of behaviour – your finer qualities – your partner will be able to respond positively, warmly and open-heartedly towards you, thus inviting a reconciliation.

It may well be that in the circumstances your partner will initiate a reconciliation, thus inspiring you to respond in your usual attractive way. Reawaken in yourself the beauty, harmony and mildness which you brought to the relationship at the very beginning. You need have no doubt that these are the qualities your partner cherishes most in you and misses most greatly. Be positive in reforging strong links. Avoid further disorientation.

25

7 What Can I Do to Put Things Right?

It is safe to suggest a reconciliation with your partner in your own way. It is safe to bring the problems gently into the open. It is safe to be accessible and open-hearted. It is safe to be honest, and it is safe to expect to understand and to be understood.

There is no need to rely on an intermediary or to entertain unconventional or unnecessary means of communication. You can be direct, providing you are true to your own nature, for it is this your partner perceives and loves.

8 What Do I Most Want From Life?

In the field of human relationships, your heart's desire is to be the perfect complement to your partner. Your joy will come through the nurturing of life, giving form to your creative ideas. For you, life itself is an enriching experience.

THE LINES

One

━━━━━X━━━━━

Nature is taking its course. The onset of winter is hinted at by the first chills of autumn. As the first green shoots springing out of the earth tell us that spring is in the air, so the first signs of decay indicate what is now to come. Note the season as its first indications appear, and take the appropriate precautions.

Two

━━━━━X━━━━━

When the receptive qualities come into proper relation to creative qualities, both together form a natural, almost miraculous third dimension, which neither quality could create alone. Symbolised here is an unalterable natural law being perfectly reflected in the relationship between *yin* and *yang*, positive and negative, male and female.

When these laws are perfectly reflected in our collective nature, something marvellous happens – apparently with the greatest of ease. Without vainglory and pomp and ceremony, actions – your actions – speak louder than words. They stand to be respected and admired in their own light. They tell their own story. You have no need to seek promotion or recognition for what you have done. There is no need for you to seek formal acclaim for your achievements. Work itself carries the momentum of change, and it should be allowed to do so freely.

The oracle advises that you now lie low, adopt a low profile, and that you cultivate an impenetrable personal reserve. You can do this either by withdrawing into seclusion and isolation away from the world, or by throwing yourself into its midst. Either way, this is a time to move unnoticed and unknown.

Three

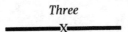

The situation pictured in this line is of a person who is doing well in matters of their work. Recognition and acknowledgement are naturally forthcoming. However, there is a strong suggestion here that you should refrain from 'blowing your own trumpet' and attracting attention to yourself.

You ought not, therefore, actively to seek recognition or fame for its own sake.

Your talents and abilities are still developing, and you should give yourself time to grow with the possibilities which present themselves, without allowing yourself to be easily distracted by vainglory.

Let your work be judged on its merits alone.

Four

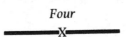

It is an inauspicious time to be drawing attention to yourself. People are already inclined to feel jealous and envious. Usually, if we are following our heart truthfully, such unwholesome attitudes in others cannot harm us, but at present, the reverse is true.

You should, therefore, take heed that the kind of attention you receive will not further your aims as you might wish. It is far better at this time, to be 'incognito', to maintain a low profile and work hard.

It does not matter whether you conceal yourself in solitude or in the crowd. The point is to repel the wrong kind of acclaim by resisting the temptation to *invite* acclaim at all.

Five

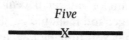

There is no doubt of the value of your personal work. Whether you are compelled or invited to assume important responsibilities in co-operation with others, you should allow your personal talents to express themselves with a modest silence, so that each nuance and intricacy is effectively communicated. The line is favourable where such excellent qualities abide.

Six

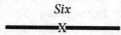

This line pictures an unnecessary and unnatural conflict between the forces of receptivity and the forces of creativity. The advice of the oracle given in answer to question 5 applies here to some extent, except that here both elements are harmed, both suffer.

The picture which emerges is that of the dark force trying to supplant the strong light force. A dark force tries to exist in the place where a light force naturally exists. It injures itself, but in the process also injures the light force. In this line we have a deliberate obstruction of a natural process manifesting as a conflict between light and dark, in which the dark element is finally overthrown, but only at some cost.

Where all the lines are sixes, they change into their opposite, denoting the hexagram *The Creative*. All the qualities depicted in *The Receptive*, changing now to *The Creative* in their positive form, exist in a fixed point of time which is sometimes called eternity.

HEXAGRAM 3

Difficult Beginnings

1 Is This Person a Compatible Partner?

In relation to a partner, this oracle is more favourable than unfavourable. It is not, however, so much the qualities and characteristics of your partner which should be looked at here, rather the circumstances in which you find yourselves. Circumstances colour the way you see other people.

At present you are going through a very difficult time, a time when you are about to embark upon certain important changes in your life. Everything is in flux around you. Things are in motion and are happening at great speed. The ground is being laid for completely new possibilities, even undreamt-of possibilities, but there is nothing certain or definite in the trends you perceive affecting you. There are so many elements involved that it is practically impossible to see a pattern in them. However, the oracle suggests that beneath all the activity that is going on around you, there is an order.

The sudden appearance of your partner in this confusing light may be the cause of some of the apparent chaos out of which new possibilities now arise. All the indications, however, are positive. In the same way that a new birth is a positive idea, though it is surrounded by new complications at the beginning, so you and your partner are surrounded by complicated circumstances.

2 Does My Partner Love Me?

At this time it is impossible to give a definite yes or a definite no to this question. In truth, it is too early to tell. However, if this is your principal aim, then you should keep it in mind when solving the necessary problems as they arise. Keep an open mind and be wary of deciding for yourself too early in the relationship.

3 Do We Have a Future Together?

As this oracle concerns itself with the beginning of relationships and with the beginnings of new activities, which are still in a state of flux, it is reasonable to believe that if these processes are passed through satisfactorily, then they will form the basis for a sound future relationship. If you do not weather the problems of this time in the proper manner, then the future will have to be based on a different foundation, under different circumstances, perhaps even with different people. The oracle assumes that you have not yet completed this process, but are just beginning it and so in this sense, forewarned is forearmed. If you follow the advice of this oracle, then you have good reason to be optimistic about the future.

4 What is the Most Important Attitude to Adopt at This Time?

If you are confronted with difficulties which you are not sure you can cope with alone, then you must have an attitude of humility and be willing to seek the appropriate help and advice. The oracle suggests that almost certainly you cannot see through these difficulties without such help, and therefore you must be inclined to search for it, and be willing to be guided by it.

5 Why Has Our Relationship Broken Down?

Since you have been aware all along that the situation is difficult and requires caution and assistance from others, there can only be one main reason for any breakdown in the relationship, and that is undue and unnecessary force. Have you been too forceful when you should have been patient? Have you been negligent in your analysis of the problems? Have you swept aside details when you should have looked at them more closely? Have you failed to take well-meant and proper advice? Have you failed to seek advice from others? All these faults, individually or all together will have contributed to the failure of your relationship.

6 Will We Get Back Together?

If you have been humble and have accepted the right kind of guidance, then there is every possibility that a reconciliation can take place. You can only answer this question for yourself in the light of what you know, and by looking at your conduct.

7 What Can I Do to Put Things Right?

There is no suggestion as yet that you have gone too far. If you had done so, then there would be nothing you could now do to put things right. If you have not already gone too far in acting forcefully and without restraint, then now is the time to seek help from others and to follow their guidance carefully and with an attitude of humility. Only in this way can you overcome the problems.

8 What Do I Most Want From Life?

Because of the profusion of difficulties at this time, you find it hard to fix the exact focus of your attentions. However, it can be said that it is your chief desire to grow through these difficulties to your own satisfaction.

THE LINES

One

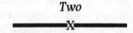

You must constantly keep your objective in mind, despite any obstacles you may be encountering. However, you do need the right kind of assistance, and you should seek it with proper respect and humility.

Two

All sorts of obstacles are now presenting themselves. You are

32

surprised by the sudden appearance of somebody new on the scene whose attitude is helpful, but whose intentions you mistakenly mistrust. You will eventually realise that you have misjudged this person, but nevertheless you decline the assistance offered because it is not the right kind of help for you now. After a good many years, or another cycle of time, you will be able to enter into a relationship with the right person who will be able to be of assistance.

This is a difficult and special situation. The essence of the advice given here is that you must not accept just anybody's assistance or help, but that you must be patient and wait until precisely the right kind of help is available to you. Only in this way will the problem be resolved in the due course of time. The proper attitude here can be summed up as humility tempered by discrimination.

Three

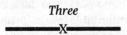

Although time may appear, on the surface, to be in a state of flux, you must remember that there is order beneath it. This order is now beginning to show itself. You are not at present in a position to be able to pilot yourself successfully through the various difficulties that still prevail. If you attempt to do so alone, you will fail. Therefore the advice of the oracle is to find a person who, as it were, knows the lay of the land.

Four

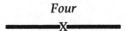

The time has come for you to act, but you lack the right resources with which to do so. There is no disgrace in asking for help. Indeed, such action would be commendable, and the results likely to be favourable, despite any residual feelings of self-effacement in yourself.

Five

You are full of the right ideas – with the best possible motives – but the other people involved in the situation are unreceptive to these ideas and fail to comprehend what you are trying to do or say. The one thing you must not do is force the issue, but there are several things you can do. You must realise that this particular idea cannot be realised without the concurrence of everyone else, and in order to obtain this concurrence, you must be free of any mistrust or bad faith in your own attitude. You must continue to work hard without distraction, and over a period of time you will become aware of how the situation gradually alters in favour of continuing the idea with the co-operation of all others concerned. If you follow the advice of this oracle, obstacles will certainly be swept out of the way.

Six

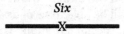

Sometimes at the outset of a new situation, a person becomes utterly swamped by the sheer weight of the difficulties that are encountered. This is one of those situations and you possibly feel dejected and miserable. Perhaps you have already given up, and have adopted an attitude of total resignation to failure. Cheer up! It is in the very nature of life itself that light follows dark and dark follows light. The *I Ching* acknowledges the one immutable law in its name: the *Book of Changes*. If you are unable to change your feelings from negative to positive by an act of will, the general forces of greater change of which you and all life are a part, will sweep across your life, and when the time is right you will experience a renewal of heart.

HEXAGRAM 4

Inexperience of the Young

1 Is This Person a Compatible Partner?

This hexagram indicates a person who is inexperienced and naive, who, when confronted with serious predicaments in life, is unable to respond in a mature or wise fashion. In general, the hexagram refers to a young person who has a great deal to learn about life and who is especially ignorant of the way in which the forces of the universe operate. In a special sense, the young person here is not so much stupid as inexperienced.

The oracle describes a special kind of relationship – that between a young person and a teacher or guide. It is important for you to be aware of your need for enlightenment, and therefore, without any presumption whatsoever on your part, you must try to find somebody who will spend time in teaching you. The two principal qualities which you must display in order to attract a teacher to you are patience and deference. You must also be aware that there is absolutely no obligation on the part of anyone who helps you. In the end you will find a guide. It is important for you to listen carefully to everything the guide says and to follow the advice given.

There is a warning here: the oracle only speaks once. Because you are without guile, your mistakes go by unchallenged. Relationships go well as long as you are *sincere*. You have the potential for enlightenment, and this springs out of your inexperience and willingness to learn, but you are advised not to persist in your questioning beyond a modest measure: you should not repeatedly consult the *I Ching* without spending sufficient time to ponder the advice it gives you. If you continually repeat your questions from a mood of dissatisfaction, you will be met with silence.

Do not abuse the patience of your guide. Your guide feels a responsibility to lead you along the path of enlightenment. You must be ready to seek clarity of understanding at each step along the way. Having said all this, the oracle favours you in so far as it is willing to respond to your present need.

2 Does My Partner Love Me?

There is a special kind of affection which a teacher or guide offers to those who seek enlightenment. In this case, you have no need to doubt it. If you are painstaking in your efforts, you will honour such affection.

3 Do We Have a Future Together?

The future offers the possibility of wisdom. If you and your guide are suited to one another, the relationship will bear fruit. There are no short cuts to enlightenment. You must pass through each stage, as everyone must. Provided you are sincere and that you do your best, success is assured.

4 What is the Most Important Attitude to Adopt at This Time?

An experienced guide deserves your respect and your trust. Your guide will have no desire whatsoever to confuse you. Such a person will offer clear explanations and a clear example. If you are wide-eyed and alert, you may be sure of success in the end.

5 Why Has Our Relationship Broken Down?

You are in the special position of being a beginner in the ways of enlightenment. If you have spoiled things for yourself, it will be largely because you have not heeded the advice offered to you – you have persistently questioned the answers which have been offered, and you have been insincere and even rude. You must understand that nobody is under *any obligation* to help or assist you. The oracle advises that you discipline yourself so that you do not waste time or energy.

6 Will We Get Back Together?

You have only to display a willingness to learn and a sincerity of purpose and you will attract favour.

7 What Can I Do to Put Things Right?

What you have left undone, be willing to do. What you have to do, do well. Your mistakes will be passed over, but the spirit in which you do things must be correct. If you act in bad faith, this will not be ignored.

8 What Do I Most Want From Life?

You have drawn this oracle at this time because your one desire is greater self-knowledge. You wish to improve yourself. If you follow this path, you will meet others like yourself, with whom you feel a natural empathy. Because yours is a worthy aim, you will attract helpers at each stage of the way.

THE LINES

One

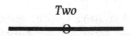

There is a need for you to impose a discipline on yourself. Only in this way can you hope to dispel ignorance. However, such measures only succeed if the manner of self-discipline accords with your own nature. Do not be too hard on yourself. Too much self-criticism is as bad as too little, and will only damage your self-motivation. Nevertheless, because these are serious matters, you must have the appropriate respect for them.

Two

The line is generally favourable. It describes a person who finds him or herself in humble circumstances, but who nevertheless has a definite aptitude for assuming authority and the initiative over other people. Being without conceit in your own nature, your strengths are less inhibited. You are thus able to suffer fools gladly. This is certainly right in the circumstances. This general attitude must not only extend to people of your own sex – the same deference should be shown to the opposite sex. The tenor of the oracle is that the positive traits in your character are developing well, and this invites favour and success.

Three

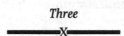

You are not strong enough to take the initiative in any situation. Because you are naive and gullible – due to your inexperience of life – you are highly impressionable, especially when in the company of people who are older, wiser and stronger, and whose personalities are more developed, and whose experience of the world is greater than yours. This being the case, you should be careful not to be too coloured by your surroundings and too influenced by them.

The advice applies equally to a young woman or a girl, who is here advised to display reticence in relation to the opposite sex in order to avoid being mistreated. However, where the proper courtesy is shown on both sides, the oracle does not rule out a relationship. At this time, people must observe the proper degree of deference and courtesy when dealing with each other, otherwise no good will come of such encounters.

Four

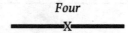

You are subject to wayward fantasies. Your mind is wandering and dreaming. You must not indulge yourself in such thoughts. Ultimately there is no point in thinking about such things, and if you persist, you will experience personal embarrassment. As a way of learning, it may not be necessary to take things this far. Nevertheless, the warning stands.

Five

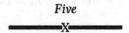

This line refers you back to the advice given in question 4 *What is the most important attitude to adopt at this time?* If you adopt the attitude advised in that answer, you will invite the assistance you need in order to find the way. Providing you retain your guileless innocence, the way lies open for you to understand the insights which you have been, and will be, offered.

Six

This is the line of someone who will not listen to good advice when it is offered. It refers to someone who has strayed so far from the path that there is only one way to bring him back – with a sharp shock. The only purpose behind such a jolt would be to bring you to your senses before things go too far. Such an event could only be justified cosmically if it helped you to regain equilibrium, or to find a new state of inner peace.

HEXAGRAM 5

Patience

1 Is This Person a Compatible Partner?

You and your partner are compatible, and the problems you are facing together at the moment do not arise from any profound difference between you. However, there is no doubt that there are problems to be overcome which will have consequences for the future.

Any problems at home, or in the family, or between you and your partner, are there because you have brought them in from the outside. Perhaps, for example, you are bringing home problems from work. It is not appropriate for you to point a finger at anyone. There is nobody to blame. Although you can see that there is plenty to worry about, the source of your concern is beyond your control. Fretting and worrying and upsetting everyone else with it is not going to improve the situation in the slightest – it will only aggravate it.

If you persist in this attitude, you might make the wrong decisions at crucial times. Despite all this, the outcome of your present source of worry is fated to be successful. This does not, however, mean that you should sit back and wait for things to happen or take their own course. That is not the way it works. You must persevere in what is right, as there is no other course of action open to you.

2 Does My Partner Love Me?

Your personal relationship is not threatened at its source. On the contrary, you should identify your family life as a source of strength at this time. You know in your heart that things are going to turn out well.

3 Do We Have a Future Together?

By now, you should be able to distinguish between things over which you have control and the things over which you have no control. Apply your best efforts to the things over which you have control, and allow fate to do the rest.

This hexagram concerns itself with matters of destiny. There is no reason to feel that your efforts are not aided by the invisible forces at work, but you must not attempt to interfere with them, for to do so would be to prejudge their effects, and this would be to act beyond your powers. Meanwhile, enjoy yourself.

4 What is the Most Important Attitude to Adopt at This Time?

The name of this hexagram is *Patience*, and this is your best attitude. Do not rush forward blindly without being completely sure of the lie of the land.

5 Why Has Our Relationship Broken Down?

Things can only have failed if you have been impatient, if you have jumped the gun, if you have acted without due caution, or if you have been busy finding scapegoats rather than taking stock of the situation as it is. It has to be said, however, that any failure in the relationship is totally unnecessary. There was no pressure on the relationship to fail, only the requirement for patience.

6 Will We Get Back Together?

A complete breakdown of communication is not suggested by the oracle; and would be extreme under the circumstances. If you recognise your complicity in bringing matters to a head, such unnecessary tension will be alleviated. Above all, you must be capable of grasping the reality of the situation. However tempting it might be, do not allow yourself to be deluded. It is imperative to be clear-minded in matters of fate, as decisions you make now will be crucial. Only in this way can you overcome the problems without underestimating the forces of destiny.

7 What Can I Do to Put Things Right?

We cannot affect the outcome of matters of fate by our behaviour. It is doubly important to avoid self-delusion by being straight and honest with yourself and others. Upon this basis you can find the necessary inner fortitude to endure the time of waiting without losing your calm.

. Concentrate on preserving inner composure. Only a self-contained person knows how to be patient at the right time – and such a time is now. This does not mean that you should do nothing, for you must do what is necessary, but you must allow your actions to be infused with the self-control of someone who inwardly-knows matters of fate from other kinds of challenge.

8 What Do I Most Want From Life?

Above all, you want a satisfactory marriage between your responsibilities at work and your home life. You want a successful outcome to the present situation. You *need* more faith in the forces which control destiny. Even now you do not *really* believe in such things.

THE LINES

One

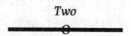

The problems and difficulties are still quite a long way off. Keep an eye on them, but act naturally in the meantime. Do not do anything you might later regret.

Two

As problems come closer, people are inclined to develop differences of opinion, pointing the finger at one another and letting the differences between them get carried to extremes. No individual is to blame in this situation. Because someone says something nasty to you is no reason for you to be just as nasty back. It only compounds the bad feeling. Just relax.

Three

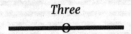

You jump the gun, and your best effort does not carry you through to the mark. You are now in a vulnerable position. This is not a time to say 'Oh well, better luck next time.' The consequences of your present predicament may be no laughing matter. Take great care.

Four

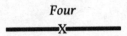

This is a life and death matter from which there is no escape. Do not panic, keep calm, do not do anything untoward which could intensify the danger. This is your only chance.

Five

This is the oasis in the desert, or, more accurately, the eye of the storm. The general endeavour is fated to succeed, but take advantage of the lull to enjoy yourself, and allow others to enjoy themselves also. In this way you will have the necessary strength to overcome the challenges and difficulties which still lie ahead, but with every certainty of your succeeding.

Six

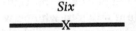

You have reached the critical point. It may at first seem as if everything is lost and that you are helpless, but due to the intervention of invisible powers, things take an unexpected turn. Whether this is for better or for worse, you cannot quite tell, but God acts in mysterious ways.

Good fortune comes in an unrecognised and inexplicable form. Such a force deserves your respect, and you must respond with suitable maturity. In the end, you are gleeful.

HEXAGRAM 6

Deadlock

1 Is This Person a Compatible Partner?

You and your partner are definitely compatible with one another, but because you both wish to assert your individuality – and because you are both highly self-opinionated – you both feel that it is necessary for you to adopt opposing standpoints on all issues, both trivial and important, without giving an inch.

This is a situation of conflict generated out of pure cussedness on *both* your parts. You are *both* strong-willed and you are *both* convinced that your point of view is the 'right' one. The oracle makes no judgement or evaluation as to who between you is right. If you have drawn the oracle in order to establish this, you have no partisan response. Instead this hexagram warns that if your contrary positions are maintained you will both end up by seriously alienating each other.

Unless you are both prepared to compromise no good will come of this quarrel.

2 Does My Partner Love Me?

It is very clear that you love each other very much – in a contrary sort of way – otherwise neither of you would consider anything important enough to argue about so vehemently. But if you take things too far, you could 'go off' each other. Under the circumstances this is not necessary! You are like two people looking at the finger which points to the stars, instead of looking at the stars themselves.

3 Do We Have a Future Together?

Now and in the future you must learn to resolve your difficulties and differences of opinion even where this means accepting compromises and, where necessary, agreeing to disagree over some issues.

Individually, you must each overcome your ever-present sense of self-importance. It is important for you both to aim at spiritual harmony. If you recognise in each other positive and valuable qualities, you will find that the differences between you are comparatively trivial. The admonishment of this hexagram is to develop a sense of proportion.

4 What is the Most Important Attitude to Adopt at This Time?

You and your partner must recognise the difference between quarrelling and argument. People who quarrel are really only interested in their own point of view; argument, on the other hand, is based upon the desire to *understand the other person's point of view*. If neither of you can appreciate the other's point of view then this is a limitation you *both* possess.

How is it possible to argue effectively if you cannot appreciate the viewpoint of your partner? How can you pretend to yourself that you really care about your partner if you do not care enough to tolerate your partner's ideas, or indeed, even to listen to them properly? In this specific sense, both your respective standpoints may be invalidated.

The other issue which must be cleared up between you is this: there is no point in having an argument if all you want to do is win it. The only justification for arguing is to enhance your understanding of the overall situation. Arguing eristically displays a weakness of character and, if persisted in, can have a very divisive effect upon the relationship.

Your best attitude, therefore, is to be open minded at the expense of feelings of self importance.

5 Why Has Our Relationship Broken Down?

Your relationship has not broken down – yet. However, out of the present situation, it is more than possible to create an irreconcilable division between you. At present you are both incapable of standing outside the situation and seeing it for what it is.

6 Will We Get Back Together?

In your case the question should read, 'Will we resolve our quarrel sensibly and amicably?' or, 'Will we agree?' In some cases, no matter how hard two people try they simply cannot see eye to eye. At such times the only thing to do is to find somebody you both respect and whose impartial judgement you both trust, to act as arbitrator between you. Although this can only assist you in a limited way, it may help you to accept a position that is less extreme in relation to your partner than your current one. Ultimately, the resolution of the real problem will only come about if you both recognise that arguing from such a selfish standpoint (a competitive attitude) implies a defect of character in both of you. Neither of you is prepared to acknowledge the other as winner on the grounds of who shouts loudest or who ultimately is the most forceful or powerful, because you both already know that these criteria are immature and amount to nothing in the end.

Ultimately the winner of the argument, if you like, is the one who first overcomes their sense of self importance, and who overcomes it best. (Nothing destroys peace – inner and outer – between two people or between nations more effectively and completely than self importance.)

You both win if you rise above the argument itself.

7 What Can I Do to Put Things Right?

If you are incapable of resolving the differences between you on your own, then you must find a completely impartial person to arbitrate. You must find someone whose authority and judgement you both acknowledge, respect and by whose decision you are both prepared to abide.

Such enmity between you is, of course, no basis for taking on important collective challenges. As a couple you are very weak at the present. You are very vulnerable. Not until you are of *one accord*, once again, can you contemplate any plans or ambitions.

8 What Do I Most Want From Life?

You think you most *want* to win. What you *need* is agreement between you, what will make you happiest is harmony with your partner. What is needed is a wider perspective – from both of you.

THE LINES

One

Stop the argument now before it grows out of all proportion, and beyond control. Yes, there might be a little last minute bickering between you, but in the end you will both be smiling again.

Two

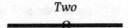

If you deliberately enter into a fight with your present adversary you will definitely lose. This is apparent to everybody. There will be absolutely no disgrace on your part if you refuse to be drawn into such an unbalanced contest. If you give ground while the situation is still contained you will certainly not regret it.

Three

If you write a poem and somebody steals it, or plagiarises it and publishes it under their own name without reference to or acknow-ledgement of its author then the question for you is this, 'Is the poem theirs or is it yours?' The answer is that even though the credit for writing it goes to somebody else (nowadays, of course, there are rules governing the ownership of copyright, but this is extraneous to the point being made here), the poem is still yours because you wrote it. The principle here is that, what is truly yours can never really be taken away from you – even though it may appear to be. Just as a copy of an original masterpiece can never be more than a copy. Therefore, do not make any claims based on a desire for adulation as there is no need to demean yourself even if others do.

Four

The fires of discontent spur you on to pick a fight with someone you

47

know you can beat. A little victory now, you feel, would do your morale a lot of good. But you also reflect that being without good cause – and not wishing to take advantage of another person's weakness – such an ungainly victory would have no value for you; it would be more likely to leave a sour taste in your mouth. It takes this caution to dispel your own private inner conflicts and you achieve a victory over yourself which you experience as a reconciliation. Such an outcome cannot help but do you credit in the future. Good fortune.

Five

This is the line of the peacemaker, the person to whom adversaries turn when they cannot resolve their own quarrels and difficulties. This person can be relied upon to give a fair and impartial judgement without any taints of bias or prejudice, and who is able to weigh the merits of both sides in such a way that both parties feel free to abide by the final decision.

Honour to the adversary who wins the day.

Six

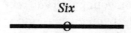

Your victory, such that it is, is ungainly, and undeserved. You cannot wear the crown of success because it is widely disputed. Why? Because you have missed the point of the argument – namely that winning and losing are not necessarily the same as right and wrong. Just because you have won the argument does not mean that you are right. It simply means that when you come up against a stronger adversary – who also happens to be right – your defeat will be all the more humiliating. Take no pride in such a victory.

HEXAGRAM 7

Challenge

1 Is This Person a Compatible Partner?

Because of the immense inner resources which you and your partner share, this relationship can only work within the framework of a rigorous self-discipline and outward discipline. By necessity, this is not a relationship of equals. You are the directing force behind the action which you both undertake. You are not only responsible for your partner, but also for other people. In order to succeed such responsibilities demand a tremendous discipline, and the power to inspire the people who rely on you for direction with purpose and moral courage.

2 Does My Partner Love Me?

The purpose of your union is to create strength and action. Such love as your partner bears you is expressed by an unremitting confidence in your powers of leadership and decision.

3 Do We Have a Future Together?

You must not underestimate the present situation and its power to be the focus and base for future challenges. Bear in mind all that has gone before. If you fully appreciate your situation, you will realise that there is a clear dividing line between victory and defeat. The future, of course, must be determined optimistically in terms of victory, rather than defeat.

Nevertheless, there is a warning implied. If this present challenge is overcome together, you must not allow such a victory to cause a deterioration in your attitude to future challenges. Maintain a strict sense of what is fair. If you transgress the rules of fair play, then you can expect defeat in the future. In this case, all your actions, in your own view, are justified by a victorious outcome.

4 What is the Most Important Attitude to Adopt at This Time?

This is the hexagram for those people who are preparing to come into conflict with others. Organisation is vital in preparing for combat of any kind, be it in sport, warfare, mental or spiritual challenge. The leading person must be capable of organising and deploying the forces in an economic and systematic way. There is no doubt that you are aware of the seriousness of your position.

5 Why Has Our Relationship Broken Down?

Any failure in the relationship arises from your inappropriateness for your position. You do not have the necessary leadership qualities; you lack the ability to evoke the love and respect of your partner and those who depend upon you for guidance, and, above all, you lack the power to clearly organise your forces in the best possible way in order to attain the ends that you desire.

6 Will We Get Back Together?

If you still command the respect of the people who follow you, there is still enough time before action. Providing you maintain a clear sense of your responsibility, and polish up your organisational arrangements, there is no reason why you should not expect a satisfactory outcome.

This is only one battle, as it were, in a long line of battles. If you are preparing to take on serious challenges, then those further challenges will depend on how you fare with this one.

This is not so much the story of a relationship as one person facing another, as what this relationship is capable of generating when, as a unified team, you take on life's challenges.

7 What Can I Do to Put Things Right?

Only a strong sense of justice and the ability to screw your courage to the sticking-place will enable you to resolve this situation. If you cannot achieve this, then defer to one who can.

8 What Do I Most Want From Life?

You most desire victory with fair play.

THE LINES

One

This line refers to the preparation for a challenge at its outset. There are two things which must be set right before taking on any opposition. Firstly, your reasons for making the challenge must be impeccable, absolutely untarnished – without blemish in every respect. Secondly, you must be able to count on the perfect organisation and adherence to the cause of the people who will actually effect the challenge. Both these conditions must be fulfilled, or the result will be failure.

Two

In making a challenge, the person who is called upon to lead and the governing force should be present in person at the place of challenge. Power should not be delegated out of cowardice.

The rewards and honours given by the government or leaders should be given to the rank and file challengers themselves, and not to their leader – to the army, rather than the general who represents them.

There is an intimation here that a leader should be present in person at the actual place of challenge. The leader should not direct from afar.

Three

Here, the situation is made critical during the time of challenge because of a profusion of leaders arising, instead of one, clear recognised leader. If orders and directions are coming from everywhere – instead of from one centre – nobody knows what to do to avoid a mass defeat.

It may well be that the government which gives power and authority to the challenging force is usurped during the time of challenge, as when a civil revolution takes place at home while the army is abroad.

Four

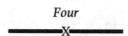

If opposing forces are so much stronger than yours that engaging with them would result in a certain defeat, then you should protect your forces by a retreat with dignity.

Five

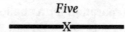

This is an almost impossible situation to master. The opposition has gone wild. Your own forces need taking in hand by a powerful leader capable of exerting a restraining and disciplining force. However, even if such a leader were to arise and take the matter in hand, the chances of success would be remote. Yet it is still of the utmost importance that everybody should be brought under control. An *experienced* leader should be trusted to restore order.

Six

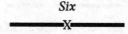

You have won victory. When it comes to paying people for their assistance in this challenge, reward should not take the form of privilege or power in case evil or divisive forces should take hold in their hands. Credit, however, should be given where credit is due, in an appropriate manner.

HEXAGRAM 8

Leadership

The scope of this hexagram embraces a wider social context than that of two people in an exclusive bond of love. It refers to people who live or work together. Perhaps they share a house, commune or kibbutz, or work in the same office or factory.

1 Is This Person a Compatible Partner?

You and your partner find yourselves in the context of a group. Your identity as a couple is either strengthened or weakened through its identification with the group as a whole. While every social or cultural group is in a sense a family, the reference here is not necessarily to a traditional family.

Within the social group, you are compatible. Your compatibility even extends to recognising the same leader to whom you give allegiance.

(If the drawer of this oracle considers him or herself to be the leader of the group, and capable of drawing others together in solidarity and unity, then the advice is to cast the oracle once again in order to receive the affirmation or denial of the required qualities.)

You must be clear in your purposes in volunteering to be a member of such a group. In addition to feeling a natural allegiance to its leader. You also feel you have something to offer the group as a whole in the form of a positive contribution.

Your sense of responsibility towards the social organisation comes from a basic empathy with the people who comprise it. The absence of such a natural calling would only make you feel uncomfortable within such a social organisation. As in the traditional family setting, the foundations upon which successful participation and personal growth can take place are the same as those for society at large, but here the distinction is that you are able to share more intimately experiences with a group as a whole, and in this way a sense of solidarity is established; giving you, your partner and each member of the group a definite and dependable social identity.

People are *drawn* together by their common empathy, but *held* together by their common interest. People will only want to join a group if they feel naturally attracted to it, and will only stay in it as long as the group's interests remain focussed and identified.

Ultimately, then, it is the power of an idea which holds people together. This applies not only to small groups of people, but also to society and the world at large. For example, an individual's belief in peaceful coexistence should be expressed in the way this person behaves in relation to the people with whom the individual lives. On a much bigger scale, such an ideal can link up the world.

The role of a leader, therefore, be they head of a small social group, of a city, or of a country, should be to embody the idea which unites the people. The fundamental principles of leadership are solidarity, empathy and identity with a group, and these principles apply regardless of scale.

2 Does My Partner Love Me?

The basis of all social solidarity is mutual affection. This is true not only of small groups, but of large groups – indeed, of all societies in the world. In the absence of affection, the inner fabric of any social organisation, regardless of scale, must ultimately stand or fall at the expense of individual free choice.

It is the love between individuals within the social group which gives the whole group its strength.

3 Do We Have a Future Together?

The kind of social set-up described in this oracle is one which is dependent upon adequate leadership. The social group can only last if its leader maintains the ability to keep the group together. However, this also implies that the group's greatest potential weakness is the leader.

By way of comment, one might add here that if, in this case, the leader is able to stand as a representative of a higher idea to which the group pledges allegiance, then such a group will not stand or fall by the leader's personal merits or demerits alone, because here the force of solidarity arises from a common belief.

4 What is the Most Important Attitude to Adopt at This Time?

If you are the leader of a group, then the correct attitude stems from an awareness of the serious responsibility which goes with your position.

You must be strong, tolerant and zealous. You cannot be effective unless you feel a sense of vocation for this kind of work.

If you are a member of the group, you must be willing to identify with the general aims of the group, if this does not mean being untrue to yourself. Providing you feel that you have something positive to offer the group as a whole, and that the group as a whole has something positive to offer you, then you will be without contradiction regarding important matters.

5 Why Has Our Relationship Broken Down?

The answer to this question is all the more complex since we are concerned here with two relationships, one between the individual and a partner, and the other concerning the individual's relationship to the group as a whole.

If you no longer feel attracted to the ideas embodied in a group, then you will no longer wish to be a part of it. If your partner feels this, you will feel the tension between you. The relationship between you cannot flourish if either of you do not feel allegiance to the group as a whole.

On the other hand, a weak leader, incapable of holding the group together – either through a lack of personal strength, or through the absence of a vocation for such work – will eventually cause the group to disunite. This in itself may put pressure on individual relationships within the group, which might not be able to survive alone without the force of a binding idea. In this case the cause for breakdown will be the loss of a common identity.

6 Will We Get Back Together?

The subject of this hexagram is the bringing of people together, and holding them together, through the common impulses of love, affection and mutual respect. Any divisive tendencies arising within the group will spring from a lack of any of these qualities in any individual, regardless of their standing. Only these qualities can recreate true bonds.

7 What Can I Do to Put Things Right?

A person who is in the position of leader cannot *manufacture* the necessary qualities by which to bring a group together and to hold it together. Such qualities must be innate. Not everyone can be a leader. There are those who feel a natural calling for leadership, and possess more than just a knack for bringing people together. Where these qualities are unquestioned, minor differences of opinion will not be sufficient to break up the group. Such a leader will recognise that it is the common experience of members of the group which is the basis of solidarity.

If people are not happy within the group, they should be allowed to go their own way without fear of reproach, and without pressure or force from the leader of the group or its other members.

No individual should be expected to go against his or her own nature. The same applies to a leader. When the person at the centre of the group feels that he or she does not possess the necessary qualities to hold the group together through force of character, that person is obliged to leave the group entirely.

8 What Do I Most Want From Life?

Your aim is a modest one. It is to be a useful member of a social community according to the integrity of your belief, and by means of unhindered personal choice, enabling you to be free to give according to your abilities. When these values are applied, they represent mankind's highest social aspiration.

THE LINES

One

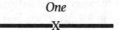

If you are honest with yourself, you cannot be dishonest with others. No worthwhile relationship has ever been based on personal dishonesty, or ever will be. When you speak, speak from the heart. In this way you set up a good chain of karma.

Two

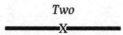

If, in order to win the approval of others, you are required to compromise your personal honesty, then you do not deserve approval. For if you win the approval of others by compromising your personal honesty, that approval is worth nothing.

Three

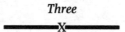

It has been said that those who pretend to false intimacies are in the end the loneliest. You cannot be intimate with every type of person, and you should not try to be. Where there is no genuine empathy between people, there is always room for courtesy and civility, or even something slightly warmer. You should therefore save yourself for those people with whom you feel a natural affinity, and in such cases, intimacy is right.

Four

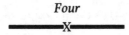

Where you give allegiance to a leader, without inner contradiction or reservation, there is no reason to hide your loyalty.

Five

This line concerns itself with the rightness of free association. When people enter into relationships openly and freely, and of their own choice, then they will be without fear or prejudice. Such associations automatically attract the right kind of people and deter sycophants and the uncommitted. In such a situation, there is no need to curry favour from anyone, or to pretend to intimacies which do not exist. Such a principle holds true for all relationships in life.

Six

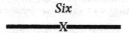

'Shall I or shan't I commit myself?' You must make a decision before it is too late, or you will regret it.

HEXAGRAM 9

Limited Persuasion

1 Is This Person a Compatible Partner?

At present, you are the weaker of the two in the relationship. Your partner is self-willed and selfish, and tends to run roughshod over your feelings. But there is nothing you can do to stop this person from going too far, except make subtle hints and gentle suggestions. Only in these ways can you quietly persuade your partner that enough is enough. You must judge for yourself in what degree your partner's actions cause harm. If you are careful and unassuming, it is possible that you may be able to persuade your partner to behave in a less dramatic and more subdued manner.

2 Does My Partner Love Me?

It is not possible to describe your partner's present behaviour as loving, or arising out of a loving attitude. He or she has a lot to learn about love, but it is not unlearnable. Your partner's best teacher at the present time is kindness.

3 Do We Have a Future Together?

As strange as this may seem to you, your future relationship with your partner lies in your own hands. It is more your decision than your partner's. If you really want a future together, you will find the right recipe for conduct through the more gentle powers in which you excel.

4 What is the Most Important Attitude to Adopt at This Time?

You will be able to achieve most if you understand that it is in the realm of subtle influence, rather than direct action, in which your power lies. Be amicable.

5 Why Has Our Relationship Broken Down?

Your power to persuade your partner to see reason was limited from the very outset. The breakdown in the relationship was probably caused more by your partner's insensitivity to your suggestions than your weakness. If, on the other hand – in your attempt to be a mild restraining influence – you placed your partner under too much moral pressure, then in this way too, arguments of a serious nature may have blown up between you causing the collapse of the relationship.

6 Will We Get Back Together?

Some degree of understanding and communication between two people always exists but there is no indication here that you can base your communication upon genuine empathy. Providing your partner has not gone too far, and providing you have not already called off the relationship, having already reached the end of your tether, then there is a possibility for a reconciliation if you conduct yourself according to the advice of this oracle. Although you may not realise it, you still have the initiative in the relationship. What is important is the way you use that initiative. If you can find it within you to be amicable, but at the same time objective, there is a real possibility of pulling this relationship back onto an even keel.

7 What Can I Do to Put Things Right?

You do not have the power to exert a controlling influence over your partner's actions and behaviour or moods. The level of effective communication and mutual understanding between you is very low, and it is not possible to make an effective impression upon your partner. A person who is bent on getting their own way and doing things their own way is unreceptive to wise counsel.

The only thing that might make any impression on your partner is a quiet, hinting persuasiveness. If you can find exactly the right balance in doing this, it is still possible to open up the doors of communication between you and to bring the relationship to the light of reason. Do not underestimate your own powers in this regard, but certainly do not overestimate them either.

Nevertheless, success is a real possibility, if the damage already done is not so extreme as to have forced you beyond your own limits of endurance, even beyond caring.

8 What Do I Most Want From Life?

You need to cultivate in yourself the capacity for greater endurance. Patience has its greatest strength in a strong will.

THE LINES

One

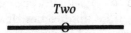

Some areas of activity are inappropriate to your best qualities. Even though you are inclined to take on challenges, in this case you would be better off doing what you were doing before.

Two

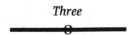

You can already see by your companions who precede you that the way forward will not lead you to your objective. You do not need to go all the way to find out why. You do not need to incur any personal approbation, so you also turn back.

Three

You have completely misunderstood the situation. You have over-estimated the power of your influence on those around you. Although the signs were there you ignored them. You attempted to make an impression on those around you with the full expectancy that things would go your way, but their reaction to you was unfavourable, and you suffered embarrassment. The essence of the problem here lies in the fact that the circumstances were considerably more complicated than you at first imagined, and your over-simplification of the issue has compromised your self-esteem. The result is in-house quarrelling.

Four

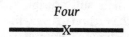

You are in a position of considerable influence, for you advise those who have the greatest power to act. On the issue at hand the stakes are high. The advice you give is crucial. See to it that the advice you offer does not compromise the objective truth of the situation. Only in this way can you steer your way through the obvious problems, without recourse to any violent methods. You can expect success.

Five

The sentiment that underlies friendship between people is loyalty. In some people, loyalty will take the form of dedication to the group; in others, in whom greater responsibility is entrusted, it will take the form of confidence and credibility. Within a social and working situation, such mutual friendliness augurs well, generating an uplifting sense of unity.

Six

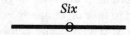

Because you have been so consistently caring, the possibility for real mutual understanding now approaches. It is imperative that you continue to care. You must avoid being over-presumptuous, and you must recognise that one of the most important attributes of a caring person is restraint. Although you have done well so far, you must not forget your objective. There is still a little way to go.

HEXAGRAM 10

Sincerity (Honest Intent)

1 Is This Person a Compatible Partner?

Your partner perceives the world in a completely different manner from yourself. This can often be deeply attractive just as sometimes it can be highly irritating, and sometimes communication is not possible. True communication is only possible between equals. Here the situation is one in which two people are so different and so unequal that misunderstandings easily arise. However, providing the partner who is 'lower' acts with good humour, the 'higher' partner is able to respond with positive feelings. Humour, then, is the basis and the catalyst for growing close in this relationship.

A word of warning: where the inequality between you arises from natural states within, the possibility remains for greater growth. Where both superiority and inferiority are merely on the surface, there is a danger that you will both deceive each other. The important thing here is that each person should recognise the true inner worth of the other, and should not impose values which may seem more comfortable to live with, but which have no basis in reality. If you share a common sense of humour, it is possible to grow through laughter.

2 Does My Partner Love Me?

Your partner is in the unusual position of understanding you better than you understand your partner. This creates difficulties of communication for both of you, making many of your respective acts seem on the surface rather ambiguous. However, if you are genuine in seeking this person's affections with a light heart, you will receive a favourable response. There are great prospects if you hold to this sincerity of feeling, but the situation is nevertheless difficult. If you act consciously in the light of this difficulty, you are less likely to make mistakes.

3 Do We Have a Future Together?

Where people are able to presume a good feeling between themselves, the growth of that feeling is entirely dependent on behaving well, that is to say, with simplicity, honesty, due decorum and due consideration for the feelings of others.

You should behave in such a way as to be able to build upon all that is already good in the relationship you have created. If you depart from good conduct, that which has already been created will be effectively depleted and worn down. The future is built upon day-to-day considerations, and so day-to-day conduct is the most important area on which to concentrate.

4 What is the Most Important Attitude to Adopt at This Time?

It is important to recognise that other people may have something very valuable to offer you, and you should respect this. By adopting a less self-opinionated attitude in the relationship, you will also open up a part of yourself which enables others to recognise your true value.

5 Why Has Our Relationship Broken Down?

The universe is full of inequalities. However, this is not as bad as it seems, since it is the dynamic interplay of tensions generated from inequalities which in turn create revolutions both in the external and internal worlds. Relationships will fail to grow where these inequalities of nature are not heeded or respected.

This is clearly a situation where you are playing at love and not meaning it. Sooner or later, love appears as a tiger, and bites. The victim in such a situation is ultimately always the one who has been dishonest.

6 Will We Get Back Together?

An honest intent is always the basis of fruitful possibilities. Where there are basic differences in personal and spiritual development, the links between people must be forged in the most lighthearted way possible. There is no point in feigning an attitude, or pretending feelings which are not present, as this will only widen the gulf between you, and will ultimately lead to greater separation or irreconcilability. Turn your mind towards a stronger recognition of what you have to give, rather than what you can receive, and in this way you will acquire the appropriate blend of seriousness enabling you to rid yourself of the selfishness which tends to make your heart heavy with grief. This is the way upward, and wherever it leads, you must follow.

7 What Can I Do to Put Things Right?

Order will only come out of chaos where feeling and thought converge on one point of rare clarity.

You must be in control of yourself before you can hope to influence another person, even for your mutual benefit.

The essence of all relationships should be natural, honest affection. This must be *felt*, and not merely thought. If you are insincere you will treat people as objects to be manoeuvred by your will. In matters of the heart, especially where the differences between you and your partner are emphasised, this can only lead to further estrangement. If you persist in this insincerity, you will find yourself without friends and companions, and you will find little inner peace. The way out of this is through the prospering of a more trusting heart.

8 What Do I Most Want From Life?

Though you are both highly conscious of the differences between you and of the fact that there is an innate inequality in the relationship, your main desire in life can be expressed as a deeply felt urge for real communication with your loved one: that is to say, equality. You know that real communication only comes from a state of true equality. When your love is matched by the other's love, then and only then is perfect understanding between you possible. The purpose of communication is to provide endless opportunities for growing towards greater understanding of yourself and the world. When you understand yourself, you will understand others. This is something you already intuitively know, and you must work towards achieving this state.

THE LINES

One

Go forward, but without the taints of a superficial ambition to drive you. If you strive to achieve important things, it must be because they are worth achieving in themselves, and not because you feel the rewards are worth having. All that glisters is not gold. You must beware of being dazzled by the expectations of rewards enshrined in shallow aims. Retain inner composure, especially where circumstances are unusually favourable.

Two

You are true to yourself, amid others who are not. You are not drawn by the superficial enticements of life, but prefer to trust in the path you perceive as being correct. You place no demands upon others because they do not see your path, and have nothing to offer or hinder you. You are in a state of clarity, and you do not indulge yourself. This will lead to good fortune.

Three

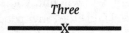

Here you are not in a good position to act with authority, although you would like to do so. Your vision is clouded and your self-awareness is far from complete. To undertake anything important at this stage might create unfortunate circumstances not only for yourself, but for others.

You should pause and take stock, lest you offend others in a way they may not be inclined to forgive.

Four

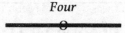

Although the situation is not entirely straightforward, you are in an optimistic mood, and not without justification. You therefore feel inclined to risk a gamble on your own abilities to make the right moves in the right way at the right time, and in this way you are fortunate in attaining your desired aims.

Five

You are determined to pursue a certain course of action that you have chosen. Sometimes being so single minded can make you suffer from tunnel vision. This lack of awareness of the effects of your attitudes and actions can make you prone to serious mistakes. The important thing here is to be aware of your own attitude.

Six

You will reap what you have sown.

HEXAGRAM 11

Peace

1 Is This Person a Compatible Partner?

Yes. You naturally see eye to eye; there is harmony between you; you both exert a very good influence upon each other.

This is a good time to put aside the cares of the past, ánd to elevate your feelings for your partner in an atmosphere of charity and general goodwill and good cheer. Already you feel the salubrious effects of the season. This is, therefore, an auspicious time to grow closer.

2 Does My Partner Love Me?

If you have doubted your partner's love in the past, then there will be less and less reason for you to doubt it in the future. If you open your heart to receive love, you will not be disappointed. If you have no fear about returning what you receive, you will attract good fortune.

3 Do We Have a Future Together?

Take advantage of the present, to sow good seeds for the future. The more effort you put in to what you are doing now, the greater will be the yield later.

You have the power now to augment the naturally fertile processes of nature. In this light the future looks very promising, and even bountiful.

4 What is the Most Important Attitude to Adopt at This Time?

Prepare for action. This is the time when the farmer cultivates the land and sows the seed, the time when a businessman winds up the account for this year and prepares optimistically for the next. This is a time to write dates in your diary to organise your life.

5 Why Has Our Relationship Broken Down?

If you are stubborn and unforgiving and judge your partner on the memory of old quarrels, and are in the habit of dragging skeletons out of the cupboard at every opportunity, then you repel the good feeling which is offered to you, and the new bloom which is trying to grow.

6 Will We Get Back Together?

If you have parted, then this is the time to reconcile the differences between you. The oracle suggests that all efforts made to unify will succeed, but if this is not a time for renewal, then you should let an old relationship go and seek for a new one, for your happiness lies just ahead. Do not be tempted to look over your shoulder. This is not the time to reflect on the past.

7 What Can I Do to Put Things Right?

Let begones be bygones.

Be open and natural with your partner. Do not conceal your feelings but share them. Encourage your partner to open up to you.

A strong good force is beginning to permeate your relationship. A great deal is possible if you act together and in harmony with one another. Make the most of this season for it will pass.

Be active and avoid brooding states of mind. Make a list of exciting things you would like to do together, and then organise your time so that you do them. Make this a priority.

A new springtime is dawning in your relationship. Shake off those pockets of complacency, learn new ways to love each other.

8 What Do I Most Want From Life?

Experience should have taught you that you get most out of yourself when you cultivate your natural talents. If you do what you are good at, and improve it, you are likely to make great strides forward. The satisfaction you will feel, will be more than words can tell.

THE LINES

One

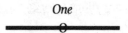

You are emerging into a very productive time in your life. You are unlikely to wait around for things to happen to you; you are more likely to go out into the world and make things happen. The effect of this is that you attract other people into participating and this augments your good fortune, as – providing you are astute – you can be sure to benefit them too.

This is a good time for achievement.

Two

The time is highly fortuitous. If you put your mind to it, here is great scope for action and innovation, for generosity and co-operation. This is even, if you plan carefully and show great foresight, a time when risks pay off.

Where you work with other people, and you organise them and depend on their co-operation, work in such a way that everybody is able to make a contribution to the work as a whole, in as positive a way as possible. In this way everyone works to the mutual advantage of everyone else.

Efforts must be made to avoid separatist and divisive attitudes from arising in the group. If everybody is clear about what is expected of them, then the work will continue apace.

The process once again describes the Golden Mean – nothing too much, nothing too little – everything just right, balanced harmony. In this way things get done.

Three

The pendulum of change in affairs of the world constantly swings

70

between the poles of good and bad fortune. In order to hold a steady course through life, one must be the master of one's own fate. This is the only way to withstand the vicissitudes of change. There is nothing we can do to affect this immutable law of change, even if we can manage to reduce its effects to an absolute minimum. However, despite the ups and downs, and swings and roundabouts, if we remain true to ourselves we can still avoid the snares of misfortune.

Four

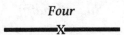

The rich and the poor are mingled together, drawn by the attraction of mutual affection. The motivating force is spontaneous good will between them. Such actions as these give meaning to the action of peace.

Five

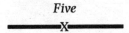

There are times in life when the social differences between people dissolve and people come together without pomp or ceremony and without affectation. Apart from natural disasters, national emergencies and the offices of the great leveller, *Death*, these times are usually very, very happy.

Six

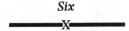

Malign forces are rising once again, and there is nothing you can do to stop them. There is no point in offering any form of retaliation, as you do not possess the necessary strength to overcome. Ignominy would be the result for you and your loved ones.

All you can do is accept your position. However, this does not imply an, 'If we can't beat them join them' attitude. This would be equally wrong. You are in a hopeless predicament.

HEXAGRAM 12

Superficiality

1 Is This Person a Compatible Partner?

The short answer is no. This person has many important lessons to learn about the work of life, and is encumbered by superficial and worthless values. In essence, this person is blind to everything else but their own petty desires. You should not cultivate association with a person of this calibre, and you must watch for any similarities you may find in your own nature.

2 Does My Partner Love Me?

Appearances in this case are definitely deceptive. The person in question is capable of an effective facade, but is not interested in evolving through love. Love tends to attract love, but if you are attracted to this person it may well be for some other reason – you must not be deluded into thinking that love is at the root of it. If love is not at the root of your attraction, then you may be certain that something less wholesome in your nature is, and needs to be very clearly understood. Only in this way will the conflict between the appearance of things and their reality be adequately resolved in your heart.

3 Do We Have a Future Together?

The time is not propitious to think of the future in terms of a truly fulfilling love relationship. The oracle is clear about this. You must not act.

4 What is the Most Important Attitude to Adopt at This Time?

The oracle advises that you withdraw into seclusion and foster spiritual strength, ignoring the demands of those less worthy than yourself. Only in quiet meditation and the cultivation of clarity of mind will you best hear what your heart is saying to you, and only when you have heard what your heart is saying can you act with strength. The time has not come. Do not act.

5 Why Has Our Relationship Broken Down?

The basis of your relationship was founded on the quicksand of material values, and fuelled by superficial desires. From the very beginning the roots of this relationship were too weak for growth. The only way to deal with such a relationship is to withdraw from it to a position of inner strength, self-reliance, and reliance on that which you know to have true inner worth.

6 Will We Get Back Together?

The present is so unfavourable as a time for growth that you are aware that decline has already set in. Certainly, this is not an appropriate time to contemplate any form of reconciliation. It is a time for personal self-examination.

7 What Can I Do to Put Things Right?

You must not allow yourself to be influenced by attractive but superficial appearances. You must hold to what is higher in your nature, even if this means breaking off from another person. Close proximity to a person of this nature at this time is not advised. This person is inclined to use other people for purely selfish motives without regard to their worth. You may be just another person being exploited. Alternatively, you may be tempted to exploit your partner without regard to inner worth. If so, you should immediately desist from this way of thinking.

8 What Do I Most Want From Life?

You want to retain your integrity at all costs.

THE LINES

One

You must safeguard your future possibilities even if this means withdrawing entirely from people who in any way threaten your integrity.

Two

You must be watchful for the guile of those who want something from you, but who have little to offer themselves. It may be that you can help them without intending to, by holding firmly to your own principles, if these are strongly based upon integrity. This is good for them, if you can bear the consequences. However, it is not advised that you expose yourself to such people.

A willingness to endure difficult times, without at the same time compromising with less worthy people, enables you to bring about success in your own life.

Three

You should know that people who require influence over others without truly deserving this position of power eventually become aware of their own inadequacy. This awareness leads them back to themselves and provides an opportunity for self-renewal along a better path of action.

Four

The situation is changing, from one of immobility to mobility, stagnation to dynamism. A path is clearing in the darkness. To understand certain important responsibilities, one must feel a calling in order to acquire the necessary control over a situation. If a person is presumptuous about his position, he may fail. If a person really has a vocation for a certain line of work, others will recognise this and support that person, because they are of a like mind, and will participate in the work and assist towards its completion.

If the work and person suit each other, success comes automatically, but there is a warning against arrogance.

Five

When things are going well and according to plan, one must be constantly mindful of hidden dangers. The danger here is specifically in the attitude of arrogance which arises in fortunate times. If one is sufficiently humble, one is less likely to make serious blunders and more likely to make better use of the opportunities offered, thereby enhancing the chances of continuing success. If one is not heedful of these dangerous attitudes, confusion may result.

Six

Certain stagnant situations can only be re-enlivened and re-energised by the right kind of person. A stagnant and lifeless situation can remain forever stagnant unless revitalised by the right kind of energy. Continuous effort of a creative nature must be made in order to stimulate creative activity from inaction. Perseverance will *earn* rewards. Do not trust to windfalls.

The important thing to note here is that the quality of the effort, together with the quality of the person, must not be underestimated. Both are essential in the creation of peaceful equilibrium and dynamic activity.

HEXAGRAM 13

Peace in the World

1 Is This Person a Compatible Partner?

You have a strong sense of the meaning of higher love. Any question of who is or who is not a compatible partner implies for you the way in which your relationship fits in with a larger social order; this will include mutual friends and family, as well as in a wider sense of society in general.

You recognise the importance to you of a peaceful co-existence and how this involves personal strength and being mutually receptive to each other's ideas and feelings. All these qualities are present at one level or another in the relationship.

This relationship has the capacity for great achievements. Together – all other things being equal – you and your partner are able to make a considerable contribution to the well-being of others in some particular area of life. Where there is a *will* there is a *way*; there is very little in the world you cannot achieve together, so powerful is your empathy. You are made for each other. As a pair you have a tremendous aptitude for organising your values in accordance with the *universal will.*

2 Does My Partner Love Me?

The love between you is profound. Together you have love enough for others to share.

3 Do We Have a Future Together?

Here the answer is contained in the question, the operative word being *together*; your private aims are also the aims of the wider social group in which you develop your identity.

Conversely, if within the social group there are many conflicting aims then the future will be on shaky ground.

Where there are agreed aims, then people naturally gather together. Thus the future is created. Common aims and common feelings unite a team. Ask yourself then, 'Do my partner and I have the same principal objectives? Do we care about the same things? Do our objectives accord with the wider aims of humanity as we feel and understand them?' and finally, 'Are these things important enough for us to live together?'

Positive answers mean a positive future and *vice versa*.

4 What is the Most Important Attitude to Adopt at This Time?

Every attitude often implies complex assumptions but here the assumption is very simple: assume that unification with others is of paramount importance. You must align your attitudes according to this idea. There is no room for anything divisive.

5 Why Has Our Relationship Broken Down?

Instead of enhancing your potential for creating inner meaning and order in your lives you have complicated matters needlessly and created confusion. You did not realise the value which could have come from this relationship as you are under a misapprehension that other things are more important. Such a misconception has created a divide between you and other people instead of bringing you together. Divisive tendencies arising from mistaken intentions always bring pain and destruction; rarely do they result in good.

There is an order in the universe; actions which transgress the law of the universe – universal principles – always do so at personal expense. We pay for every transgression. Life participates in the prevailing order for good or for ill. Herein lies the human choice – for good or for ill? The moral development of mankind will have universal consequences. Clever self delusion could cost more than it is possible to pay except by life itself. (In universal terms this is not a price we ought to pay for the propagation of deliberate misconceptions.)

The oracle states, 'if you create divisions in the world, then you create divisions in yourself.' Division in the self is painful confusion. It is difficult to withstand such a predicament for very long and certainly no relationship can survive for very long like this.

6 Will We Get Back Together?

At the outset the relationship was on a good course and you both recognised the potential in it, but then the relationship degenerated into chaos due to a confusion of conflicting values. Perhaps the downfall began when you began to cast your net too widely. Perhaps one or both of you began to want things which you knew the other could not give; perhaps your expectations outstripped the basics of happiness; perhaps over familiarity has grown into ugly contempt.

This hexagram is about unity with others, including your partner. You have drawn this oracle because events are tending towards unity and not division. Therefore there are excellent grounds for optimism – providing you both perceive the relationship in its wider context and do not view it as exclusive. A reconciliation will only succeed if you allow it to grow.

7 What Can I Do to Put Things Right?

You must understand that in order to achieve a true union with your partner and others you must abolish secrets between you immediately. *You must be prepared to trust each other implicitly and explicitly.* All dark secrets must be brought out into the light of day and openly *forgiven.*

Joy arising from unity with others must be shared. Anything which tends against this is potentially divisive and harmful. Trust is the basis for ordered possibilities. Truly great things comes from such trust.

You must prepare for relationships before they are entered into.

Talk more *with* your partner directly, person to person, face to face, and not through intermediaries. Do not speak *at* your partner or others. The difference is crucial. Speak as human beings, not as important people.

8 What Do I Most Want From Life?

Your heart's desire is a noble one – namely that you wish to fit in with a larger social order and be of use, so that organically, it may function towards higher objectives, not only for yourself but for the world in general.

THE LINES

One

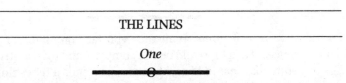

You have to be clear about your reasons for wanting to work with others – in clear, unequivocal terms – *before* you begin work. Assume others want to work together. As long as this remains a true desire things will go well.

Two

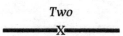

Often within a larger working organisation smaller groups form. If these smaller groups form around ideas which do not accord with the overriding principles and aims of the larger group a faction is created.

A faction which opposes the common interests of the group as a whole is always based upon selfish and malign motives. This is a dangerous situation, for it de-stabilises the whole group and threatens to break it down.

The idea of creating a faction or allowing one to subsist must be wholly opposed. A small faction can grow stronger and the result will be that the whole group will be brought into disrepute. The whole group will therefore be humiliated and weakened.

Three

A faction within a group which is based upon selfish motives is like a cancer which slowly eats away at the whole group. You are under a misapprehension, about the nature and aims of the whole group in your attempt to oppose this cancerous faction by becoming a member of a cancerous faction yourself. This means going about in a perennial state of mistrust towards the whole group. You do the whole group no good by holding to your position and by entertaining ideas of taking the 'other side' by surprise.

If the situation persists you will achieve only one purpose, that of alienating one another and bringing about the destruction of the whole group. No other outcome is likely if one participates in such an inimical process. Cease from this course altogether and demonstrate to others the wisdom of so doing.

Four

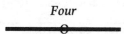

You and your protagonist realise as you face one another that the consequences of a fight would be the complete and total destruction of all you both hold dear in life. This awareness puts a refreshingly sane light upon your predicament.

Acting upon this mutual awareness the doors open from both ends, offering the possibility of an alternative solution.

A genuine reconciliation brings good fortune for all concerned.

Five

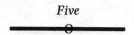

The possibility of a peaceful and satisfactory reconciliation presents itself, but the circumstances are frustrating. One side cannot fight the other without both sides losing. This is a contest where neither side has even the remotest chance of winning.

The realisation of this by both sides enables you both to adopt a responsible and sane attitude, and this has the effect of safeguarding the possibility for a genuinely peaceful agreement, based upon a change of heart and a sincere open-handed trust.

You realise that beneath the conflict over details you are all of *one accord*. If you all keep this in mind and make it the basis for working towards a real reconciliation, eventually you will overcome all the difficulties.

Joy will succeed the sadness of your hearts; and, as Confucius puts it '. . . when you come to understand what is in your inmost hearts your words will be sweet and strong, like the fragrance of orchids.'

Six

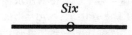

At heart we are at one with everybody else, but at present there is a nagging hollow feeling. This is because we are on the fringes of events. We need to feel the warmth of true accord by participating in the scheme of things. Although the situation is not perfect, our hearts are in the right place and because of this we can grow closer to the higher aim of mankind as a whole, which is perfect unity.

We can take real comfort from the fact that where the heart is willing, there is a way and that elusive warm feeling will come in the end.

The experience of life is complete only when there is peace in the hearts of all peoples in the world. When this peace is achieved mankind evolves to a new plane of awareness. Many people in the world already know what this awareness means.

NOTE: One of the principal assumptions of the *I Ching* is that nothing and nobody in the world is expendable, except evil.

Only within a group can an individual hope to find a suitable sphere of activity. The *I Ching* has a basic *postulate* and a basic *requirement* for all those who come to it for wisdom and guidance and help.

The *postulate* is this: All situations are in a constant state of change; nothing is fixed eternally.

In every situation (and so in ourselves), there lies the seeds of growth and change. A new situation is constantly being born. Hope, love and joy can never dry up.

The *requirement* is this: We must always be capable of adapting to new situations and of finding the appropriate answers to every problem; we must forever seek new food for the inner feast and be ready to digest it.

True fellowship is only possible when the world – all countries, cultures, systems of belief – is at peace. The inmost hearts of all peoples in the world speak the same language, this is the language of peace.

The broken hearts of the world can only be healed with the love of us all.

HEXAGRAM 14

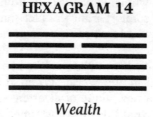

Wealth

1 Is This Person a Compatible Partner?

You are fortunate indeed to encounter such a person. Although outwardly this person may seem ineffective – and perhaps too self-effacing, even self-deprecating – nevertheless he or she is possessed of great qualities of inner strength and modesty. This person is unselfish by nature and has cultivated this quality, and is also wise in the ways of the world.

2 Does My Partner Love Me?

Yes, your partner is very well disposed towards you, but there is room for growth. Stress your most positive feelings more strongly.

3 Do We Have a Future Together?

Certainly you do, but it won't be easy all the way. You must be aware that you will encounter difficulties and retain those good qualities which you have between you in order to combat them.

4 What is the Most Important Attitude to Adopt at This Time?

Many of the difficulties you have experienced arise from your attitude towards wealth and the way this has affected your attitude towards other people. Through your conceit you have become blind to the feelings of others. The value of material things has increased in your mind beyond the value of individual people, and negative influences taken hold in your heart. These will manifest themselves as unfeeling arrogance and wastefulness, and are therefore the cause for great blame attaching to you.

The proper attitude for you to hold at this time is one of humility based on an understanding of your own blindness. It might do you good to entrust some of your wealth to other people for their use.

5 Why Has Our Relationship Broken Down?

Although great inner qualities such as unselfishness and modesty are present, they can only be maintained by a constant battle against their opposites. If such a relationship as yours has broken down, it is because of such opposite qualities manifesting in you, in your partner or in both of you as selfishness, arrogance, greediness and conceit at your good fortune. All these characteristics bring darkness into a relationship, and also – less importantly – lead to bad administration of possessions, which will ultimately be the reason for their loss. If the relationship has broken down, you have only your greed to blame.

6 Will We Get Back Together?

If you and your partner have actually separated, then any possibility of a reunion will not be based upon considerations of material wealth, but rather of spiritual values. In times of unhappiness, material possessions can be very cumbersome and it may well be that you wish this particular aspect of your life did not exist. The test for you and your partner at this time is to see through these material attributes to the spiritual side of life which is the true foundation of a relationship.

7 What Can I Do to Put Things Right?

What is required from you if you are not to bring further harm to yourself and others is a revolutionary change in attitude. The advice given in answer to question 4 sets out the appropriate perspective for you to adopt in bringing about such a change.

If up until now you have been selfish with your money and

possessions, reluctant to share your wealth with friends and family, then now is the time to change. Greedy people who hoard their wealth tend to lose it in one way or another, and rarely, while they still possess wealth, does it bring them any joy. Where wealth is shared and is used to bring others happiness, it tends to increase itself. Here we do not speak of profligate spending, but of a genuine desire to be *kind*.

8 What Do I Most Want From Life?

Your chief desire is to acquire even more wealth than you already possess. If, through your wealth, you can express a kind spirit, you will discover a new and not displeasing dimension to life; not only will you find that others will be more kindly disposed towards you, but also that your fortunes will improve.

THE LINES

One

The position of wealth is new to you and you have yet to tread on anyone's toes. It is important for you to remember that your situation naturally attracts difficulties. If you retain your modesty and humility, it is unlikely that you will make any serious mistakes.

Two

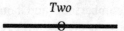

Useful possessions attract useful and able people. You are warned against setting too much store by fixed property.

Three

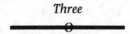

You are warned against being grasping in material matters. You are not asked to give your wealth away, but you should understand that wealth is to be shared. Only by sharing your possessions will they bring you any joy.

Four

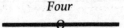

Do not make the mistake of comparing your wealth with the wealth of your neighbours, as this will only lead to envy or greed, or both. Such an attitude will complicate your life beyond belief.

Five

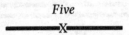

You are a good-hearted person, and your attitude towards others is wholesome and kind. However, you should temper your benevolence with sufficient awareness and respect for other people's methods of doing things. If you do this, then you honour your good fortune.

Six

You put your wealth and position at the disposal of a good and wise person. In this way you benefit from this person's wisdom, and ensure your continuing good fortune.

HEXAGRAM 15

Modesty

1 Is This Person a Compatible Partner?

Your partner is attracted to you because you are by nature a modest person. This is a very desirable characteristic in any individual. That you are modest does not mean that you are self-effacing or self-deprecating, neither does it mean that you are a fool. A person with a modest disposition is able to view other people with clearer vision than is, say, a conceited person.

A boastful, arrogant person is unlikely to attract you. You are more likely to get on with a person who is of a similar disposition to yourself. Such people do not make great demands on others. It is highly likely that your judgement of your partner is clear and accurate. Confidence in your appraisal of your partner's character is justified.

2 Does My Partner Love Me?

Modest people are the easiest to love. You offer nothing that stands in the way of the honest affections of others. Modest people always attract respect from other people and respect very easily grows into love.

3 Do We Have a Future Together?

The oracle's attitude towards you is extremely favourable. The future is placed in your hands, and from your partner's point of view it is in a very safe place.

You are not the sort of person to allow good fortune to go to your head. As a worker, you try to take an interest in everything you do. This provides a very firm foundation for the future.

4 What is the Most Important Attitude to Adopt at This Time?

A modest person is in a very good position to view the world objectively. Since you are free of conceit, you act with a certain clarity which commends you to other people. Sustain your attitude, as it will enable you to carry through even the most difficult problems in life with greater ease.

5 Why Has Our Relationship Broken Down?

Wilful, less balanced people may find the modest person easy prey. It is not difficult for someone who has the will, to exploit you or to take advantage of your pleasant disposition. It is possible that if you have been the object of such mistreatment, you have become aware of it and have reacted very strongly against it.

So rarely does modesty inflict harm upon others, that it is much more likely that harm has been inflicted on you, and you have taken the appropriate measures to extricate yourself from the situation. This indicates, superficially at least, the reason for the breakdown of a relationship.

6 Will We Get Back Together?

Modesty does not necessarily imply self-consciousness or shyness (which is quite a different characteristic). Modest people are people of great integrity, and they also possess a tremendous capacity for forgiveness. If your perception is not clouded by an inflated sense of your own importance, then you do not take advantage of the weakness of others.

Your modesty is your strength. If you are inclined to be forgiving, then a reconciliation is always possible. However, under the circumstances, you may well be the kind of person who is once bitten, twice shy. You can trust your own wisdom.

7 What Can I Do to Put Things Right?

You have a tremendous capacity to restore things to their proper place and create harmony and balance once again. If this is what you want in this case, it is well within your power to achieve it.

8 What Do I Most Want From Life?

Modesty is a quality which brings out the best in people. Your desire is to live your life to the full in the light of wisdom, and above all you have a strange but wonderful hankering to be of service to others. Chiefly for this reason, the oracle highly favours you.

THE LINES

One

━━━━━X━━━━━

The cardinal quality in your character is that you are profoundly unassuming. This quality enables you to undertake even the most difficult of challenges. As you do not inflate issues out of due proportion, you are able to cope with very difficult tasks with what seems to others to be considerable ease.

Two

━━━━━X━━━━━

There are times when, because of your modesty, you have a profound influence on other people. This is one of those times, and acting from the heart brings you good fortune.

Three

━━━━━O━━━━━

You have achieved something for which you have been recognised. Your continuing modesty inspires greater affection from others and enables you to continue the good work, for which you will receive just rewards.

Four

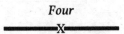

Excessive modesty can lead to an attitude of self-deprecation. Modesty in a person shows itself best in the context of work and doing things for others. Nothing is too much trouble for you, even minute particulars. The person who is too modest does not believe himself to be important enough to attend to such things. Do not underestimate your own worth, and certainly do not do so as a means of disclaiming certain responsibilities.

Five

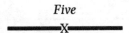

A truly modest person is not a weak person who allows other people to exploit him. This is a time when modesty should be combined with firmness to achieve what needs to be done without arousing resentment in others. The quality of the firmness in this situation is impersonal. There is a need for you to revitalise the meaning of modesty within you. You need to discipline your attitude towards yourself.

Six

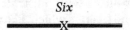

You know the difference between the pretence of modesty and real modesty. Only by being truly modest can you hope to dispel the illusions that other people have about themselves. It is very important that you act in this light in order to bring about these ends. There is no doubt that the situation deserves your attention, though you may feel reluctant to do anything about it out of a sense of modesty. Do not use this as an excuse.

Above all, modesty teaches by example rather than by explanation.

HEXAGRAM 16

Musical Harmony (Enthusiasm)

1 Is This Person a Compatible Partner?

This hexagram concerns itself with music. It is also concerned with those inspired actions and feelings which, like water flowing down the mountain, seek the paths of least resistance.

Music is an arrangement of sounds which are structured and ordered according to a time signature. The power of music is to draw elements together. Music – like no other language – has the power to speak directly from your heart to the hearts of others. Music has the power to absorb emotional tensions and to clarify feelings which would otherwise remain dark and obscure. Above all, music is the natural language of the universe. Within its inner symmetry and structure lie many of the secrets of life.

The universe itself is constantly moving and changing. Musical expression mirrors this movement best.

In music lies not only the power to express the common feeling of people but also to evoke common feelings which draw people together into a common identity. In this sense music is a potent catalyst for social unification. People are able to identify each other through a common taste in music; nations identify their culture through the music they produce.

For the person who draws this oracle, music represents an

important part of life. You are already aware of this and if you are not a composer yourself, you still enjoy in music the purer clarification of your own deeper feelings. This suggests that you possess in your nature a certain innate fluidity, a genuine willingness to follow the law of the universe. This will reflect in the way you experience life in general and in the ways in which you treat experience, especially in relations with people in general, not only your partner.

You are not one to consciously seek obstacles and difficulties; to follow the *Tao* of music is a natural tendency. So with your partner you will find the easiest and most natural means of communication and unity. You are compatible with your partner where you both allow for the spontaneous expressions of your mutual affections.

You are only likely to make a mistake in your choice of partner in life if your natural enthusiasm for uniting with others arises from an over exertion and distortion of your own deeper feelings.

However, the meaning of enthusiasm is to be filled with happiness, exuberance and joy. For a person like you it will be difficult to delude yourself about the feelings of others. You are naturally alive to other people's feelings, you can easily align yourself with them.

With you it is always the spontaneous expression of your joy which reaches home, reaches your partner's heart, bringing with it a wonderful, wordless understanding between you. All this allows for the release of tensions and the growth of love in the *spaces* between you.

2 Does My Partner Love Me?

You need to be attracted to a person who expresses their feelings for you in a subtle and uncomplicated way. The natural language of the emotions is music; the language of the body is dance; the language of the heart is its rhythm; the language of joy always expresses itself through enthusiasm. You are attracted best to highly positive, fearless people.

While these languages may express themselves with the precision of mathematics they can only be truly understood intuitively. Music (some music) has mysterious and invisible ways of communicating subtle ideas to all of us, ways we can only grasp through intuition.

The challenge in love for you is to find still purer, more subtle ways of expressing your feelings for your partner and for others.

3 Do We Have a Future Together?

The future of your relationship with your partner promises still greater possibilities of growing closer. Music is the medium which can connect you to still higher manifestations of love. Between you, you are likely to develop a higher notion of the meaning of time. In the popular sense 'the future' does not excite the usual anxieties because you have a better grasp on the possibilities of the present.

There is a tremendous potential for a beautiful flowering between you.

4 What is the Most Important Attitude to Adopt at This Time?

The word 'attitude' implies the conscious framing of a world view. The meaning of enthusiasm is that your world view is conditioned by an innate feeling of joy with which, across the panorama of experience, you are constantly in touch.

If you have drawn this oracle at this time, it is because you have already become aware of the part of you that tunes in and harmonises with the more profound order of the Universe as it is expressed in deeper human feelings.

Consciously or not, you tend to harmonise naturally with your partner and the world at large – the better feelings in the world.

5 Why Has Our Relationship Broken Down?

The laws which govern nature are inviolable. If you oppose nature you oppose yourself. If you disturb nature's balance you disturb your own balance. We cannot escape our preternatural connection with everything else in the world. All we can do is distinguish objects in the world and select modes of activity according to our awareness of choices and our perceptions of the world.

Music has the power to express love. It has the power to unite soul with body. It has the greatest propensity to link the consciousness of the left-hand side of the brain with the consciousness of the right side. It has the greatest power to act as a medium through which the invisible communicates with the visible world; it has the power to mediate in the dialogue between creator and humanity. In this sense it is mankind's supreme achievement. Through music mankind is able to share one voice in song.

In the human heart music has the power to release feelings as opposed to locking them up, the power to evoke emotions, to bring them alive.

These are the powers, in whole or in part, which govern your relationship with your partner. If your relationship has broken down – and this oracle makes no suggestion that events have come to such a pass – it is because you have transgressed these powers, abused them in some way. Discordance has been permitted to supplant the laws of harmony; time and experience have fragmented into a chaotic disunity.

The pertinent emotion aroused between you will be resentment. It is the divisive power of this emotion which will have caused a rift between your love for each other.

6 Will We Get Back Together?

The path back to mutual understanding is the path of least resistance; follow the path which most naturally suggests itself to you. Do not go looking for unseen obstacles where there are none. It is in your most elevated feelings that you best understand each other, appeal to these in each other. Only natural inspiration can suggest the way. There are no cut and dried rules, no automatic recipe. Only through these higher feelings can humanity be united. These are the feelings you understand to be sacred, or special, beyond doubt; it is the 'alive' feeling of meaningfulness.

7 What Can I Do to Put Things Right?

Resentment is the emotional tension which arises out of pride and intolerance. You cannot be reconciled, you cannot hope to heal the divide until you both overcome the resentment between you. Music and dance, a shared activity, are the languages of reconciliation; these will form the bridge back to each other's hearts.

8 What Do I Most Want From Life?

You are an aspirant for the highest joy. You want to attain the most elevated spiritual feelings with your partner. You want to touch with your heart the beautiful unseen symmetry of love in which you are enfolded; you will fly here on the wings of inspiration.

93

THE LINES

One

You have misunderstood the meaning of enthusiasm and this is expressed by an ugly display of arrogance. Enthusiasm is an expression of emotional joy and not a footstool for one-upmanship games. If 'enthusiasm', as you understand it, is a means by which you create divisions between people, then you eventually will attract misfortune.

Two

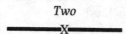

You are at peace with yourself. Since you do not swing between emotional extremes you can perceive things as they are, while others around you may be dazzled by the light of day.

A new time is dawning, but those around you cannot read the signs, as you can. Act upon what you see. You possess a rare gift of insight upon which others may depend. You understand good and bad, light and dark, weakness and strength; this perception lends a peculiar potency to your decisions, for which others admire you. Good fortune will be the result.

Three

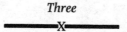

You are relying too heavily upon another for your cue to action. There is nothing especially reprehensible in this. What is significant for you, however, is a sense of timing. The right thing must be done at the right time if it is to have the right effect.

You must be decisive at the decisive moment to act.

Four

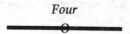

You are endowed with the rare quality of a completely positive self-belief, unhindered by misgivings and limiting doubts about your own abilities. You inspire confidence in others, raising their enthusiasm to meet the challenges at hand. By arousing the spirit of co-operation in others you enhance an already certain success.

Five

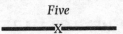

Your enthusiasm does not meet with the corresponding energy of approval from others. The atmosphere is like a wet blanket over a flame. Oddly enough this has a salubrious effect upon you as it prevents you from being carried away by your enthusiasm. Had you been, you would have landed yourself in trouble.

Six

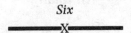

Your enthusiasm is entirely misplaced. However, it is unlikely that you will go too far, and this will enable you to haul in the reins, as it were, to avert any damage which might have been done.

HEXAGRAM 17

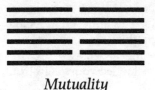

Mutuality

1 Is This Person a Compatible Partner?

Deep in your heart there is a willingness to give the best of yourself, but you are encountering some difficulty in doing this. The problem does not hinge upon the rightness or wrongness of your partner, but on how best to accord with the circumstances in which you find yourselves. There is a need for give and take in any relationship. This hexagram, in general, emphasises this give and take. The accent is on your ability to receive the initiative from your partner at times when you most feel inclined to be the person who initiates.

It takes a very open-hearted person to be receptive to the initiatives of another, but in your case everything depends on your being very receptive to your partner. This means avoiding the strong temptation to elicit responses by devious or underhand means.

A greater trust in your partner is called for, and in this you must be consistent. That is to say, it is not enough for you to make concessions, or allowances 'just for now', but to perceive that you can only gain access to the more precious parts by a willingness to listen attentively and consistently to the feelings your partner has. If you are seriously trying to achieve this trust, your fundamental willingness to give more is rewarded by a deeper appreciation of your partner's feelings. In this way you grow closer to each other, and follow each other, rather than one following the other. Both lead and both follow. Joy may express itself in this paradox of love.

The warning implied is that by failing to adapt to the signals you receive from your partner, you fail also to register the appropriate time to lead or to follow. You therefore lose the sense of the relationship altogether. However, by being adaptable, you learn to receive affection as well as to give it, and so the cycle between you is maintained.

2 Does My Partner Love Me?

One can never demand to be loved by another, and it is a mistake to try.

All one can do is to inspire such love by a willingness to listen and to feel the needs of another person, and to let that person act upon you. But this willingness must not be inspired by craftiness or sly manoeuvring and manipulation. The willingness must come straight from the heart of the other person and from your heart, if it is to be of any value.

If these conditions are fulfilled, then one can expect to deserve at least what one is giving.

3 Do We Have a Future Together?

For some people, the most difficult thing in the world is to learn the art of patience. There are times when things must move quickly, and there are times when things must take their own course. This is a situation where time must take its own course, and you must be patient.

The future is seeded in the present. Each passing moment has a rhythm and a pattern for the perceptive eye to behold, either joyfully, or with fear. It can be said, however, that the tendency here is positive, but you are warned that the future is most inviting when you demand least of it.

4 What is the Most Important Attitude to Adopt at This Time?

Optimism.

Your optimism can be based on two foundations. One is false, and one is true. However, optimism is favourable if you are sure that it is based upon the right foundation.

The tendency of the circumstances is towards a state of joy, rather than sorrow and, on balance, the oracle suggests that you are well equipped to respond to the feelings of your partner. As this is the natural tendency, you should follow it and this will bring you closer together.

5 Why Has Our Relationship Broken Down?

The natural state between people is dynamic harmony. Whenever this harmony is wilfully and deliberately disturbed, the relationship automatically breaks down.

The situation here is that the breakdown of the relationship is the direct result of failing to adapt to the initiatives of your partner. This means failing to be receptive to the affection of your partner. Such selfishness has blinded you to your partner's feelings. This failure to follow where you most desire to lead is brought about by a constantly repeated habit of mind, wherein you place more importance on yourself than others, in this case especially your partner. Your sense of self-importance makes you rigid and unreceptive, inflexible, and therefore incapable of adapting.

All this means a lack of breadth and clarity of perception, both of which are required to understand the circumstances as they move and change around you.

6 Will We Get Back Together?

Once the cycle has been broken, it can only be repaired with the help and consent of your partner. However, the I Ching makes no promises in this regard since each circumstance carries its own complex implications. You must perceive these intuitively.

7 What Can I Do to Put Things Right?

The first requirement is to be aware that separation has occurred because of your own inflexibility and lack of receptivity to the person you desire most.

The way back from this state is to recognise the importance of learning to adapt according to the circumstances which surround you, and then to be willing to adapt. Action from the heart is sensitive to the actual circumstances and this affords a proper stance on the world, which is the most valuable beginning to the process of putting yourself back into perspective.

It is imperative that you are consistently adaptable. There is no weight in flighty considerations.

You must mean to be receptive; you must want to understand.

8 What Do I Most Want From Life?

Your heart's desire can best be understood in terms of your greatest fear.

Your fear is that by yielding trust to your partner, you will be harmed.

This fear is unfounded. You must find a way to dispel it, in order to arrive at the knowledge that by yielding to your partner you will not be harmed. Until you actually risk trusting your partner, you will never learn the truth.

THE LINES

One

The only way a person who holds a prominent position can grow is to seek out and find people outside his or her usual circle to challenge those ideas and beliefs which have been held so long. A person cannot grow by seeking their own reflection exclusively in those who act as faithful mirrors. One must not be deluded by the praise of sycophants.

The willingness to allow the widest possible range of views to enter our considerations is the way to grow in wisdom and understanding and so advance our position in the world.

Wisdom often comes from unlikely sources.

Look for people beyond your circle of friends. Do not rely solely upon the agreement of people with whose pattern of thinking you are familiar and in accord.

Two

You are urged to choose your friends with care. We are coloured in life by those people who share and condition our experiences. This is perfectly natural, but we must be discriminating.

Some people are more impressionable than others – the oracle emphasises discrimination as a means of warning.

If we share ourselves with others who display unworthiness, we may become like them. We should learn to discriminate between those who truly wish to be with us and those who wish to be with us for some other reason.

Three

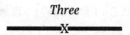

For a long time you have been aware that your life has been guided by an implicit search for a true direction. You have arrived at that point of awareness and now know the path to take. This brings you a sense of relief, but unfortunately, you are sad to leave behind some of those with whom you had some empathy in bygone days. But now that a new, higher path suggests itself, you must follow it without distraction.

It is at these times that you must not give way to wayward ideas. You must be resolute.

You will attract the kind of people who follow this path and similar paths, and in the end there will be no regrets.

Four

Influential people very often attract sycophants. These are people who court the attention of an influential person for personal gain, and through no common feeling.

Relationships which have no basis in common feelings are mutually harmful. The only way to deal with sycophants is to speak clearly of your intentions, making certain that they understand you. It is imperative that you leave no ambiguity in their minds concerning your convictions. This is best for them and their growth as well as for you. In order to effect this, you must be clean of all selfishness. You cannot afford to stand on pride, as pride clouds your personal honesty.

Five

You are following a star of love with utmost faith. You will be blessed for your constancy, for such a calling is rare indeed.

Six

———X———

When a person is determined to act in the world through his work, he often calls upon wisdom in the form of some other, older and wiser, to assist and advise. This is well appointed. The work and the spirit join these two people, and so the follower acquires dignity in the eyes of those in authority.

Good fortune comes when the wise and the willing share a common feeling.

HEXAGRAM 18

Work on What has been Spoiled

1 Is This Person a Compatible Partner?

Lately you have been developing a line of activity in an inflexible environment; either a person or the general atmosphere has impeded your progress at a crucial time. This, coupled with your own present lack of fluidity has rather upset the work, or the basis upon which you are doing the work.

Your partner is involved in this state of affairs in a deep way, but for you, personally, he or she has a positive effect on the situation, enabling you to begin to get the situation once again under control. In this way, your partner has a beneficial influence on you.

2 Does My Partner Love Me?

Your partner expresses love by being supportive, but nevertheless, the initiative at the present time in all working activities, lies squarely upon your shoulders.

3 Do We Have a Future Together?

What determines the future here is the energy which you put into your work.

No work no future.

We must distinguish here what we mean by work. Work in the conventional sense is generally understood to mean gainful employment. This is not necessarily the work implied here, but rather energy which is used in a constructive way in order to produce finished results.

4 What is the Most Important Attitude to Adopt at This Time?

If you have been temporarily stopped, you should nevertheless recognise that the work must go on. The best attitude is a relaxed and cheerful openness of character, which does not allow itself to be distracted by external influences. You must move gently forward in the work to break your inertia. You have a reasonably free atmosphere in which to work, and you must be resolute in setting about working.

An energetic start soon lifts the spirits but, to some extent you must be self-reliant, and you should not rely too heavily upon your partner for the time being.

5 Why Has Our Relationship Broken Down?

Any failure now is due primarily to a lack of discipline and energy in sustaining your efforts in your chosen direction.

After a period when you have been halted, you must retain your decisive attitude. It may well be that you have not made the decision to carry on and you have allowed the situation to deteriorate. This is likely to be at the root of any collapse.

6 Will We Get Back Together?

Herein lies the challenge.

Wherever there is a challenge there are attendant difficulties, but in this case, if you do not take up the challenge, then it is possible that you will become prey to the corrupting influences of society.

The only way to combat personal apathy is to reinvigorate interest within yourself. The only way to combat apathy in society is to stir up public opinion. It is a matter of energy.

7 What Can I Do to Put Things Right?

If it is not too late, then you must find it within yourself to muster the energy and decisive power to get down to the work. Hopefully the situation can be remedied.

Certainly it is proper to be busy at this time: this is *not* the time to be lazy.

8 What Do I Most Want From Life?

Your main object is to put right what has gone wrong, in order to continue with a process that started well and promises to end well. The general implication of this hexagram is 'stop your dilly dallying! Get on with the work!'

THE LINES

One

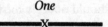

You are in danger of being trapped by outdated and out-moded ways of behaviour. You should dispense with them, which will not be difficult as they have not become so entrenched that you are unconscious of them. You cannot blame your father if you are spending your time trying to put right what he has allowed to go to waste.

What is required here is a complete reordering of the basis of your actions and the reinvigoration of the moral principles by which you lead your life. The oracle suggests that such a restructuring of your life will go well, if you take the matter seriously enough.

Two

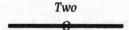

The deterioration of the situation is symbolised by the phrase 'what has been spoiled by the mother'.

However do not be over-zealous in putting things to right again. Remember that other people have difficulties and problems of their own with which they must wrestle, and so be correspondingly good-natured while picking up threads and continuing with your own work.

Three

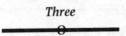

Sometimes it is possible to be a little over keen and over zealous in rectifying past blunders. This is likely to have an antagonising effect (but this is not serious). It is, however, certainly correct that a vigorous attempt to put things right is better than a wishy-washy attempt, and no real harm can be done.

Four

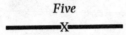

Problems which are not solved immediately often grow roots, and produce ugly flowers later. This is happening now. If the ugly flowers are allowed to blossom, you will regret it.

Five

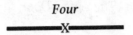

Any attempt on your part to put right what has now been allowed to become a corrupting influence attracts help and praise from other people. Good fortune.

Six

Not every person who is in possession of a highly developed moral character is duty-bound to give effect to his wisdom by becoming involved in politics or social life. Some people prefer to work on greater self-realisation, and any work in this direction serves mankind in general without the necessity of participating in the details of social politics.

However, refraining from participating can never be justified if a supercilious or over-critical attitude is adopted towards the world from which you have detached yourself. If you really feel strongly about something then you must be prepared to do something about it, and not content yourself with idle criticism of other people's ineptitude.

HEXAGRAM 19

The Open Door

1 Is This Person a Compatible Partner?

The influences on the present time in your life indicate joy and effectiveness for somebody concerned with helping and teaching other people. This is a time of approaching growth and light. The import of this hexagram stretches over a period of months to come, and since it is generally favourable, it may indicate that any connections with people, either on an intimate level or in professional circles, are well favoured. There is no indication whatsoever that you should be particularly suspicious or cautious about any particular individual, but at present your mind is focussed on finishing particular work. You already perceive that you must work hard and with dedication, but because of this illuminating time, your work will go well.

Your relationship with your partner will be successful, prosperous, and it will flower. Your ability to blend wisdom, work and tolerance for all people who come under your influence proves to be highly beneficial. All this helps in the general process of keeping negative and malefic forces under control.

You are a person who has a tremendous amount to give to others, with the ability to give it in matters concerning the way they behave towards each other in their daily lives. The *I Ching* has a high regard for such people, and calls them 'sages'. They have a special part to play. Your influence upon your partner is highly positive; you are accessible to each other, you see eye to eye on many of the important issues between you and, above all, you can work together as well as live together. You are highly compatible.

2 Does My Partner Love Me?

Since you display such a readiness to be of help and assistance – as a guide and as a teacher, as well as a companion – you cannot help but attract admiration.

Your presence imparts a natural sense of security which can be depended upon by others, and naturally your partner feels this and is reassured by it. Your partner feels a very strong attachment to you, a profound empathy and loyalty which it would be very difficult to undermine.

3 Do We Have a Future Together?

Periods of ascent are always followed by periods of descent, and although this hexagram concerns itself primarily with a period of light and growth, the qualities of the person described are not subject to the same transcience. The person here is aware that times change, that periods of darkness follow periods of light and that light follows darkness, and prepares for them. Such a person's wisdom encompasses as many possibilities as experience can give. However, if your future with your partner is based on past experience, you may certainly anticipate a future together which will be, on balance, more rewarding and positive, sustaining and caring. It is precisely because you do care that the oracle looks so favourably on you, your life, friendships and works. There is nothing to fear in the future.

4 What is the Most Important Attitude to Adopt at This Time?

Since you are a person who feels a keen sense of responsibility to those people who have been placed in your care, and since your authority is respected by those same people, you are best able to honour such trust with a renewed sense of kindness and increased willingness to place your wisdom at their service.

Having this sense of clarity of purpose, you will not only be able to take full advantage of the propitious time, but also to justify the trust that has been placed in you. Thus you provide for less propitious times through constantly building up goodwill.

5 Why Has Our Relationship Broken Down?

This is a time when the forces of light are growing steadily all the time. If, as is unlikely, you are encountering serious problems with your partner and with other people, then these are likely to be short lived.

There is no real cause for alarm or fear that what has already been achieved will be spoilt. Any upset is fleeting, and will almost certainly right itself. However, the oracle does underline the importance of being consistently hard working and at the same time maintaining a consistent tolerance of others. There is no suggestion of blame attaching to any individual or situation.

If there are any particular circumstances to which you should pay close attention, then these details will emerge in the lines. If you have received any moving lines in consulting this oracle, the situation will be clarified there, and you must interpret your fortune accordingly.

6 Will We Get Back Together?

As indicated by the preceding question, it is unlikely that there has been any division or parting, and if there has been one it will only have been a temporary and fleeting thing, and certainly nothing upon which serious attention should be placed. Unless the oracle indicates otherwise in any moving line, there is nothing to suggest that an optimistic attitude towards your partner is not appropriate. Certainly if you perceive the possibility of unsavoury influences coming to power at some later point, you should move against them immediately and without delay.

7 What Can I Do to Put Things Right?

Your role in life is to help and teach others. By persevering in this task, and by having faith in your own ability and wisdom, your influence will continue to be beneficial to others. Nothing of any importance should have gone wrong. If there has been a mishap it will right itself with a little prompting.

8 What Do I Most Want From Life?

You are principally a teacher of wisdom for all, without discrimination. Your gift to mankind is your untiring readiness to teach and care. This is a noble heart's desire and the oracle looks very favourably upon you.

You need to feel that your time with people is worthwhile; that the seeds you plant will grow into beautiful ideas in other people's minds, and that the guidance you give will foster new levels of awareness.

THE LINES

One

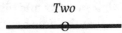

Throughout the various strata of society there are various levels of influence.

The situation here is that an opportunity arises for you to join with other people in a good cause, and you come to the attention of those people in more influential circles who have an affinity with such matters. The warning implied in this line is that despite such beneficial influences and intentions, you must guard against allowing yourself to be carried away. Good fortune is indicated.

Two

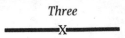

The portents of this line are excellent for you because you possess the necessary inner qualities of steadfastness and resolution, and an awareness that the things of this world are transient and fleeting. Therefore you are able to pursue your life's objectives with courage and fortitude, without misgivings or loss of perspective.

Three

X

This line describes a person who, because of his favourable position in relation to other people has, or may become, headstrong and frivolous. Such attitudes are dangerous because they threaten the integrity of your actions and ultimately lead to no good. On the other hand, if you are aware of this possibility, you may avoid abusing your situation by becoming more keenly aware of the responsibilities which have been entrusted to you.

Four

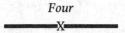

The situation is very favourable for a person of influence and position, able to recognise a person of ability, who is taken into confidence without due discrimination.

Five

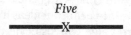

This line describes a person with great responsibilities.

The advice given is concerned with the wisdom to delegate matters to appropriate people who have the necessary power and ability to conduct affairs with efficiency and correct conduct. Everything depends on the ability to properly assess character. Having delegated the power effectively and appropriately, you must have sufficient faith in your delegates to let them do their own work.

Without such faith the wrong delegates may be enlisted. The outcome implies a judgement of your abilities.

Six

The subject of this line is a very special and wise person. Hitherto you have not felt it would be appropriate to join in the affairs of the world and give it the benefit of your insights and visions. The situation has now changed, and you feel that the time has come for you to re-enter the sphere of activity. Approach others with a suitable humility for the benefit of helping them in their work. This is a matter of good fortune for those you help.

A View of the World

1 Is This Person a Compatible Partner?

In matters of love you are very discriminating; you have a way of attracting to yourself people who are also highly discriminating. Both you and your partner are likely to possess wide ranging sympathies. Neither of you place great store by shallow gratifications; you are looking for a deeper, richer empathy. You dream of growing, expanding, giving: your perception of the human heart is profound. You are a difficult person to deceive where true affections are concerned as you have a keen sense of the true and the false, the sincere and the insincere, the affected and the unaffected. You treasure your partner's spontaneous expressions of love towards you.

You have a tremendous capacity for viewing society in a broad panoramic spectrum, you may even be gifted with second sight; you are instinctive about important issues, intuitive about other people's motives, and you already understand many of the secrets of the human heart; you have a way of influencing others without their being aware of it just by your presence. When you are at your best, love and wisdom emanate from you – others sense this and are attracted to it – you breathe hope into people's despair and people become attached to you, sometimes even emotionally dependent upon you while they are learning to have faith in their own love. You bring confidence into people's lives by filling up their loneliness even when you yourself feel lonely. The irony in all this is that you often take refuge in your own ivory tower. You need to be alone sometimes to contemplate the things that lie between heaven and hell.

2 Does My Partner Love Me?

If you are already involved in a relationship then you are already aware that your partner loves you very much, and he or she is likely to express this not only through innocent spontaneous expressions of love but in practical ways.

If you are not involved with any particular person and there is a relationship in the wings, then the attitude of your partner is one of deep admiration for you. This is indeed a very strong basis for love to grow and prosper between you.

3 Do We Have a Future Together?

For a person who cares as much as you do, the future can never be closed. You derive energy from your awareness of death. If you are young you know the value of overcoming your fear of death.

You will give and receive much love in your life, as you have in the past. Your life will stand as an example to others. You may have a tendency towards asceticism, but the joy of human contact lures you into the world of people.

Your future will be peaceful at the deeper levels of love with your partner. You will bring great joy to others by your mutual strength and openness of heart.

4 What is the Most Important Attitude to Adopt at This Time?

You are engaged in the work of developing your powers of concentration and thereby strengthening your powers of communication. This is a process which cannot be rushed, since it involves the gradual elevation of consciousness. You should take time to record your thoughts. Your inner life is rich with insights. Reach out with your mind.

5 Why Has Our Relationship Broken Down?

It is unlikely that your relationship with your partner has irretrievably broken down. If anything, there is a slight problem of communication between you. You may not have taken the trouble to communicate your special love for your partner recently, and this may have caused some distress; or it may be that your insistence, at the moment, on developing your own line of thought has caused a feeling of alienation in your partner. Even if sharing your insights is inappropriate at this time, the absence of human contact for extended periods can be disturbing for both of you.

6 Will We Get Back Together?

If you have made the wrong choice of partner then it is unlikely that you will reunite. If, on the other hand, you have not made a wrong choice, but there has been an estrangement between you, then a reconciliation is definite.

7 What Can I Do to Put Things Right?

You are already in the formidable position of being able to balance head and heart. Although your heart does not rule your head, your open sincerity and honesty evokes the best possible responses from others in any given situation. You have a way of making people want to give their best. Your own deepening awareness of universal forces has a mysterious way of attracting beneficial, protective and salubrious energies.

8 What Do I Most Want From Life?

You often underestimate your personal value, but this will do you no harm in the end. Since your present work involves the development and strengthening of your powers of concentration you are able to direct it specifically at thinking through social and political problems in minute detail. Your basic kindness of heart enables you to understand the true nature of the forces which govern the human condition. You are developing the happy knack of finding simple solutions to problems which affect vast numbers of people.

Your heart's desire is to be a participant in a peaceful, loving world.

113

THE LINES

One

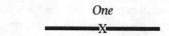

You are required to develop your understanding of social forces and to deepen your awareness of the inter-dependencies of people and institutions. Understand the connections between ideas, institutions and people.

You already know that nothing shallow from you is acceptable. Give your very best.

Two

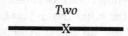

It is wasteful for a person of such insight to indulge in introversion. You should be making the most of your gifts, placing them in the service of others who are in need of your help. Failure to do so will only lead to frustration and excessive limitation. Neither is necessary, and should not be encouraged.

Three

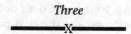

As Socrates said, 'The unexamined life is not worth living.' During such times of self examination a deepening of awareness is inevitable. Self improvement is best justified when others can benefit. They too may learn how to develop their own potential with your guidance and help. Place your knowledge and experience at the disposal of others.

If your reasons for self improvement are purely subjective you will encounter inhibition and self contradiction.

Be objective about your own potential without undue cynicism.

Four

People of ability and insight should not be compelled to suffer abuse through crude exploitation. Their abilities should be acknowledged and they should be offered the opportunity to work according to their initiative. Such people deserve the respect of others, especially where their work has a social value.

114

Five

You have been entrusted with important responsibilities, and you realise that you must find it within you to live up to their moral and social implications. This occasions self-scrutiny and, of course, this is demanded of you.

Six

You have reached an elevated level of objectivity. You can see the world clearly through the polished lens of your insight, and you realise the possibility for high spiritual attainment.

HEXAGRAM 21

Decisive Action

1 Is This Person a Compatible Partner?

The difficulties described in this hexagram require that you take formal legal remedies rather than take the law into your own hands, where any harm or wrong has been done to you by others. The time for considering the suitability or unsuitability of your partner has probably passed. Indeed, this issue is irrelevant under the circumstances, as what stands between you is probably a matter of law, either in the form of certain criminal charges about which you should take advice, or in the form of general wrong-doing such as deceptive or clandestine arrangements, adultery, hypocrisy or profound dishonesty.

You should make a special effort to swiftly and cleanly clear the obstacles that separate you from justice, you are warned that you *must not* take the law into your own hands.

The oracle also hints at mistreatment and malpractice in relation to your affairs. If you are personally responsible for these things, then you will be confronted by a legal force. If you are not responsible, then you have a legal remedy. The circumstances in which you find yourself generate considerable tension. The general harmony of life is disturbed. Lies, deceits and cheating prevail in your social life, and you may be sure that at least one person, known or unknown to you, is spreading nasty, unkind and untrue rumours which do nothing to help your situation.

2 Does My Partner Love Me?

In your present mood, it is unlikely that you will be interested in the answer to this question. It is because of your partner's actions that the present situation is tense and difficult. Any love which you might bear each other at the present time is so buried under difficulties and complications that its light cannot shine through.

3 Do We Have a Future Together?

If both you and your partner are found to be innocent of the difficulties generated by other people's unkindness, and if you have taken the advice of the oracle, then harmony will be restored to your lives, and all the obstacles will be overcome in the proper way. If, however, only one of you is innocent, and while the other the principal cause of the difficulties, then of course you can expect no future together at all.

It looks as if one of you may come under the jurisdiction of the court, in one way or another, and through this you will be separated.

4 What is the Most Important Attitude to Adopt at This Time?

In order to put things back on an even keel, and to return order to your life, you must now be decisive, active and vigorous. If you are to overcome the difficulties, you must not be rash, rude or insulting; but neither is there time or room to entertain doubts about your position and what must be done. This is not a time for ifs and buts.

5 Why Has Our Relationship Broken Down?

This hexagram concerns itself with the way in which you can solve an already difficult problem by recourse to the law and legal measures. The reason for the breakdown between you and your partner is a deception on the part of one of you, perhaps adultery or some other kind of infidelity. The breakdown may also be due to a misunderstanding between you caused by rumours, which may not be true. In this respect you must suspend your judgement until you find out the truth through formal means.

6 Will We Get Back Together?

Nothing good will happen in this situation unless you yourself take the initiative to bring about a resolution. Certainly the oracle makes no promise of a reconciliation between you and your partner, as tensions in the environment are too extreme. Only when the general violence of emotion has subsided will this question be within the bounds of your contemplation.

7 What Can I Do to Put Things Right?

The source of the problem is definitely the person who is spreading the unkind and untrue rumours. Whatever the truth *might* be, it is certainly being distorted in a way which is unfavourable for both you and your partner. The truth can only be brought to light through recourse to criminal proceedings in law. Whatever is preventing you from taking the appropriate measures, you must now cut through and take those appropriate measures without further delay. You are warned that if you do not take action, the matter will become increasingly complicated and more and more difficult to unravel, and the people responsible for causing the harm which has already been done to you may do even further harm.

8 What Do I Most Want From Life?

This is the hexagram concerned with justice and punishment. Your main objective is that justice should be done.

Justice can only be done in circumstances where the law is clear and where its spirit and purpose lies in the strict, swift reconstruction of social harmony, where it has been disturbed by misdemeanours. The law cannot command respect if justice takes too long in coming. Punishments and penalties have very little moral value if the gap between crime and punishment is so long that the clarity of the law is muddied and the effect of punishment is dulled.

Where punishment is necessary, it should come swiftly after the crime and as a sharp shock. In that way it is effective. Beyond this the law loses the poignancy and the clarity it needs in order to maintain the values of social harmony and to command respect.

THE LINES

One

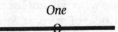

A first time offender should not be severely punished. The point of punishment in this case is to warn the offender against a more serious crime.

Two

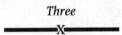

Here the offender has pushed providence beyond its normal limits of endurance. Although leniency is not deserved in this case, it should at least be considered, if not acted upon. Even if any offers of mitigating circumstances are not sufficiently convincing, you should endeavour to keep your temper.

Three

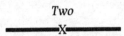

Your power, in this case, to mete out punishment to offenders is quite properly called into question. You meet with a barrage of well-aimed antagonism. Nevertheless, in the circumstances the punishment itself was justified, but the general experience is unsatisfactory.

Four

You are confronted with a difficult situation, which you would do well not to underestimate. This situation calls for deep concentration and determination in the face of serious odds. You will succeed providing you do not waver.

Five

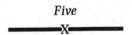

The problem with which you are faced contains no subtle ambiguities. The rule to follow is that of the Golden Mean. That is to say, straightforward honesty, without erring too much on the side of either severity or leniency. You must be as flexible as the tempered steel in the blade of a sword.

119

Six

This is the line of someone who will not listen and, as a result, simply continues to repeat a mistake of the past. Since such mistakes, at one level or another, affect the general harmony of other people, things cannot help but go wrong. Such a person attracts misfortune.

HEXAGRAM 22

Aesthetics

This hexagram describes the role of art and aesthetics in human relationships and culture. It points specifically to the form in which ideas and sentiments are expressed. It does not focus on the conflict between inner reality and outer form, although where the aesthetic expression of an idea truly reflects its inner worth, then all forms of art (for example, painting, sculpture, music, architecture) are acknowledged as having great value.

1 Is This Person a Compatible Partner?

The partner most suited to you is one who has definite artistic leanings, and for whom feelings are expressed in some kind of creative representational art. Even the way in which a person dresses might be important; for example, where colours and fabrics are chosen with care. While aesthetic considerations do not exactly govern the relationship, they are nevertheless very important to you both.

You both appreciate the outward appearance of things, you are both sensitive to the outer appearance of each other. You appreciate the care and effort that goes into creating pleasing sensory effects. Neither of you is oblivious to the fact that it is only through the expression of ideas in a tangible form that people come to comprehend the inner structure of the meaning of the universe. Art has the capacity to express our inmost thoughts and feelings.

Nevertheless, you are also aware that aesthetic beauty is a transient thing, whereas spiritual beauty is eternal. For this reason, you should not place too much emphasis on your mutual interest in the representation of ideas, for when divorced from their inner meaning, they are only empty shells of expression.

It was because of the transcience he perceived in aesthetic art that Confucius felt most uncomfortable with this hexagram, for he intuited that although art is the manifestation of the intangible spiritual impetus, it must not be forgotten that it only *represents* the feeling or thought, and should never be mistaken for the feeling or thought itself.

However, the power of aesthetics cannot be denied its place in our world, because it enhances our sense of the beauty within us.

2 Does My Partner Love Me?

So far as your mutual interests are concerned, you certainly regard each other with affection. The problem is, how deep do your feelings really go? There does seem to be a need to explore the potential depths of your relationship.

3 Do We Have a Future Together?

Where your mutual appreciation of art is the main connection between you, then the following principle will apply to the future of your relationship: the deeper are your real feelings for one another, the longer your relationship will last. If your perception of your partner is merely cosmetic, then your feelings will be correspondingly skin-deep, and the relationship will not last very long. If you only find your partner's appearance attractive, then the relationship will only last for as long as the appearance remains attractive to you, and no longer. The conflict between surface appearance and inner worth is sharpest where feelings are concerned. This is the cutting edge of love, and as the basis for a future relationship, this is where we walk on thinnest ice. Nevertheless, the oracle does not pre-judge your possible depths, and neither does it doom the possibility of a future relationship. It merely describes a way in which to contemplate the situation.

4 What is the Most Important Attitude to Adopt at This Time?

If you accept that the role of aesthetics in your life is to enhance the beauty of your inner feelings, and at the same time you recognise the relative importance of the beauty of a form, it may be possible for you to harness your mutual creative energy as a means of exploring reality.

Reality also encompasses those feelings which are not easy to reconcile, but the process of comprehension involves a difficult transcendence of mere aesthetics, to the realm of creative art which endures in time as opposed to the transient art of fad and fashion.

The acceptance or rejection of this challenge will not necessarily determine the success of the relationship, but the awareness of alternatives will assist you in the cultivation of the right attitude towards your partner.

5 Why Has Our Relationship Broken Down?

The kind of creative representation alluded to in this hexagram is not in itself powerful enough to hold a relationship together; although it is capable of beautifying a relationship, where its seeds are deeply planted. If the strength of your relationship lay in your mutual appreciation of beauty and aesthetics, then this alone cannot sustain it. The causes of any breakdown, then, lie far deeper than your mutual appreciation of art. Perhaps you have placed too great a value on the appearance of things, and now that your relationship has had to bear the weight of more serious issues between you, you have found that art in itself is not a strong enough foundation upon which to build.

Artistic appreciation and creation has the power to illuminate the depths of feeling between two people, but it must not be mistaken for the feeling itself. Perhaps the essence of your problem lies in this distinction.

6 Will We Get Back Together?

Providing the relationship has not already been shattered by a profound disillusionment with each other, then it is of course possible to repair it. It may well be, in aesthetic terms, a much more profound creative challenge for you both to put the pieces together in a new way, making the outer form correspond more exactly with the inner form and to restructure your feelings for each other. This is the challenge of creativity in action, requiring a much more serious application of willpower and great determination.

7 What Can I Do to Put Things Right?

Explore your deeper feelings, and if possible communicate these to your partner in a creative way.

8 What Do I Most Want From Life?

If creative art is the process by which you have chosen to express your feelings, then it is where art expresses love that you will derive your greatest joy in achievement and appreciation. The value of aesthetics lies in the beautification of form, not of meaning.

THE LINES

One

At the outset, you feel that travelling by the path of least resistance may not, in the circumstances, bring the best results. You feel that to compromise on your self esteem at this stage would belie your integrity and seriousness of purpose, and in this you are absolutely correct.

Two

You enjoy life, in a *dilettantish* sort of way, but although your pleasures titillate your senses, they are superficial. There is no harm, of course, in wearing a mask. But take care to remove it once in a while, as this kind of mask has an unhappy habit of adhering to the wearer's face by the operation of a mental process called vanity.

Three

The good things of life are yours to taste and enjoy. Your social life is full of the grace and ease and refinement which brings you satisfaction. It is fine to take a goblet of wine with friends, and to spend time in charming and enchanting pursuits, but take care not to fall into the wine vat itself, or allow yourself to become submerged in bubbly trivia, devoid of sense and feeling. Your happiness may well depend upon heeding the oracle's gentle warning.

Four

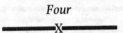

You are already aware that the social trappings of the high life lack the depth of meaning to which your mind is naturally attracted. The temptations of comfort and safety, recognition and adulation are strong. How easy it would be to allow yourself to be lionised by society.

You can have an excellent time cavorting among acquaintances, but you already know that you will miss your true friends. Your thoughts are even now travelling towards higher aspirations than mere social recognition.

Five

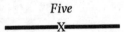

You know that many people are obsessed with the acquisition of money, and the material goods this will buy. You once shared this aim, but now you understand that there is more to life than the amassing of possessions, and you seek spiritual treasures at the expense of material treasure.

You now want to comprehend the meaning behind the form. You wish to communicate with the feeling beneath the tinsel surface, but in applying yourself to these aims you feel desperately lacking in the qualities needed to pursue your quest and cultivate the friendships of those people whose lives bear a hallmark of a higher quality than your own.

The sincere seeker will always find a friend. There is no need to feel dejected. A new way lies ahead.

Six

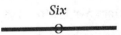

Here, the contradiction between inside and outside is reconciled in feeling, in form and in art. In affairs of the heart, you feel meaningful inside at last. In the field of art, you have achieved personal excellence. So far as this hexagram is concerned with the state of the spirit, you have tasted grace.

HEXAGRAM 23

Separation

1 Is This Person a Compatible Partner?

There is no real depth to your present perception and therefore this is a bad time in your life to make decisions about a possible partner, especially one you are considering for life. The principle influences are negative, and your world is full of darkness, which may lead you to despair. Whoever you see through this dark glass will not appear attractive, this is not because they are unattractive in themselves but because the atmosphere inside your mind makes you unable to discern their subtle nature.

You are prone to prejudice. You cannot trust your own judgement at the moment.

2 Does My Partner Love Me?

The true situation is that the heart does not know itself. Love seems further away than ever, but whether this is due to your own blindness or the truth, can only be determined by patient, watchful and docile quietness. Nothing more will bring this answer closer. You cannot assume that your partner does not love you, however. It is simply that the question of love has not yet arisen.

3 Do We Have a Future Together?

If you have received any moving lines in drawing this oracle, then you should consult those lines.

As ever, the seeds of the future lie in the past. If those seeds were not well cultivated or deeply planted, then it is likely that their growth will be stunted.

If you address yourself honestly to this question, the answer may be apparent to you even now. The tendency of this oracle is, however, to point towards the need for patience, and if you are feeling empty and dejected at present, then you should be aware that this will certainly pass.

On the positive side, you are at heart a generous person, and in the past it has been within your capacity to give a great deal to those you love, which has commanded their loyalty and respect. The future of any relationships you hold dear – from those closest to you, to those with the world at large – springs out of your gentleness and generosity of nature. Through these attributes, you are well able to assume responsibility and sew something to make your relationship secure even in times of adversity.

4 What is the Most Important Attitude to Adopt at This Time?

The depth of your thought is giving way to shallow consideration. This process is likely to continue, as this is the condition of the time. You should not act when your understanding is so imperfect or when you tend only to appreciate the surface appearance of things rather than their inner reality. Your present attitude should be one of open-mindedness and, if in doubt, you should be generous rather than selfish. You should not impose your views on your partner.

Above all, you must learn patience. This is the most valuable attitude of all at this time, as there is so much darkness and conflict surrounding you. There is very little you can do in an active way to put things right, and any attempt at positive action might end badly, and cause a negative reaction against your will, against even your better nature. However, the time will change, and you can gain confidence from this knowledge.

Rarely must we place our trust in the natural operation of the cosmic forces which govern the universe, but this is such a time.

5 Why Has Our Relationship Broken Down?

From the outside looking in, it probably appears to you that your relationship broke down rather suddenly – almost collapsed – but obviously the reasons for such a collapse run much deeper. It is possible that the fault lies in the way you perceive things.

As this is not a time for perceiving the meaning of things in their inmost meaning, your life may well seem empty to you and devoid of meaning. Again, this is only how things appear. The truth, as usual, is quite different.

You should ask yourself if you have been impatient, if you have assumed you had a deeper understanding of your partner than you really possess, if you have in the past acted with force when you should have acted with gentleness, or if you have in any way acted out of tune with the time. These could all be very good reasons why the relationship has broken down.

6 Will We Get Back Together?

The answer to this question will probably lie in the lines. If you have received a moving line, consult the meaning of that line.

It is unlikely that your intuitions at this time will give you any insight into the future, but after a period of time you may see more clearly. Be patient.

As a matter of caution, especially with regard to matters of the heart, you should guard against taking advice from people around you whose judgement may not be any more trustworthy than is your own at present.

7 What Can I Do to Put Things Right?

Wait. Be patient. Do not act.

You must trust to the time. You must submit entirely to the forces of the universe without even a hint of opposition. You are feeling empty, and any movement will accentuate rather than dispel this feeling, which will pass of its own accord. You must not indulge yourself either in self-pity or in any self-deprecating attitude. In a time of quietness you must not make noise. This is not the reaction of a fearful person, but of a wise one.

8 What Do I Most Want From Life?

You most want lightness and clarity to be restored to your private inner world. You feel dejected, at a loss, in a state of darkness. You are aware of your predicament, but you are powerless to change these things. You desire once again to experience control over your own destiny, the power to make light what is now dark.

Paradoxically, your heart's desire will change as your circumstances change. If you are aware of this, and do not confuse your heart's desire with superficial expectation, you will come through. You already intuitively know that this time of darkness will pass.

A word of warning is appropriate: you must guard yourself especially against exploiting superficial qualities too quickly, and then being satisfied with a quickly growing fruit which just as quickly decays.

THE LINES

One
——————X——————

You cannot trust the people around you, and those in whom you can place trust are threatened by the same rumours and unkind lies, deceits and slanders which undermine your own position and your happiness.

You cannot stop these people from being harmful. All you can do is to exercise the utmost patience and outwait this dangerous period.

Inaction is your very best action.

Two
——————X——————

The danger around you persists, and is growing closer. You can feel its presence, and you feel discomfort. There is no haven of refuge in the form of friendly advice or help from any quarter. You must rely entirely upon yourself and remain watchful.

You must be ready to change and adjust your position at a moment's notice in order to avoid the sudden appearance of danger. Failure to be alert will lead to a bad defeat.

Three

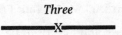

The people around you are having a bad effect, both spiritually and morally. You are aware of their bad influence, and you seek to escape from them. Unfortunately, you cannot do this – due to circumstances currently beyond your control – but your determination not to be led from your true self makes you aware of the deeper affinity you have with another person. Through this truthful relationship you are able to resist the malevolent influences successfully. This has the effect of turning the other people against you, but your position is strongest because in this case you are right and they are wrong.

Four

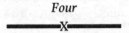

There is nothing you can do to prevent complete disaster. It has already touched you personally and in an extreme way. Nothing more can be said.

Five

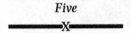

When dark forces grow close to light's strong forces, they change automatically. This is the law. They no longer remain dark with intrigue and malevolence, but transform into forces of light. Here it does not matter what form the strong light force takes, whether in the visible or in the invisible world, but in its presence darkness has no dominion.

The effect of all this on everyday life is to create an atmosphere of greater happiness and forgiveness around you. Nothing bad need be expected in this new light.

Six

There are limits even on misfortune. Now you have reached rock bottom, you cannot come to any greater harm. Your circumstances cannot yield any more disfavour.

Now higher forces once again take control over your affairs. This is apparent to everyone and brings a great deal of relief to you. A principle of cosmic justice inevitably comes to bear on these circumstances. Just as it is always the case that light follows dark and dark follows light, so the negative forces always destroy themselves, and the bad that people have caused returns to themselves in equal measure.

It is well to understand the nature of evil forces. They prey not only upon the good, but upon themselves, while at the same time depending on the strength of good to sustain them.

When evil is controlled by good, affairs come under the control of order. The reverse is never true.

The principles of order and chaos obey a moral law. The heart of the universe is a unifying idea – this is why it is said that one must act blamelessly at all times.

HEXAGRAM 24

The Moment of Transition

1 Is This Person a Compatible Partner?

This is a time of new growth, fresh undertakings and natural stirring of new energy. A period of stillness, even stagnation, is now coming to an end and is being replaced by a time of gentle re invigoration of the life forces within you.

The main characteristics of your relationship with your partner over the last few months have been quietness and almost bland emotional exchanges, taking place in a period of decay and darkness when compared with what is coming in now. Already you feel an upsurge of hope, energy and vigour.

While there is no indication at all in this hexagram that your present partner is in any way unsuitable, if you have been experiencing loneliness, it may intimate the possibility of a new companion coming into your life. The process of change will be natural, slow, regenerative and completely beyond your own control, but nevertheless good for you. It marks a definite improvement in your feelings in relation to yourself and to society at large and to your everyday life. The tone of the oracle is at once optimistic and hopeful, and portends the coming of joy and prosperity. The important thing to note here is that while you will feel an impulse to greater action, this does not mean that you should force circumstances to change.

132

The season is changing. You are at the edge of a brighter time, and over the coming months you will notice that it will become even brighter. If a new relationship forms during this time, you will be well suited and it will bring considerable and lasting joy to both of you.

2 Does My Partner Love Me?

In the recent past you may have felt unloved, but this was due to the very quiet time and the very quiet emotional relationship you have been conducting between you. However, the oracle indicates that this quiet time, now being displaced by a new growth of warmth and invigoration, was as much a seasonal period as is the new time approaching.

In the coming months you will have good cause to believe in your partner's love for you, and in return, your own feelings will naturally become warmer. Any good seeds you have planted in the past will now blossom, but the oracle warns that you must not force anything. Do not overnurture what is good, but allow it to blossom naturally, caring for it in the usual way but with a new enthusiasm and hope.

Because of the transition you are now undergoing, everything in your life will now improve considerably, not only in terms of your relationship but also in every other aspect of your life. This time in both your lives is a renewal and a new beginning. Everything that once lay inert will now be divinely inspired and will grow naturally. Emotionally, you will feel a greater warmth and confidence.

3 Do We Have a Future Together?

Almost without reservation the oracle answers this question in a positive way. It is a time of growth and flowering. A period of decay gives way to a period of growth, in the way that spring follows winter. You did nothing to begin the process and there is nothing you can do to stop it.

The future is inevitably bright for you now. You can view it with optimism. You will find that even old differences will be easily healed in the midst of such a gentle change of fortunes.

The oracle does warn that no attempt should be made to speed up the natural order of things. Bear in mind that the period of renewal is still in its very early stages. Time must be taken to store up energy for future action. The saying 'haste makes waste' applies.

4 What is the Most Important Attitude to Adopt at This Time?

You may already have noticed that your attitude is subtly changing, almost without conscious effort on your part. You are naturally beginning to feel more optimistic, more light-hearted, more in the mood for giving. All these subtle changes in attitude are in complete accordance with the time. You should merely follow them. There is no necessity for artificial restraint on your energy. You will feel an automatic impulse to move forward in a positive way. If you act in accordance with the energy you possess, you will remain in harmony with the season.

5 Why Has Our Relationship Broken Down?

As the nature of this hexagram points towards the period of transition which you are now undergoing, you may have recently experienced the gradual decay of one relationship followed by the gradual growth of another relationship. If the old relationship has broken down, it is through a process of natural decay, a natural withering away of energy, spontaneity, optimism and the invigorating emotional exchanges which keep all relationships alive. At the point of transition all those influences are passing out.

New life is being breathed back into your emotions. Therefore, if an old relationship has ended, you must let it pass. Let the new in. You must not dwell on the past but look forward to the future. If, in the first stirrings of a new relationship, you are already encountering difficulties, it can only mean one thing. You are trying too hard and moving too quickly, and the advice of the oracle is to slow down.

If you have received any moving lines in drawing this oracle, you should pay close attention to their meaning in order to establish your exact position in the transition.

6 Will We Get Back Together?

As this is a time of personal renewal for you, it may well be a time of reconciliation. Old divisive tendencies which have lingered in the past will now have a chance to heal in the ambience of a new spring-like energy. If you feel that there are sound reasons to expect a reconciliation with an old partner, then this will unquestionably happen. If, on the other hand, you have already entered into a new relationship, you must not force any issues, but allow events to evolve their natural course.

If a reconciliation with an old love is truly what you desire, the old seeds of your love lie dormant. Now is the time that they are likely to sprout new shoots and give your relationship a new lease of life.

Above all, you must not force things to unnatural conclusions. It is proper to treat new life with the gentleness, care and attention which is appropriate to it.

7 What Can I Do to Put Things Right?

The whole tone and quality of this oracle addresses itself to the idea of a very *natural* flowering because the time has come. There is nothing in the oracle to suggest deliberately willed and conscious action in relation to problems. If things have gone wrong in the past, they will gradually find their own resolutions. Events will arrive at their own natural conclusions, almost without conscious intervention on your part.

The power of the season is very great. All you can do is trust in the new light now emerging, in the same way that you trust the sun to rise. If you have been ill, then health will come. If you have been alone, then you will find companions. This will not be by any deliberate act of will on your part, but because it is the time for such things to happen.

The only thing you can positively do is to see that you get plenty of rest, so that whatever is now beginning may be strong later.

8 What Do I Most Want From Life?

The new period of growth brings joy with it. After so long, life which was comparatively dormant now takes on new and exciting possibilities. You already feel that the time of waiting has passed and the qualities for which you have been waiting are now entering your life.

THE LINES

One

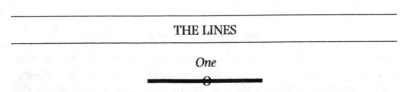

The good path is straight and narrow. If you are tempted to digress and you feel easily distracted from what you know is the correct way of acting, now is the time to take hold. In a time of personal growth and development of character, it is important to be mindful of pitfalls and temptations and to take action to avoid them. You will certainly regret any failure to check evil tendencies.

Two

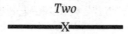

During this time of transition and growth, there is a need for humility and self-control. Show a willingness to be guided by wise companions.

Three

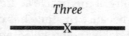

There is a need for a much stronger resolution than you have hitherto shown in following the path which you know to be the right one. The difficulty you are experiencing is caused by a fundamental lack of inner composure, which is expressing itself in your failure to resist obvious temptations. The oracle does not suggest that you are making no effort to stick to your resolutions, but warns that you must be more serious-minded in this respect.

Four

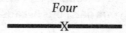

The general law governing this line is that, 'Like tends to attract like, and like tends to dwell with like.'

You are associating with people who are not good for you, but there is a person beyond this circle with whom you do have a strong and well-founded affinity. It is the thought of this person and the influence of this person which makes you resolve to unite with those who are your true companions. This is the right thing to do, and although the oracle does not promise good or bad fortune in making such a change, you realise that only good can come of it because it is the right action.

Five

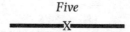

This line means that the time has come to make a clean breast of it. Even though this might be painful, you really have no other choice. Such a resolve requires a stalwart heart, and does you credit in the end.

136

Six

X

You have missed a golden opportunity. The reason for this lies in a completely inappropriate and misplaced conception of the world.

Because of your outright stupidity and your unwillingness to heed reason and good advice, you suffer a misfortune from which you may draw a lesson for the future. You must spend time developing a correct attitude towards the world.

HEXAGRAM 25

Innocence

1 Is This Person a Compatible Partner?

This hexagram concerns itself with the highest good in human nature, namely innocence and simplicity. The law here is that people are endowed with an innately good nature.

Goodness manifests itself in human nature by its simplicity and innocence, untarnished by impure motives, cosmetic desires or anything that thwarts natural spontaneity of action.

Simplicity and innocence are the hallmarks of a person who is natural and true.

Here, the question of the suitability of a partner turns more on the way you project your own nature. If you act in accordance with your own true nature, which is spontaneous without being carefree, then it is natural for you to attract the same purity in another.

Like attracts like.

You will know that your partner is suitable by the absence of certain qualities. If you yourself are innocent of self-deception and of guile then you may be sure that you will be doing the instinctively correct thing. Here it is important to guard against conscious purpose.

If you seek to achieve some outward fulfilment in order to fulfil any sense of inadequacy in yourself, then the natural innocence of this relationship will automatically be lost. This is a relationship which is founded on innate suitability, not on created suitability. Here lie the seeds of a joyful commitment with a partner with whom you feel true empathy.

2 Does My Partner Love Me?

In keeping with the spirit of the oracle, it is this kind of question which you should avoid. By asking such a question you are purposefully trying to create or generate some response.

Perhaps unintentionally, you are in some way allowing your own nature to degenerate.

Follow the original impulses of the heart, for they can always be trusted.

3 Do We Have a Future Together?

As with the last question, this is the kind of purposeful intellectualising in which you should not indulge at the present. It automatically places you in a mental stance which is inappropriate to the conduct of innocence.

The warning here is that if your future actions are tailored to a specific end, then your motives may already be sullied with a selfish intent. Hence the answer remains subtle and inconclusive, and asks of you something which you already know in your inmost heart. Very simply, the answer to your question is that your future existence together depends upon your not consciously expecting one.

4 What is the Most Important Attitude to Adopt at This Time?

By persevering in the absence of impure motive, you will naturally adopt the correct attitude. By not creating any unnatural intent, you will automatically be left with the correct intent.

If you are experiencing a sense of loss, but you are not sure what it is you have lost, then the oracle is suggesting to you that you have lost your sense of guileless innocence.

The only attitude which is proper for you at the moment is one which can only be characterised by a childlike state of trust. This state cannot be consciously manufactured. You must allow this part of you to surface naturally.

5 Why Has Our Relationship Broken Down?

If everything in your relationship has turned on being natural, and on spontaneous action, then a breakdown in the relationship will have come from departing from a natural way of acting. That is to say, if you have acted with impure motive, or with ulterior designs, or if your real reason for wanting a relationship with this person is in order to satisfy superficial desires, then you will naturally have attracted misfortune to yourself, and communication will automatically break down.

Look at your recent past and ask yourself if you have been thinking too much about what you want from this person, rather than allowing the natural course of things to flow. If the relationship has deteriorated, it is almost certainly because you have forgotten that this person's nature and your nature are governed by a natural state of innocence. Perhaps you have both been trying too hard, and have therefore created an unbearable and stifling atmosphere between you.

6 Will We Get Back Together?

The original impulses of the heart are always good. This is the essential meaning of this oracle. If you are not naturally inspired towards the person in question, then you will not be reunited or reconciled. If you are, then those actions, thoughts and feelings of the heart will tend towards a reconciliation of their own accord.

Any forces brought to bear upon your partner which are designed to effect a reconciliation will not achieve their purpose. Everything depends upon a natural course of things.

7 What Can I Do to Put Things Right?

All action in the world arises from a spiritual state.

If things have gone wrong, it is because you have acted from the wrong spiritual state, and in order to put things right you must first correct your own spiritual stance in the world. In this case, the situation is more difficult because you cannot consciously re-acquire a sense of innocence in your perspective on the world. You must simply let go and allow your sense of what is natural and honest to gain control of your actions once more. Paradoxically enough, the

140

best thing you can do at the moment is somehow *not* to do anything in an obvious or purposeful way, but to allow the natural flow of spontaneous action to give you the guidance you need. This way, it is the unintentional and the unexpected which declare the path towards the heart. If your concentration is directed at achieving something, you will not achieve it.

You have no doubt heard it said that the way of truth is a narrow way. This oracle is a perfect metaphor for that spiritual state. You cannot comprehend it except by allowing it to comprehend you. It is a paradox which can only be understood in an unintentional, unexpected and unpurposeful manner. You must cultivate a higher self-trust.

8 What Do I Most Want From Life?

If a person has strayed from the path of purity and natural innocence, then that person's strongest desire is to become uncomplicated and clear once again.

THE LINES

One

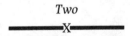

Follow your heart, not your surface thoughts. This will bring good fortune.

Two

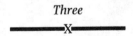

Act without intent, that is to say, act as if there will be no tomorrow.

Three

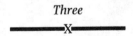

Sometimes a person suffers misfortune through no fault of their own. Nevertheless, that person must still act with purity, despite such misfortune. Even though what has happened is not your fault, you must not bear any grudge. Remember that it is not only important for you to avoid misfortune – you must also not be the agent of misfortune for others. Under no circumstances must you allow yourself to be coerced into acting in a way that leads you away from

141

yourself. It is vital that you incur no blame, and invite none, despite any pressures from your environment.

Four

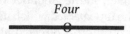

There is no real basis for your feeling of anxiety. Do not indulge in worrying just for the sake of it.

Five

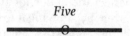

Where you suffer by some accident of circumstance, provided the cause lies outside your actions you must not act unnaturally to put it right, but must let nature take its own course. This is very much an act of wisdom through an act of faith.

Six

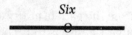

This is a time for patience. You must wait for an outcome. Do not impose your will on the situation. The warning here is that if you interfere in the present situation, you will not succeed in creating progress, but will only forestall progress.

Do not act. Do not interfere. Do not intervene.

HEXAGRAM 26

Held in Check

1 Is This Person a Compatible Partner?

You have tremendous aptitudes and abilities which you would like to express with all the power and force of your personality, but for your own good you are being held in check. If at this time an outlet was provided for you, you would not be able to make the most if it, even though you feel that you would. You are therefore being controlled despite yourself.

None of this implies that the quality of your life is being diminished in the slightest. Such a situation should not change your relationship with your partner. If you recognise that you are, as it were, being saved for a more propitious time, then the build-up of energies should not inwardly be experienced as frustrating. This is important from your partner's point of view, as the effect of such restraint in your life might make you difficult to live with. This need not be so. You can afford to take the time to develop yourself and carry on your relationship with your partner in a perfectly amicable way without placing unnecessary stresses and strains upon it.

2 Does My Partner Love Me?

You are a strong and potent force in your relationships, not only with your partner but with others. Because there is not a lot going on at the moment you might be tempted to charge around like a bull in a china shop, unintentionally causing all sorts of harm to yourself and to others. Therefore, it is imperative to exercise self-control on the one hand, and to occupy yourself with interests that keep your life fresh on the other. You must be careful to remember that it is not your partner who is the restraining force, and therefore you should avoid any unjustified feelings of resentment. Your partner's attitude towards you is one of admiration and respect. Your partner recognises that you have great potential for creative action in the world, but you must not let this be a reason for neglect.

You should make a habit of taking your partner into your confidence during less busy periods, and continue to do so when you are taken up with weighty matters. Guard against treating your partner as an appendage to your life. You must return your partner's special love for you in full measure. This means giving time and energy to your partner's needs.

3 Do We Have a Future Together?

You and your partner have a very fulfilling and productive future ahead of you. You have a great deal to offer, not only to yourself but to others. You must not be impatient. This is the time for nurturing your possibilities, not exhausting them.

4 What is the Most Important Attitude to Adopt at This Time?

Do not dwell too much on future possibilities, as such thoughts will only drain your energies. It is particularly important for you to concentrate your energies on the demands of today. Conserve your best energies for future challenges, and make ordinary, mundane things your top priority at the present time. Redecorating the house, for example, would be a more significant way of spending time than sketching out the next ten years of your life. Accepting your present limitations is a good test of character for the future.

5 Why Has Our Relationship Broken Down?

If there *has* been a breakdown in the relationship (and certainly the circumstances do not suggest it), it will have been due to you straining at the leash and creating unnecessary tensions which have nothing to do with your partner. It is highly unlikely, however, that you will have had the opportunity to take things too far. The situation is that despite yourself, things remain under control. Although there is a slow build up of creative pressure within you, the power is not great enough to force off, as it were, the tightly-fitting stopper. Thus the relationship is kept within reasonable bounds, in spite of any tendency of yours to go to extremes.

6 Will We Get Back Together?

The answer to question 5 describes the situation as it is, and where there has been no parting, there is no need for reconciliation. However, there is need to improve the relationship. You can cultivate a more loving personality. This will have the paradoxical effect of making you feel inwardly more refreshed.

7 What Can I Do to Put Things Right?

It is unlikely that anything of importance will have gone wrong. The powers keeping your energies in check at the moment are inestimably greater than your power to do any harm to yourself or to your partner. Therefore, despite your urge to push ahead and achieve great things, you are effectively held in check, much as a racehorse eager to run is kept in a horsebox until it is time for the race. You cannot axe down the walls which keep you from escaping because you do not have the room to swing the axe. In this case, you simply have to wait until the door opens, but you can be sure that there is wisdom in all this.

8 What Do I Most Want From Life?

You want achievement. You are being held back so that you can generate the necessary energy to meet the real challenges that lie ahead.

THE LINES

One

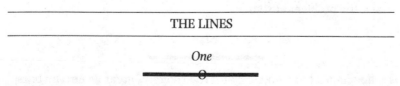

The pressure within you to rush out into the world and get things

145

done is building up. If you take the stopper off now you will only find that you do not have the necessary energy; that now is not the right time to act anyway; that your lack of control would cause havoc. This would reflect back on you with full force. Therefore control yourself, and wait.

Two

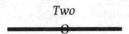

The difference between your power of forward motion and the power that impedes you is huge. You know that it is futile to attempt to make an impression on such a formidable restraining force. You cannot win. You are forced to wait for your own good.

Three

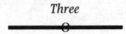

It is time to meet the challenge. The trainer opens the door of the horse box and leads the racehorse out. You can take confidence in your natural prowess, though this does not mean that you will win the race. The other horses also want to win. Nevertheless, you know what you want, and this gives you a greater impetus towards attaining it.

Four

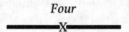

You are in a position to take definite precautions against a *potential* danger. By taking the precautions, you win, well in advance.

Five

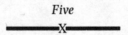

Put your energy into neutralising the cause of the problem rather than attempting to protect yourself against the effects. It is, for example, far better for us to find peaceful ways of coexisting than to find ways to protect ourselves from the consequences of nuclear war. Attack the problem at source.

Six

The floodgates have opened, and the rivers of creative energy burst forth, generating tremendous power for change.

HEXAGRAM 27

Health (Body and Mind)

1 Is This Person a Compatible Partner?

This hexagram refers to an important aspect of the relationship, namely that of nourishment. This involves the proper intake of food as well as stimulus through ideas and stimulus through interaction with others. Here we are concerned with the nourishment of the *whole* person, the *whole* relationship. Nourishment in this sense is the mainstay of a balanced life.

A great deal can be learned about a person by observing which parts of the body are nourished and which parts are neglected.

The compatible person here pays attention to diet. Without doubt, what is consumed in the way of food and in the way of ideas, contributes to the whole person. Your responsibility to your partner at the present time lies in the fostering of care, first in matters of physical health and then in matters of the spirit – through love and kindness. You should give your attention to the problem of correct food and drink in their proper measure, having special regard to quality.

2 Does My Partner Love Me?

By attending first to your partner's most fundamental and natural needs, you express your love and affection. Nurture your love through a caring disposition and you will attract a spontaneous, loving response from those who depend upon you.

In some degree, the oracle advises a greater need to pay attention to this particular area of your life. Especially where you neglect parts of your body or indulge yourself in others.

3 Do We Have a Future Together?

The essential requirement of any relationship is physical care. Provided you look after your body adequately and to the best of your ability throughout your life, you will be in a better position to take advantage of life's offerings. Eating and drinking, as a specific aspect of self care, are in themselves a life force. Eating is an active process, digesting a passive, quiet process. Both are fundamental for good health.

4 What is the Most Important Attitude to Adopt at This Time?

First you must recognise the importance of nutrition. Be prepared to look after life's basic needs before all else.

5 Why Has Our Relationship Broken Down?

If the relationship has broken down, the primary cause is a lack of proper sustenance or an over-indulgence in harmful 'sweets' or 'candies'. Nature left unhindered is capable of providing sufficient for all of life's needs in a completely balanced way. If you are eating too little or indeed, too much, or indulging in foods which are either harmful in themselves or non-nutritious, then you are going against nature's balance. (The warning includes over-consumption of synthetic foods.) There is a general warning against harmful physical and mental habits which can become obsessive.

The abstract qualities of a relationship find their roots and their health in the basic biological needs of the body. Love is the nourishment of a relationship. Just as a body will starve if deprived of food, so a relationship will starve if deprived of love. Here you must ask yourself: what nourishes love?

Deprivation of spiritual food – kindness, love and affection – coupled with dietary deprivation, brings about moral and physical weakness. There is no joy in weakness.

6 Will We Get Back Together?

Nature, left to itself, is balanced and is a balancing influence. From the point of view of health, one must be careful to sustain a balanced intake of nutritious food and drink and at the same time, one must adopt a balance of spiritual practices. In this way, you and your partner will be able to bring yourselves back into a state of health. If you pay close attention to the advice of the oracle, then the answer to the question is positive.

If you ignore this advice, then you go against the processes of nature. When a person goes against the processes of nature, they throw themselves upon chance.

7 What Can I Do to Put Things Right?

If you yourself enjoy sustained good health, then it follows that you will be able to provide your partner and others with the basics of life, their daily bread. In the same way, if you nurture your inner development, you will be able to love others better.

You have drawn this oracle at this time because your chief concern is health and general well-being, not only for the sick who need their health restored, but also for the well who need to sustain good health. This is the principle aim of proper care.

Certain areas of your body need greater care and attention than others. You must discern which areas these are (if necessary, take advice) and see to it that they are properly cared for and receive sufficient attention. You should recognise that if the most important areas of your body are well looked after, then the *whole* person attains a healthy radiance. If you neglect this, your mind as well as your body will suffer.

8 What Do I Most Want From Life?

What is adequate is enough. To overeat, for example, is to be glutted, to undereat is to starve. Your aim is to do neither. Thus you maintain the perfect balance of nature in yourself.

149

THE LINES

One

It is unnecessary and wrong for you to covet, envy or be jealous of the quality and quantity of other people's possessions. You have all that you need for self reliance. If you fail to appreciate your own independence and excellent position you will find yourself acting discordantly with others.

Two

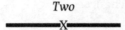

You know that you can take care of yourself, nevertheless you do not, due to a wavering fear, an inner timidity. The import of this line is that you should turn your mind to ways in which you can support yourself, or at least go some way towards doing so.

Three

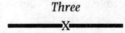

You are abusing your body by partaking of addictive substances or indulging in obsessions which are having a destructive and deleterious effect upon mind and body. You will fall into ill health unless you bring such habits under strict control. (If you cannot achieve this alone, then you should accept the assistance of those best qualified to help you.)

Four

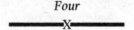

Your aims are high and good, but you cannot achieve them alone. You know this, so with an upsurge of zealous energy you seek ways to achieve your aims with the help of others. Normally such an aggressive approach is not advised, but in the circumstances, your efforts are justified.

Five

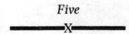

This is the line of someone who is aware of his or her responsibility to provide sustenance for dependants, but for some reason is unable to do so. Seek help from those who can give material help, by asking for it. You are especially advised to avoid strenuous or heavy work which would compromise your own health and well being.

Six

This line represents someone of tremendous wisdom and character whose influence has the effect of making others feel spiritually uplifted. By sustaining a responsible attitude to the possession of such a powerful influence on other people, any great, but difficult undertaking succeeds. This will have an extremely salubrious effect upon other people.

HEXAGRAM 28

Under Pressure

1 Is This Person a Compatible Partner?

From the outside looking in, it would appear that you are an unlikely couple to form a successful relationship. It is true that the situation is out of balance, but it is possible to make the appropriate adjustments in order to make the relationship more tenable.

Perhaps the situation may be that of an older woman with a much younger man, or an older man with a much younger woman. There is no doubt that if things stay as they are, the relationship will not work. There is too much pressure focussed in one place. The weight must be spread out evenly across the emotional spectrum. Important adjustments must be made.

2 Does My Partner Love Me?

If you cannot unequivocally answer this question for yourself in the affirmative, then there is no purpose behind your present strategies – surely?

3 Do We Have a Future Together?

If the answer to question 5 applies, then this question does not. On the

152

other hand, if you have proved to be equal to the demands placed upon you, then you will find some appropriate arrangement which will make the relationship more enduring.

4 What is the Most Important Attitude to Adopt at This Time?

If the worst has happened, then all you can do is to adopt an attitude of resignation and acceptance.

If there is still hope, you must quickly appraise the situation, recognise it for what it is, and take note that it is unusual. Do not underestimate the importance of your next move or the fact that it will have consequences. Be prepared to act in such a way as to relieve the points of greatest tension. Your watchword should be delicacy. Cultivate lightness of touch, self-control, precision, economy of movement.

5 Why Has Our Relationship Broken Down?

You must have known from the very outset that the odds were stacked against you. From your own point of view the relationship was implausible – there were too many contingent factors crowding in and the responsibilities were too heavy to bear. In effect, the boat was overloaded and you did not take the necessary precautions. You did not spread the weight and you were insensitive to the demands of the situation. The differences between you were too great to reconcile. From the beginning the line between the improbable and the impossible was extremely thin, but very clearly drawn.

If the foregoing has not already happened, then let it describe the warning you must now heed.

6 Will We Get Back Together?

This question does not apply. If question 5 is relevant to you, and if things have not yet reached that critical point, then you are still in the position of making the current situation operable.

7 What Can I Do to Put Things Right?

If the answer to question 5 applies to you, absolutely nothing can be done. All you can do is to cheerfully accept the situation.

If things have not yet come to such a pass, then you must now take care to recognise the salient qualities of your unusual relationship.

The burden of responsibility is focussed on one place, and as long as this is the case the structure of the relationship will be unstable, the fabric likely to tear. If you are heavy-handed in trying to redress the balance, you cannot forestall disaster. Be delicate. Be subtle. You must adapt yourself to the situation in order to adapt the situation itself.

8 What Do I Most Want From Life?

You have been forced by circumstances to abandon the sinking ship, as it were. In so doing, you have thrown yourself wilfully upon your inner resources without help, assistance or sympathy coming to you from the past. You face the world openly, honestly and alone, but you do face it, and herein lies your good fortune.

THE LINES

One

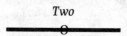

Weighty situations should be handled in the same way as weighty objects, with special care and proper preparation. First ensure that the shoulders on which you place the responsibility have the strength to carry it.

Two

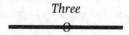

If you are an older man about to marry a much younger woman, the situation augurs well, although it is out of the ordinary. It has the effect of giving the heart a new lease of life. In the case of the younger woman, there is no need to be anxious about the future, for odd as it may seem, you are compatible.

Three

The circumstances described in the answer to question 5 of this hexagram apply here. They have been brought about by a failure to heed warning. If you do think you know better than everyone else, you are about to be proved wrong.

Four

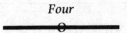

Your affability has won you the promotion you deserve. If you abuse your position by taking advantage of the situation to save yourself at the expense of others, you will damage yourself.

Five

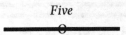

The line may describe an older woman marrying a younger man. The oracle implies that this is all right, so far as it goes, but for the woman the demands of another marriage will only wear her out. The relationship is so unbalanced that there is no possibility of mutual love.

Six

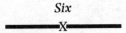

Well, you did your best. Indeed, you still want to do your best but there is nothing you can do. The hand of fate is involved. Here you sacrifice yourself in order that the path may clear for others to achieve the good where you could not. Such a sacrifice brings a blessing in disguise.

HEXAGRAM 29

Twilight of the Spirit

1 Is This Person a Compatible Partner?

Some people learn their most important lessons when the sword of death is hanging over their heads. This is not, necessarily, a situation where your life is threatened but you certainly feel a profound pressure engendered by those circumstances in which you find yourself. You feel imprisoned within your own mind, trapped by your own reason. Taken to extremes, this would become a state of paranoia.

You are trying to make sense of your life and yourself. You are trying to think your way out of the bondage of thought, which is of course difficult and dangerous, not to say impossible. You feel the urge to let your spirit fly.

In general, this is a time of spiritual crisis rather than emotional crisis. You are walking through the twilight world of the soul. You feel an impulsion towards freedom of the spirit. Your heart is imprisoned by your mind in your search for deeper sincerity. You may feel called upon to express your struggle in some creative way. You are trying to align inner feelings with outer activity, but because you are walking in an unknown world, your prevailing sense of danger makes you extra careful and doubly cautious. Yet these circumstances bring out something special in your nature. Your mind is being flooded with subjective impressions of the world. The inherent challenge is to look at yourself objectively, to understand yourself, no less.

In your struggle to instil in yourself an intrinsic and lasting strength of character, based on a good-heartedness, you are trying to overcome the fool within. You are trying to give your wisdom edge by learning how to be consistently good. This is a very high aim. In your attempt to dismantle worthless values, you are trying to build an edifice of inner truth. For some this is the sink or swim in the search for God, the acid test of a future seer.

Although your partner may well be highly compatible with you, your present experiences are not easy to share. This is by no means the easiest period in your life, but certainly if your partner can bear the stresses and strains of your path to inner discovery, it will be worth it.

2 Does My Partner Love Me?

You may not be an easy person to live with at the moment, but you are not a difficult person to love. People find you naturally endearing in your present situation and this has the effect of being highly supportive and helpful.

3 Do We Have a Future Together?

If you emerge from this 'bubble in eternity', you will be a better person in every sense than when you entered it. You will have found a deeper and more durable good in your own nature. You will be even more sincere, you will have even more to offer. You will make a better partner than you could ever have done before. The future definitely augurs well.

4 What is the Most Important Attitude to Adopt at This Time?

You have chosen a dangerous path to enlightenment. If you survive the tests which your own mind sets you may gain some brilliant insights into the meaning of death, and also therefore, of life. These are not times to be fickle with yourself. The circumstances will sharpen you up and clarify your vision. Only a fool would not be cautious at this time.

5 Why Has Our Relationship Broken Down?

Your partner may not have been able to relate to the details of the demands you make upon yourself and the world. Perhaps you have appeared foolhardy in your desire to risk life and limb in your quest for enlightenment. Certainly, you are not in a position at the present time to make any meaningful commitment to your partner, and this may have caused or forced a parting of the ways, not without some regret on both sides. In such circumstances this parting may only be temporary. Providing you do not fall foul of the dangers into which you have deliberately plunged yourself, there is no real reason to believe that your relationship has been demolished. It is much more likely that it has been suspended for the time being, while you dive for pearls of wisdom.

6 Will We Get Back Together?

You may have taken leave of absence in mind, body and spirit for a short period of time, but this is not the same as a separation. You will be reconciled and reunited with your partner at the appropriate time. You did not part over differences of opinion between you. The situation described in this hexagram is of quite a different order. Although probably true to say that your partner is deeply significant in your life, he or she is not deeply significant in this situation.

7 What Can I Do to Put Things Right?

While your mind is being deluged with subjective impressions and feelings, there is a corresponding need to be objective in your view of the world and in yourself if you are to avoid taking this to excess. In order to avoid paranoid confusion, and self-obsession, you must, as it were, keep moving. Cultivate fluidity in your nature. Be honest with yourself, but not hard on yourself. Treat your own insights and perceptions with caution, and above all be impeccable in everything you do. Make each of your actions deliberate. Fortify your consciousness with a stalwart sincerity. Share your experiences with your partner, but only at your partner's invitation. You must not expect your partner to understand your feelings, however. The people who understand you at the moment require no explanations.

8 What Do I Most Want From Life?

You most desire to find your true self, to reconcile your duality, to open your third eye, to see.

THE LINES

One

A dangerous situation can serve to sharpen our instincts, to clarify our intuitions, to elevate awareness where the normal routine world dulls the edges of perception. Here, you are becoming too accustomed to the situation for it to have an uplifting effect. You are therefore in a highly vulnerable situation.

Two

Do not try to bite off more than you can chew. Do not run before you can walk. Do not try to do too much – content yourself with one step at a time and make each step a good one.

Three

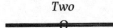

You are caught between the devil and the deep blue sea. This is a highly precarious situation, and if you move you will sink up to your neck. Therefore resist all temptation to make any impression on the situation. Keep perfectly still. The way forward will present itself in due course.

Four

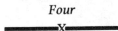

You have found a shelter in the storm. You have found a friend who offers you amenities and hospitality. There is natural empathy and honesty between you.

There is a strong suggestion in this line that you both have something to learn from each other. You are both, in your individual ways, seekers after the truth, but because of the inherent complications in communicating such ideas to each other, you should first explore the ideas which are mutually understood and build upon those.

Five

Resist the temptation to over-complicate your life with too many plans and desires for the future. Coping with the present should be sufficient to absorb all your energies. Take each day as it comes.

Six

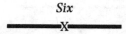

All your problems have combined together, and for the time being have made a prison of your mind. You are in a state of confusion. The initiative has been taken out of your hands.

HEXAGRAM 30

Fires of the Heart

1 Is This Person a Compatible Partner?

Your partner is well suited to you, but that suitability is conditioned
by your respective characteristics. You are a creative, fiery person,
who is able to illuminate thoughts, ideas and feelings in a way that is
beneficial to your partner and to others. However, you must inwardly
acknowledge that your brightness, like that of fire, is dependent on
certain qualities in other people which act as fuel. This is the nature of
the relationship between you and your partner. By a modest
awareness of this, you will be able to sustain your brightness. While
you shine, you know that your partner's influence is your motivation.

2 Does My Partner Love Me?

Just as fuel is the source of flame, so your partner is the fuel of your
brightness. By recognising this, you will adjust your attitude accordingly to one which is modest, acknowledges your dependence in this
sense and displays an unpretentious quietness and inner calm. These
are the correct attributes of your character. You should cultivate
them, and you will be able to shine with a steady light.

3 Do We Have a Future Together?

Although there is room for a great deal of sharing on many levels between you and your partner, your relative positions to each other are clearly defined by your own inner natures. There is fertile ground for love, but the durability of a bright relationship depends very much on your respective awareness of each other's specific roles. If you are able to dovetail together, then your love is potentially very durable.

4 What is the Most Important Attitude to Adopt at This Time?

All words and deeds should bear the mark of a person willing to compromise, willing to listen, willing to learn, willing once again to give and take in an equal and fair proportion. You are not in a position of force, but must accept the natural outcome either way.

5 Why Has Our Relationship Broken Down?

If your relationship has ended, then it is more likely to have burned out than broken down, and the failure will be largely on your part. The reasons will stem from an improper attitude towards your partner's position in your life. You have taken too much and not given enough in return. You have grown too self-willed. You may have allowed yourself to become forgetful of the fact that your partner is very squarely behind your drives and ambitions. You may have exploited too much and you have probably been selfish.

6 Will We Get Back Together?

If the fire of the relationship has burned itself out, that may well be the end of it. However, it is sometimes possible to rekindle new fire from ashes.

7 What Can I Do to Put Things Right?

Assuming that the relationship has not burned itself out, and that both partners recognise their positions in relation to each other and the uses they can make of each other for their mutual development, there is something to be done. If a person of fire and imagination realises his or her dependency on the partner for inspiration, guidance and assistance, then the relationship has a future.

There must be a genuine desire to reconcile yourself to your partner, and this desire should express itself above all in a quiet and unassuming manner.

8 What Do I Most Want From Life?

Your main desire is to generate sufficient self-discipline for the day to day consistent self-renewal of your inner light.

THE LINES

One

This line refers to the attitude you should hold at the beginning of an activity, which is symbolised by the beginning of the day, the morning. There is a lot to be done, and there are a lot of confusing impressions and details to be organised into a coherent pattern of activity. The line warns that you will not be able to cope with the complexity of the situation unless you remain cool and calm. If you sustain this attitude from the very beginning, this will condition the results at the end.

Two

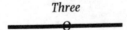

This line points out an auspicious condition in your affairs. Everything is balanced in harmony, poised between the extremes. This is an excellent position for you, both internally and externally.

Three

The line refers to the end of the day, or the evening time of life, old age. At these times, we often turn our minds to the thought that we are going to die. These thoughts are often tinged with unhappiness and our hearts feel constricted. Or we may feel overjoyed and take our celebrations too far. Neither state represents the correct attitude for this time.

You should be aware that death is the fate of every living thing. You cannot know whether death will come soon or late. The proper attitude is to spend your time developing your spiritual awareness. In this way you can honour your fate.

Four

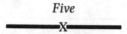

A bright fire can illuminate the darkness. If we burn too brightly, too quickly, we will not last. The oracle's advice is that the outpouring of energy must be regulated. Make a more economic use of your inner resources and their benefits will be more enduring.

Five

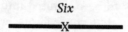

You have now reached the high point of your life. At this level, you perceive that everything in the world of Man is folly. The forces within you should blend in a perfect harmony now, and you should resist the temptation to swing like a pendulum through the poles of fear and hope, joy and sorrow. This is a time of genuine transition. Your heart swells up to perceive the larger universe.

Six

Nothing too much is once again the rule, especially where self-improvement is the aim. Too much self-discipline is as bad as too little. Too much self-criticism is as bad as too little. Too much severity is as bad as too little. The aim is to remove the bad in order to make room for good to develop. All that is bad is harmful to the spirit. Cut away only the bad part of the root and not the whole root.

HEXAGRAM 31

Natural Attraction

The basis of all that exists is heaven and earth. Heaven and earth are the subjects of the first thirty hexagrams in the I Ching. The basis of all social relationships in every society in the world is marriage. Hexagrams 31–64 are concerned primarily with social relationships.

1 Is This Person a Compatible Partner?

There is undoubtedly a strong mutual attraction between you and your partner. All the qualities are present in both of you to advise marriage.

2 Does My Partner Love Me?

This is one of those rare circumstances where the love you bear for each other is equal and mutual.

3 Do We Have a Future Together?

You should cultivate humility, be receptive to your partner and to others in your social group. This relationship has the possibility of being a warm, affectionate and fertile one within the context of marriage. The future promises the opportunity to develop the bond between you into something stronger and more enduring.

4 What is the Most Important Attitude to Adopt at This Time?

Keep to what comes naturally to you both. A relationship which contains the possibility of a fruitful marriage does not happen instantly, but must be worked at. The basis of your attraction is a natural empathy and affection for each other. Providing you are both consistently caring, this relationship will certainly blossom.

5 Why Has Our Relationship Broken Down?

The expression 'broken down' implies something sudden. If your relationship has come to an end, it is more likely to have simply withered away, worn down or dissipated to nothing because of a lack of consistency in displaying affection courteously.

Outside influences cannot be blamed. Any breakdown in the relationship has been within your joint responsibility from the very beginning. Have either of you been fickle?

6 Will We Get Back Together?

If you listen to good advice and you are not too strong-headed a reconciliation will happen. The strength of your mutual trust and belief in each other will ultimately bring you together.

7 What Can I Do to Put Things Right?

You and your partner have a natural attraction for each other. In order to allow nature to take its own course you should not impose any unusual restraint or make any special effort, but simply allow that spontaneous attraction to operate freely between you. You are both attracted to each other for genuine reasons and therefore should just act naturally.

You both admire in one another an unaffected quality. No unnecessary adornments to personality and character should be worn.

8 What Do I Most Want From Life?

You already know what you want of yourself, your partner and your life. You seek to improve on the quality of sharing which you have already achieved.

THE LINES

One

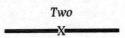

You have not made yourself suggestible enough to good influences and therefore you are unable to take them into your own life, or make sense of them in action. Because of this failing, there is no change in you.

Two

You are not in a position to act independently. Patiently await guidance if you are to avoid mistakes.

Three

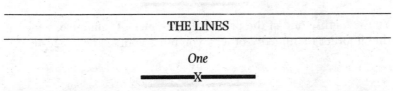

The advice here is to exercise more self-discipline. Do not allow yourself to be influenced by everything that goes on around you. Conversely, you must not attempt to influence everybody that comes into your circle. Perhaps you should look a little more closely at your motives for action. Sometimes subtle pressures from the environment are distracting.

Four

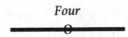

Your heart is good. Actions inspired by the feelings of your heart are good. If you act from the heart, you will have no cause for regret. People cannot help but be influenced by a person who acts in truth, but any attempt to control or adopt feelings which do not s ring spontaneously from your deepest self will only inspire confusion in yourself and others.

The usual rule in life is that love is a discriminating emotion. Only in special cases – and this is one of them – is it possible for a person to love all-embracingly. The basis of your influence is honest, and comes from the heart. The marriage of head and heart infuses your actions with a special and invigorating power.

Five

You recognise one of the principal dynamics of influence, which is that in order to influence others, you must yourself be suggestible.

Six

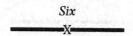

Some people merely satisfy themselves with talking about action, while others simply *do*. Here, you are talking more than you are doing, and the end result has no quality. To be effective, you must be more self-contained.

HEXAGRAM 32

Duration (Compatible Partners)

1 Is This Person a Compatible Partner?

This hexagram describes the union of two people who are highly compatible, and who, if they have not gone through the formality of marriage, live as a married couple. The symbol of the hexagram is the marriage of the eldest son with the eldest daughter, and signifies a relationship which has all the durability, strength and consistency desirable in the state of marriage. You both have everything you need to sustain a well-integrated life with one another. You and your partner complement each other very well. The weaknesses of one partner are balanced by the strengths of the other, and vice versa. You are both able to adapt to the challenges you jointly meet in life, and it is in your respective abilities to be adaptable that the strength of the relationship lies. It is your ability to be consistently strong in the ways that your partner expects of you that gives the relationship the power to endure, but this does not mean that you live boring, predictable lives together. Indeed, it means quite the opposite, for inherent in the meaning of this hexagram is the idea of momentum.

If you are inflexible and dependent upon one another, you cannot adapt to the challenges that you face together. On the other hand, if you are too independent and too flexible, the relationship will lack the necessary consistency of direction and inner strength which it will need in order to survive. Since you are naturally compatible with one another, you have found the right balance between you. You can both be true to yourselves, while at the same time be happy in each other's company and, as a pair, capable of meeting the demands of life.

Together, your sense of purpose in life is reinforced, and it is from this sense of purpose that your power as a couple is derived.

2 Does My Partner Love Me?

This is the hexagram of the truly compatible couple. You are able to *do* things together. Your love for each other expresses itself in down to earth, practical ways, and is not confined to sentimental expressions of endearment. This relationship has tremendous potential to flower into full maturity without either of you compromising your individuality to the other. Your love for each other is based upon a recognition and appreciation for each other's talents. You admire each other's strengths and tolerate each other's weaknesses. Your love is mutual and capable of carrying responsibilities.

3 Do We Have a Future Together?

The oracle focuses on this question more than on any of the others, in so far as it emphasises the ability of the relationship to subsist in time. Unquestionably, the answer is favourable. Truly compatible partners in marriage have other dimensions to their relationship. You consider each other as friends, as workmates; you have a natural desire to co-operate with each other in meeting life's demands and challenges. Without being glum or over-serious, you are capable of taking joy in achievement together. The oracle describes a marriage which lasts: all your strengths lie in the right places. You have stability where you need stability, adaptability where you need adaptability. As a couple you have the necessary strength to meet adversity, and the necessary fluidity to take advantage of changes as they arise. All the important qualities are balanced. You may be assured of a long life together.

4 What is the Most Important Attitude to Adopt at This Time?

You have a natural advantage in your relationship with your partner. Your complementary qualities of strength and resilience, creativity and receptivity are innate in your natures. In order for any relationship to last, there has to be a high degree of give and take. The ability to give and take is not something that you have had to master, or learn, it simply arises out of your fundamental compatibility. Strength supports weakness, weakness does not undermine strength.

There is no intrinsic need for you to artificially improve the quality of your lives. There is no special attitude to cultivate that is not already natural. The value of this oracle for you is that it reflects something you already know, namely that the relationship is on an even keel and that everything is under control.

If there are any specific circumstances to which your attention should be drawn, you will find these in the lines.

5 Why Has Our Relationship Broken Down?

Your relationship with your partner has not broken down. Nothing untoward or surprising will have happened to you. There have been no events to cause either of you to doubt the other. The rhythm of the relationship continues undisturbed. There is no basis for concern at this time.

6 Will We Get Back Together?

In accordance with the previous question, it is unlikely that your interest will need to be directed towards a reconciliation with each other. The quality of your relationship is displayed in the practical affairs of everyday life. Your ability to take on responsibilities as a team assumes togetherness.

7 What Can I Do to Put Things Right?

Do not be misled into thinking that the tone of the oracle implies that there is no room for improvement in your lives. While everything is in balance, and while you both possess the necessary qualities to keep things in balance, even through changing circumstances, this does not mean that everything is perfect all the time. Consistency is the secret of success, or rather consistency is the secret of continuing success. You are a highly motivated couple. Keep your specific objectives in mind. Providing you continue to do this, you will be able to resist attractive distractions.

There are times when you may feel that the pressure placed upon you by others to be dependable, compels you to express your individuality a little more strongly than is usual. If this does not distract the flow of your lives, there is no harm in it. You may, of course, go to the opposite extreme, and react to others by allowing yourself to become staid and too resistant to change. This will be harmful, since it will damage the momentum you have managed to build up.

As a couple – all things being equal – you will be able to weather changes and grow old gracefully.

8 What Do I Most Want From Life?

Among all the things that you value in life, you most value your stability. You maintain the harmony in your life well, but if you are going to go to extremes you are much more likely to err on the side of over-familiarity and over-predictability for your partner. There are times when you will both find yourself wanting a little more excitement in your life, a little more out of the ordinary.

In spiritual matters, you are not likely to take risks, but this does not imply a narrow-minded view of the world, more a single-minded approach. The difference is crucial. The important thing is to be aware of the existence of the possibilities that you reject in life, and not to assume that they do not exist or have no validity. Your road may be different from others, but all lead to Rome, as it were. The words *safe*, *predictable*, *true* and *harmonious* are not synonymous, but for you they may well have become so, and this is your road to a certain future.

THE LINES

One

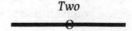

No city was built in a day. An artist cannot produce a work of art in a hurry. Do not bite off more than you can chew, nor travel in two directions at the same time. Still waters run deep, the freshest waters move swiftly. The best lasts.

Two

What you want to achieve is beyond your abilities and capacities at the present time, and you know this, so you are reluctant to try. However, such ambitions are long-range plans, you can take the time to develop your powers without wasting them.

Three

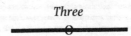

You are the kind of person who is dependent upon the weather. When it is sunny, your spirits are high, when it is cloudy, your spirits are low. That is to say, you allow yourself to be too easily affected by what is going on around you. This makes you extremely vulnerable. If you are not self-contained, you are not in control, and not master of your fate.

Four

There are methods and procedures you must go through in order to achieve the things you want. If you want to score goals, you have to play football. If you want to be with people of your own kind, go to places where they meet. Look around. Learn from the experience of others who do the things that you want to do. If you want to catch fish, first you must cast your net into the water. In other words you must act appropriately, relevantly, or you will only succeed in creating greater frustration and contradiction in yourself.

Five

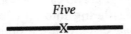

Do what you believe is right, and do not allow yourself to be so easily led by your partner. Do not wear blinkers, however. Be single-minded, but not narrow-minded. Give your will a chance.

Six

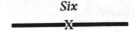

Relax. If something is worth doing, it is worth doing well. The work suffers if you are in a constant state of agitation. Intolerance and impatience may become habits.

HEXAGRAM 33

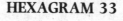

Strategic Withdrawal

1 Is This Person a Compatible Partner?

The relationship is in jeopardy. An immense and overwhelming opposing power threatens to overcome you. In such a predicament, you cannot possibly hold your ground. You do not have the necessary strength for a stand-up fight. You cannot hope to win in open battle.

Your relationship is entering into an extremely difficult time. If your partner is the adversary, then the situation has arisen from a long build-up of mutual antagonism. If your partner is not your adversary, then there is something outside the relationship which threatens to divide you. You must decide which of the two circumstances is applicable. There should be absolutely no doubt in your mind which is the true position.

2 Does My Partner Love Me?

Love could not be further from your mind.

3 Do We Have a Future Together?

You are surrounded by hostile elements at the moment. Follow the advice of the oracle. From your present point of view, the future is completely irrelevant, and so it should be. Take care of today and let the future take care of itself.

4 What is the Most Important Attitude to Adopt at This Time?

In the face of such a sudden attack and such overwhelming odds against you, your immediate reaction might be to turn and run in a state of panic. This would be completely disastrous. The best attitude for you at the moment is to recognise that winning and losing are not predetermined. You can still gain the advantage by strategically retreating to a position of greater strength.

If you retreat far enough into yourself, your defences will be unshakeable. Sustain your dignity and remain alert, and although you are retreating, in this way you will be able to keep the pressure on your opponent, making every corresponding advance on their part difficult and dangerous.

5 Why Has Our Relationship Broken Down?

If your partner is the encroaching power detailed above, then the reason for the breakdown is that you are fundamentally incompatible in your natures. At present, your partner is stronger than you, and it is impossible for you to withstand the pressure being placed upon you alone. Make no effort to do so.

If your partner is not the adversary, or antagonist, then the malignant forces approaching and threatening to divide you come from somewhere beyond the relationship. The reason for such hostility is not known, but you do not have the time to sit and wonder why.

6 Will We Get Back Together?

You must refuse to become entangled in negative emotions. Do not make the stupid mistake of being tempted towards feelings of hatred. If you do, you will become so deeply emotionally involved that you will not be able to extricate yourself. Look at it like this – if you want to conceal yourself physically, you will keep very quiet. You will not light any matches, and you will switch off your torch. In the same way, if you wish to protect your secret, you do not publicly proclaim

that you have a secret to protect. In short, keep yourself to yourself. It
is not pertinent to consider reconciliation at this time.

7 What Can I Do to Put Things Right?

The advice of the oracle is precise. From the point of view of your
antagonist you are a clearly visible target and because of your
antagonist's greater strength you cannot hope to put up any kind of
resistance in open battle. You must therefore give ground, fall back.

In emotional terms, this means that you must withdraw into
yourself. Do not be tempted into argument, do not lose your inner
composure and do not lose your temper, but calmly and strategically
withdraw into a place of safety. The *way* in which you do this is all-
important. Do not panic, do not run, do not be overcome by fear.

You are still in a position to make some impression on your
antagonist. Once you have become inaccessible, you will be less
vulnerable to attack. Herein lies your advantage. When your king is
threatened in a game of chess, and it is apparent that you cannot
counter-attack with similar potency, it is nevertheless possible to
protect the king in such a way as to put yourself in a position to
effectively damage the full effect of the opposition. You can only do
this with a cool mind, however.

8 What Do I Most Want From Life?

All you wish to do is to survive the time. If you do so, you will have
learned something very important.

THE LINES

One

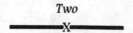

You are in dire straits. Attempt nothing. Do not go forward, do not go
back. Keep perfectly still. The situation was brought about by your
total lack of foresight.

Two

You owe your salvation to cowardice in the face of danger. By clinging to somebody of stronger temperament than yourself, without being invited to do so, you are both carried to safety, but not by your own volition. This is barely forgivable even as an act of desperation.

Three

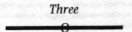

You are caught, as it were, between the devil and the deep blue sea. Your only source of rescue is unacceptable but – in a choice between two evils – you are compelled to follow even the slightest glimmer of hope, even though it leaves a nasty taste in your mouth.

Four

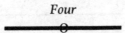

It is time for the better man of the two to go his way. He realises that no good could come of his influence if he stayed any longer. He withdraws gracefully, leaving the other to contemplate the significance of his unwholesome predicament.

Five

When it is time to leave, it is time to leave. Wisdom lies in recognising the appropriate moment to do so. Here, it is best to leave with a genuine smile. Do not allow yourself to be embarrassed by any last minute pleadings. It is time to go.

Six

You are aware that you are free to leave. You feel good about it. The future looks inviting. You say your goodbyes in an excellent spirit.

HEXAGRAM 34

The Leading Initiative

1 Is This Person a Compatible Partner?

This is a time of great energy and power for you. You are almost in a position to bend others according to your will, but in choosing a soulmate or a partner, this could be fatal. Unless you are patient, you may rush into things. In affairs of the heart, you are certainly the strong one, but you must temper this strength and energy with patience at this time. You must consciously hold yourself in check, though not to the point of frustration.

2 Does My Partner Love Me?

A time of power is a special time.

You can achieve a great deal now. Your partner cannot help but be led by your initiative. If you are of a loving disposition, then this is likely to invoke precisely the same reaction from your partner. Because you are the initiator at this time, any move will follow your pattern. A positive, affectionate attitude in matters of the heart will evoke the best response from your partner, and provide a fruitful environment for your relationship to grow.

3 Do We Have a Future Together?

The oracle tends in your favour. The gentle application of great energy contains tremendous possibilities for you. Harmony implies participation in your environment. If you allow your partner to participate, you will be able to take greater advantage of the present time. At the moment, you have the power to do a lot of good, if you work within the scheme of things.

4 What is the Most Important Attitude to Adopt at This Time?

During times when you possess great energy, it is absolutely imperative for you to combine a sense of purpose and direction with the concept of fairness in the way you treat others. It is all too easy at the moment for you to take the initiative without consulting the feelings of other people. While this initiative may not, in itself, be wrong it is important for you to join your energies with those around you, especially with those of your partner. Combine great energy and a sense of fairness in everything you do.

In essence, the oracle advises that you cultivate a greater sense of co-operation with your partner and those around you.

5 Why Has Our Relationship Broken Down?

Energy and power must be tempered with good principles. Any breakdown of communication between you and your partner will have come about because of a complete and total misuse of this energy.

The implication of this oracle, however, is that your power is positive and good. Only an unusual absence of self-control on your part will have caused the relationship to go off the rails.

At this time, you are entirely responsible for the direction of the relationship. If it has gone wrong, then you must look to your own behaviour for the cause, for it is unlikely that your partner will have been in a position to guide the relationship in the way that you have.

It is well to note one of the main precepts which should concern a great power: the greater the power, the correspondingly greater must be the control. If the relationship has gone wrong, its failure can best be understood in terms of the lack of harmony between you. If there is any bad feeling between you, you must accept the responsibility.

6 Will We Get Back Together?

If the present situation is one of turmoil, then only by directing your energies towards creating harmony can the correct environment be created for any reconciliation to take place. However, the initiative does lie with you at this time.

7 What Can I Do to Put Things Right?

You must avoid doing anything which will create disharmony between you and your partner. It is appropriate for you to adopt a kindly disposition, making yourself accessible, willing to listen, easy to approach, gentle in your responses, careful and thoughtful in your choice of words.

8 What Do I Most Want From Life?

If you can resist the temptation to abuse your responsibilities and avoid being the cause of misery and upset and do not act for personal gain or from a false sense of pride or indulge in conceit, then the circumstances are highly auspicious. You want to make the most of propitious times in your life.

THE LINES

One

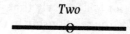

Do not confuse power and energy with rash force. If you act with energy and care, you will achieve your ambition. If you act with force, the results will be unfortunate.

Two

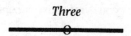

Things are looking up, but do not let this go to your head or cause an arrogant or blasé attitude. Maintain that sense of inner harmony and all will be well.

Three

Any display of arrogance is a testament to others of your unworthiness for your position. The person who is truly worthy of power accords it the proper respect. On no account does the wise person revel in it.

Four

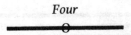

This is a time to plod on consistently. Through bringing energy consistently to bear on events in an unostentatious way, you are in a position to achieve considerable feats.

Five

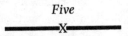

The time when you had to show a hard face to the world has passed. You can now safely pursue your course without opposition.

Six

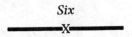

You are caught between the devil and the deep blue sea. If you force things in any direction whatsoever, you will only trap yourself. If you realise your predicament and maintain a sense of inner harmony, the situation will untangle itself. You will be able to move forward again. Without inner composure, you will not be able to extricate yourself.

NOTE: Inner composure arises from a state of relaxation. This means not allowing external events and circumstances to create inner tensions.

HEXAGRAM 35

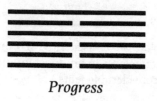

Progress

1 Is This Person a Compatible Partner?

This is an auspicious relationship between two generous people who have implicit trust in one another.

2 Does My Partner Love Me?

Can you not see the love light shining clearly from your partner's eyes?

3 Do We Have a Future Together?

You should continue confidently in this relationship without fear.

4 What is the Most Important Attitude to Adopt at This Time?

The best thing to do is to maintain a smiling, optimistic attitude and just carry on. You should, however, avoid soliciting favours from people in order to extricate yourself from a difficult situation, as this might involve you in emotional ups and downs which would mar the rapidity of your progress.

5 Why Has Our Relationship Broken Down?

Perhaps you are taking slight setbacks too seriously. If there is any breakdown in the relationship, it is due to a neurotic twinge. This oracle, however, indicates that this is unlikely and any setback is unlikely to be serious or of long duration.

6 Will We Get Back Together?

With specific reference to a personal relationship, this question should not have been asked. The assumption here is that you should not have parted under the present circumstances. If, in fact, you have, then it is beyond the scope of this oracle to address itself to such a problem.

7 What Can I Do to Put Things Right?

This is a time of progress. Take advantage of this time to develop yourself and your relationship on all its levels. No doubt you are very conscious of creating your future at the present time, and this is auspicious.

8 What Do I Most Want From Life?

The meaning of progress in this context is the development of personal clarity. Growth and clarity are your principal aims.

NOTE: Spiritual development is the work which underlies all mankind's activities throughout life. Only the values of the heart can subsist in time, and this is the cornerstone of reality.

THE LINES

One

You are developing your situation with a good heart. If other people do not live up to your optimistic and good-natured approach, there is nothing for you to do but to continue. Do not, however, be tempted to enter into any conflicting situations.

Two

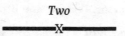

You have been forced to a halt, due to something getting in the way of your contacting the gentle, kindly and authoritative person with whom you have a definite empathy and strong affinity, and this upsets you. You must not give up. The relationship is right, and the contact will be made for no other reason than it *is* right.

Three

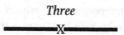

With the support of others, you are able to take positive strides forward. You may wish, however, that you could have done it alone without help, but the fact that you have been helped and that this has enabled you to make progress considerably enhances your positive feelings.

Four

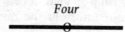

It is often the case in life that people of forceful disposition abuse their authority in order to acquire wealth by dubious and deceptive means. In times like these, especially when events are moving quickly, morally reprehensible and highly suspect methods tend to fare well under the cloak of darkness. Evil must be brought out into the brilliant light of day. Evil methods should be openly condemned and, if not checked, such atrocious standards of conduct must inevitably bring about the downfall of these people.

Five

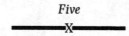

You are now in a strong position from which to exploit your advantage. It may well be that you will suffer a loss by not so doing, but this is not important and you should not attach too much weight to it.

Your good nature wins esteem in the eyes of other people, and this enables you to bring positive influences to bear upon their lives. Far more importantly, the people to whom you are close know that you care about them.

184

Six

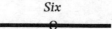

Because of the closeness of this association, it is certainly right for you to redress any wrongs which may have been committed. Normally it is not appropriate to use such force and energy as one is often in danger of overdoing things. Here, unless acting in such a way is justified, you are likely to offend and make a fool of yourself. The presumption of the oracle is that you are invested in a position where wisdom and discrimination are *expected* of you. The focus of your concern should be the manner in which you fulfil these expectations, having regard to what is 'appropriate force'.

HEXAGRAM 36

The Encroaching Shadow

1 Is This Person a Compatible Partner?

You are already intimately and inextricably bound up with your partner. There is no escape from the situation. As a couple you are completely incompatible. Your partner is totally oblivious to the values you hold to be dear and important in life. The sheer force of your partner's personality makes it dangerous for you to take a stand in a situation which you know is appalling, disgraceful and outrageous. Your partner, however, is not aware of the way you feel, and this complicates matters considerably.

2 Does My Partner Love Me?

In the light of all that follows, you may feel that the answer here should be a definite 'no', but this is to miss the point. It is quite possible that your partner, in their own way, loves you in the only way they can. The important thing to note here is that he or she is completely insensitive to the way you feel about the things which are important to you. In this sense their love is selfish and even childish, certainly immature and distinctly lacking in depth. All this is very unfortunate for you.

3 Do We Have a Future Together?

By no stretch of the imagination could you describe your future as being together. The values by which you separately live your lives, even under the same roof, are so disparate and so different in quality and meaning, that there is no common ground for sharing.

Providing you do not provoke your partner to any kind of violent response, you may be able to withstand living in a state of estrangement. Unfortunately there is no joy in this relationship.

Beyond the relationship it is quite possible for you to make a fulfilling life for yourself. Because you and your partner do not see eye-to-eye in matters of the heart, you cannot anticipate any genuinely enriching emotional exchanges taking place between you.

4 What is the Most Important Attitude to Adopt at This Time?

By now you will feel the situation is completely hopeless, but bear in mind that this is a time which will pass. At present things are going from bad to worse, which is why you must make sure that your feet are planted firmly on the ground. Do not compromise those inner values from which your life derives meaning.

By being externally submissive, you deny your partner a foothold. Evil tendencies must not be given the opportunity of undermining your true value. In these matters be absolutely clear with yourself.

Do not volunteer any information which could conceivably be used against you.

The kind of person with whom you are now involved is one of the worst possible examples of humanity. This is augmented by the fact that these types are quite powerful people and so you must not underestimate their power. Nevertheless, you do hold the winning hand. Do not forget that; but do not show it yet. (Under the circumstances this includes the utmost discretion in the use of this book.) This is a time, then, of extreme caution and extreme reserve. Sustain these attitudes.

5 Why Has Our Relationship Broken Down?

There is no real communication between you and your partner. The ideas and the feelings which bind two people together in a common empathy are missing completely in your relationship.

The relationship by no means lives up to your ideals. What makes your predicament worse, is that your partner appears to you to be completely blasé about it. He or she is oblivious, uncaring, unnoticing and, above all, insensitive. However, because of your circumstances, you are inextricably bound up with one another.

The breakdown in the relationship can be understood more in terms of a break in the spirit of empathy than an actual separation.

6 Will We Get Back Together?

Unfortunately circumstances have not allowed you to part ways in any physical sense. Unless your partner shows a miraculous improvement in attitude, then you will have to consider the ways in which you can live your life without compromising your ideals. Although this is difficult, it is not impossible.

7 What Can I Do to Put Things Right?

There is nothing you can do to put things right, but there are certainly things you can do to protect yourself from being further aggravated by the situation. Firstly, you must be secretive. You must – as the proverb says – hide your light under a bushel, and not allow yourself to be compelled by your partner into doing things with which you disagree. Refuse to go along with any compromising suggestions in order to avoid ultimately being taken in by them. All the same, you should not feel impelled to force your partner to see the error of his or her ways. By no means pretend to have all the answers. At the same time, do not allow yourself to be fooled by any quicksilver-tongued self-justifications which your partner may offer. Do not be tempted into arguments over differences of opinion. Let potential sore points go by.

The point to note here is that your partner's evil ways feed on anything and everything, but most of all they feed on your opposition. Do not provide any obvious opposition. Ultimately, people such as this consume themselves, without any help from others.

8 What Do I Most Want From Life?

In your heart of hearts, you most probably wish to extricate yourself from the relationship completely, but for one reason or another this is impossible at the moment. You want from a partner all that is missing in your present relationship, mutual affection, understanding, warm emotional exchanges, a companion and friend, someone with whom you can share deeper feelings. You would prefer to live with somebody with whom you can behave naturally without being constantly on your guard. Although none of these things are obtainable at present it is possible that you can make a better match at some time in the future.

THE LINES

One

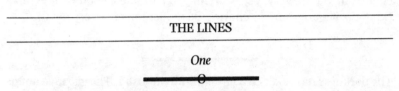

You are finding in all your tremendous efforts that the price of personal honesty is high in friendship and in money. Although times are hard, you should not abandon your personal integrity. You must simply reconcile yourself to the fact that there are times when personal security – emotional and otherwise – costs you more than you bargained for.

Two

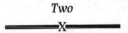

This is the line of the moral hero. Although the odds are stacked against you, persevere in what you believe is good for the benefit of others.

Three

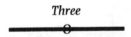

You are doing your best to put right what has gone wrong. In the process you encounter an unlooked for golden opportunity and make a powerful impression on the person or people behind all the trouble. Do not expect to eradicate all the faults in one swift blow, in the way that Alexander the Great sliced through the Gordian knot. The difficulties here run deep. Complications are more profound than they at first seem.

Four

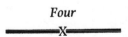

As if by chance, you gain an insight into the power of the malevolent forces which surround you. You realise that there is nothing you can do to stop them. All you can do is escape unnoticed before order breaks down, which it certainly will.

Five

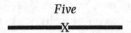

You have no choice but to escape from the situation. It is how you do so that decides your success or failure. Difficulties are coming to a climax. If you are very, very careful you can make good your escape. Do not leave anything to chance, be meticulous in every detail.

Six

The darkness has reached its maximum intensity. Things have got as bad as they are ever going to get, and now they can only improve. When evil forces have no further good elements to prey upon, they destroy themselves. When evil has nothing more to fight, it fights and destroys itself. Evil does not know the meaning of self-restraint, and this is its downfall.

HEXAGRAM 37

The Family

---

1 Is This Person a Compatible Partner?

This hexagram concerns itself with the relationship between parents – mother and father – and their children. The scope of the hexagram also embraces the relationships between the children, to each other, and also to in-laws of both parents.

The basic assumptions which the *I Ching* posits for the family are as follows

1 The family unit is the fundamental bond between people all over the world.

2 The nature of authority and power in every family lies with the parents jointly.

3 The influence of authority in a family setting comes primarily from words which are supported by good examples.

The *I Ching* places a great emphasis on the example which parents give their children. If the parents themselves do not set a consistently good example to their children, they cannot expect their children to follow in matters of courtesy, good conduct, trust or affection, or in regard to the moral principles which form the basis of society. If there is any disparity between the words and conduct of the parents, then this will only produce confusion and contradiction in the children, who will ultimately turn away from their parents.

Therefore, the solidarity of the family comes from the solidarity of the parents themselves in their relationship with one another. The basis of such stability between parents and the children is affection.

The family is the microcosm; society at large is the macrocosm. All the principles which apply to the family, apply also to the society at large. Provided that respect and integrity are based upon real affection, then all differences within that group can be amicably accommodated.

Parents should show respect for the friendships which their children form with other people, as the friends of their children should show respect for the parents. Therefore the loyalty which binds a family and a society together, arises from true affection and true respect. Where either of these two elements is missing in the individual attitude, then this will affect the whole family as well as the whole of society in a display of weakness.

2 Does My Partner Love Me?

Affection is the basis of all mutual and interdependent relations in the family and in society at large. It is reasonable to assume that parents will love their children and will love each other, and that children will love their parents.

At the highest level, affection is the basis of the greatest awareness. Therefore, it can be said that those who are most aware of the interdependence of people in the family, in institutions, and in society at large as it extends all the way around the world, are those who by their conduct and by their example display the greatest care. The only way that true care can be demonstrated is by setting a good example.

3 Do We Have a Future Together?

The future of the family and the future of society, indeed the future of the world, are intimately interconnected. As said, the principles which sustain the family are the same as those which sustain the world. Where these principles are ignored at the family level, divisive tendencies creep in and take hold. Divisions in society will only erode when divisions in the family also erode. The basis and central unit in which society's cultural assumptions are shared and communicated is the family. If the family unit itself is divided then whose example are the children to follow? How do they decide which is the good example, and which the bad? In the same way, if family unity is not based upon genuine heartfelt affection, then wherein lies the good example of the parents? The future of family unity and therefore the future of the world depends on the answers to these questions.

There is no promise of either good or bad fortune. It is the quality of the example set which determines the quality of future inter-relations and inter-dependencies in the family, in society, in the world.

4 What is the Most Important Attitude to Adopt at This Time?

The central idea of the hexagram is that parents must set a good example, as must the leaders of society. Where a parent feels that his or her conduct is wanting, he or she must be willing to improve in order to set a better example. The same applies to the leaders of society, for whom setting a good example is the basis of credibility. The best attitude for children to adopt is to follow only good examples: children are not obliged to follow a bad example. Where children do not follow the example of their parents, they must a) have good reasons for doing so, and b) be willing to communicate these reasons to the parents. Hence it is a willingness to seek out the best basis for conduct which forms the correct attitude. Not caring is reprehensible in an individual, and can only have the effect of being divisive, not only in the family but in society as a whole.

5 Why Has Our Relationship Broken Down?

If children hold their parents in contempt, or parents hold their children in contempt, or if the parents hold each other in contempt, then all affection and respect breaks down, and the family splits up. The same rule applies to society and its leaders. If the father is weak, the son will hold him in contempt, if the son is weak, the father will hold him in contempt.

In both cases, contempt is wrong: in both cases self respect is missing. The roots of contempt are the lack of self respect and a disproportionate sense of one's own self importance. Taken too far, these qualities are always divisive in a family and in society.

It is easier to respect someone we like. It takes strength to respect someone we do not like. It is upon this strength that the differences between people can be accommodated. It is the absence of this strength that is the cause of any breakdown in the relationship.

6 Will We Get Back Together?

The answer is definitely conditional.

There is nothing in this hexagram to suggest the outcome one way or another. If parents set a good example, their children will choose to follow it. In the same way, if the moral conduct of the leaders of society is not found wanting, then their laws and policies will be accepted. If the standard of care is sufficiently high, and the standard of conduct corresponds to it, the outcome will almost definitely be good fortune.

Each individual has a personal responsibility to set personally a good example. There is no other basis for a reconciliation which is likely to endure in the family or the world.

7 What Can I Do to Put Things Right?

Blood is thicker than water, as they say. It is always possible to achieve a reconciliation between members of one family. The cornerstone for reconciliation is tolerance and the strength to accommodate differences of opinion, attitudes and ways of life. Such strength arises from an expansion of awareness in the individual.

Awareness must come from within.

The same principle of blood tie applies for mankind as a whole. The reconciliation of differences is based upon a strength to accommodate and tolerate.

So long as people are willing to understand, there is always the possibility of reconciliation. This can never be taken away. Parents can only teach children tolerance by being tolerant themselves, in the same way that leaders of society can only be credible where they set a good example of tolerance. As always, actions speak louder than words: actions must support words. It is the example which gives the explanation its real meaning.

Where children listen to their parents and parents listen to their children, the best grounds for a relationship are developed. The doors for a reconciliation are constantly open. The best leaders are those who constantly consult with those whom they lead, in order to find the best ways of reconciling the differences in society. The basis of such a dialogue is, of course, mutual understanding and respect based upon affection. How can one find the solution to a problem if one has not enquired as to its source, or made every effort to genuinely understand it? Therefore, the first step to putting right something which has gone wrong, is to make enquiry, to consult, to be willing to learn and to be willing to accept the advice that you yourself give, and to set a good example.

8 What Do I Most Want From Life?

Your heart's desire is family unity based upon true affection and world unity based upon the expansion of individual awareness, mutual trust and a greater spirit of sharing at home and around the world.

THE LINES

One

Within every family there are shared rules and assumptions. Everybody in the family knows where he or she fits in and what is expected. The authoritative example for this comes from the parents. If a child is not offered a definite guideline as to how he or she should behave from a very young age, that child will grow up disenchanted and disillusioned with his or her parents. Until a child is old enough to evaluate experiences, the child is wholly dependent on the values inculcated in it by the parents. If these values are not clearly understandable to the child – and reasonable within the child's frame of reference – then the parents will have cause to regret this later.

This particular line warns against spoiling a child. That is, indulging it in every conceivable way. If a child gets his or her own way in everything without discrimination, how can the parents expect him or her to understand at some later stage when they do draw the line? How can you then blame the child for not accepting where the line has been drawn?

Two

The responsibilities of husband and wife should be evenly distributed in the running of day-to-day affairs. Neither should attempt to take on the responsibilities of the other, except under extraordinary circumstances. How the responsibilities between husband and wife are divided is entirely a personal affair, based upon a personal agreement.

It will become apparent to parents where their individual talents and abilities have the best effect.

Three

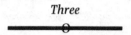

The advice of the oracle here is to err on the side of discipline rather than on the side of indulgence. Where differences of opinion within the family are causing quarrels and arguments, and where the discipline of the family breaks down, something discreditable tends to appear in its train. The basis of mutual respect is mutual accessibility to reason. The blind imposition of authority for authority's sake is as bad as indulging a family's every whim. There is no suggestion in the oracle that discipline should be imposed in the form of physical violence.

Four

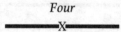

This line refers to the management of household accounts, which is traditionally the responsibility of the wife and mother. Whoever is responsible for running the household finances, the wisest course is to balance the income with expenditure. The oracle suggests that you already do this very well.

Five

The essence of your authority in the family comes not from your ability to generate fear, but in your ability to win the confidence of the members of that family through kindness and natural endearing affection. The benefit of your influence comes from your own good character and from your own good example.

Six

The added responsibilities of running a household and raising a family require special abilities. If the parents love each other, the children will love the parents. This is the basis upon which a strong family unit rests, and the only basis capable of sustaining the family through the many difficulties and problems encountered over the years.

HEXAGRAM 38

Opposition

1 Is This Person a Compatible Partner?

While this person may be fundamentally different from you in approach to life, this does not necessarily mean that they are unsuitable as a partner. Very often opposites have a curious and productive attraction for each other, which is not to say that this is definitely the case here, but it is a possibility to be considered.

The potential for attraction in this case is strong, although certain points must be borne in mind. Firstly, your differences can be used to establish a workable order for daily life which is perfectly acceptable for both of you, though nothing of great moment should be attempted between you. Secondly, the tenor of such a relationship must encompass gentle consideration of each other, especially of basic differences. Thirdly, only by cultivating your higher natures can you both attain true individuality, while at the same time experiencing a real sense of unity.

You are both very much individuals, and you both hold on to your own individuality. Your respective lower natures bear no resemblance at all, and therefore cannot mix without conflict, harming the relationship as a whole.

2 Does My Partner Love Me?

This kind of person expresses love for you through a willingness to create order between you based upon a deeply felt respect for your special individuality. As this order is expressed in everyday terms, so the love which is true love, is measured.

3 Do We Have a Future Together?

The future is always constructed out of the present scheme of things. If order is the fruit of your opposition, then there is much between you to portend a constructive and mutually respectful future.

It is vital that you both recognise each other's fundamental differences and reconcile these in an ordered way. Thus your natures blend at a higher level, though your achievements will always be modest when they are undertaken together.

You must not place too much pressure on each other to conform against your natural inclinations, for this can break down the necessary tolerances which make unity between you possible. All unity, especially between people so different, depends upon respectful tolerance.

Tolerance in a relationship is very much the mark of maturity.

4 What is the Most Important Attitude to Adopt at This Time?

You must first give serious consideration to the differences between you and your partner, and you must develop a deeply felt respect for those differences. In this way you relieve the tensions which your different natures naturally generate. A moderate and temperate understanding blended with a tolerant decisiveness will avoid the unnecessary rashness which is always harmful to your relationship.

5 Why Has Our Relationship Broken Down?

The main reasons for breakdown between you are fundamentally opposed natures. While these contradictions need not necessarily result in a breakdown, they will do so if one side is insensitive to the nature of the other. Insensitivity may be expressed in this case by overwhelming crudity, which is an attribute and expression of lower nature, and by trying to achieve too much too quickly in an unsuitable and dramatic style.

Any pressure placed on the weak points of an opposite lower nature is likely to make the higher nature collapse. This is what has happened, and the resulting loss of the sense of individuality in your partner's nature has caused a breakdown in the sympathies and affections which are the lifeblood of any relationship. When we are attacked, whether rightly or wrongly, we are like to feel less tolerant of the attacker. It is well to remember that without such sympathies and affection, the tensions between two opposed natures cannot be absorbed. The relationship therefore becomes brittle and cracks under the least strain.

6 Will We Get Back Together?

There are no guarantees where your natures are so directly opposed, especially where the cause of the initial breakdown has been due to insensitivity on one side, or both. The meeting point, for there must exist a meeting point, is always in the higher self, so the relationship represents a challenge for personal improvement. It can only be reached by gentle and undramatic means. The way to achieve such mutual reconciliation, is by attempting small reconciliations on minor matters and by avoiding the larger differences between your natures. By placing too heavy an emphasis on your differences, you will only increase your difficulties. Your only chance of reconciliation is through the things you have in common.

7 What Can I Do to Put Things Right?

You can best avoid making mistakes by using no force or unsavoury means of persuasion or coercion. The advice here offered is to act according to your own individuality in its higher manifestation – in this case with gentleness, tolerance and spiritual awareness – and by trying to understand the importance and meaning of true affection. To ignore this higher manifestation in your own nature will only increase the present divide, and will generate further misunderstandings which can only be overcome in the natural course of time.

8 What Do I Most Want From Life?

At present your main desire is to reconcile the opposing forces in your own nature.

You tend to perceive the world in terms of opposites: black and white, positive and negative, *yin* and *yang*, love and hate. You polarise the extremes and act according to them. At the lower level, you are a pawn to your own thoughts. At the higher level, you seek to bring these opposing forces together into a systematic way of behaving. This brings you to a truer view of the world which embraces more possibilities, thus attaining a true and lasting peace of heart.

THE LINES

One

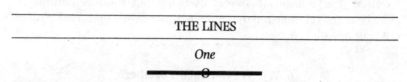

The most important element here is to resolve differences of nature not by force, but by being unremittingly tolerant and true to yourself.

If force is used, unhappy consequences will arise which will inevitably generate conflict and resentment in your partner.

Those who naturally accord with you will be attracted to you. You must trust this fact. Those who do not naturally accord with you must be allowed to go their own way without hindrance. Like the 'tar baby' principle, what you attack attaches itself to you. If you restrain yourself from attacking, the opposition naturally withdraws and causes you no harm.

Two

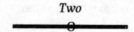

There are times when untoward circumstances keep you from the people who are most like you. In these times a chance meeting with like-minded people may assist your purpose.

Three

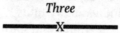

In the face of what often appears to be injustice and unfair opposition, you must be resolute in your choice of companions and friends.

Do not compromise. If you put your faith in your true companions, matters will go well for you, but if you do not, matters will go badly for you.

Four

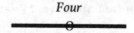

Among people, like attracts like. This is a universal law. Where you are surrounded by those with whom you have no inner affinities, you will feel no empathy.

It is natural to feel isolated and unsure of your footing, but those with whom you share a genuine feeling are naturally attracted to you, and you to them. By being true to yourself, you will inevitably encounter these people, and through the resolute application of your willpower you will achieve your purpose; but only that purpose is consistent with your true inner nature.

Five

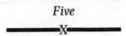

Very often, a lack of vision prevents us from recognising our true companions at first sight. Now, however, such a companion recognises your true nature, and this person acts positively towards you. By this, you come to realise the similarities in your respective natures, and on this basis the possibility of mutual work is created. You are advised to avail yourself of the opportunities provided by such a fortunate encounter without any further mistrust.

Six

Your own inner turmoil creates an ambiguous state of mind which results in an attitude of deep mistrust towards those whom you call your friends. You cannot decide whether the people around you are to be trusted, and you vascillate wildly between trust and mistrust. This brings a great deal of confusion to you, and your heart is sore. However, despite your own inability to reconcile your attitude towards those people, they approach you with honesty and clarity. In this way they bring you to your senses, enabling you finally to recognise their true worth in your life.

HEXAGRAM 39

Impasse (Difficult Obstacles)

1 Is This Person a Compatible Partner?

This hexagram describes either a situation wherein you are trying to make contact with a potentially compatible partner, or one in which you are trying to overcome some hindrance which lies between you and your present partner, but you encounter a direct block or impediment which completely thwarts forward movement. This is more than a hitch or a snag.

You feel frustrated in your attempts to find a way around the object of obstruction. It is as if you have been confronted by a huge abyss, and you have no means of getting across. You are stymied. However, the oracle implies that the obstruction is not entirely defeating. You do not have to give up the ghost, or give up your intention of reaching your desired objective. Although you have come to this head and realise that to overcome the difficulties will require a special solution, nevertheless your intentions are honourable, and you must keep to them.

The import of this hexagram is to suggest a way in which you can confront this difficult block to your progress, so that you may eventually overcome it and achieve your aims.

2 Does My Partner Love Me?

The oracle is neutral on the question of your partner's love. There is no suggestion of ill will on either your part or that of your partner. The nature of the obstruction, however, may hint at the need to reinforce your growing awareness through the development of your character.

3 Do We Have a Future Together?

The advice given in this oracle focusses specifically on your present situation. It asks you to look at the future in terms of the difficulties to be overcome. At this time, the future of any relationship with your partner is entirely dependent upon your overcoming the drawback, whatever it might be. This definitely does not mean that the future is closed – it merely places a necessary condition upon it.

4 What is the Most Important Attitude to Adopt at This Time?

You cannot confront the difficulties directly at the present time. You must therefore be prepared to take a few steps back. Continue with your life as usual, but be prepared to confront these problems when the appropriate time comes. There is no doubt that you are intended to overcome them.

In order to resist the inevitable build-up of tension or frustration, you must recognise that the delay which has been forced upon you is part of the preparatory process. Keep your eyes on the problem, but from a distance. In this way you can learn more about it.

5 Why Has Our Relationship Broken Down?

There are two possible interpretations of this situation, only one of which will be appropriate to you.

First, it is possible that the relationship has not broken down at all, but has merely been impeded because of the need for personal development on your part and the need for you to take stock of your situation. You may regard it as a timely block, a blessing in disguise, saving you from making a gross error such as would ultimately destroy the relationship.

Second, it is possible that you have attempted to overcome the obstacles alone, and without pause for thought, without realising their magnitude or the possible consequences. By acting so thought- lessly, you will have seriously compromised yourself in the relation-

THE I CHING ON LOVE

ship, in such a way as to have caused a complete breakdown in communication between you.

The former interpretation is likely to be appropriate, however, for the spirit of the *I Ching* is to assist a person in making progress and to give where necessary timely warnings of impending difficulties.

6 Will We Get Back Together?

The nature of the present obstruction presents an unusual challenge for you to overcome in order to effect a reconciliation, not only with your partner but with certain elements of yourself.

The focus of the advice given is to point out the special way in which you can overcome the obstacles in order that such a reconciliation can take place. Forward progress here can mean the reintegration of yourself at a higher level of experience. This is why you are advised to accept the assistance of a friendly guide who is well disposed towards you, and would like to see you overcome your difficulties.

7 What Can I Do to Put Things Right?

The advice of the oracle is clear. You must pause and take stock of the situation. You must rule out any possibility of a direct approach: it is only in very special circumstances that you are required to meet an obstruction head on. You must realise that the check on your progress does not spring from something outside you; external expressions only make the nature and scale of the difficulties apparent. Your problem is an internal one.

Though the drawback may inconvenience you, you cannot overcome it alone. You require the assistance of trusted friends, and specifically the guidance of one person more experienced than yourself in finding ways to overcome the obstacle.

Just because the situation is difficult, you must not allow yourself to be distracted by some other objective which will lead you away from the present encumbrance. It is necessary for you to overcome your present difficulty.

There is no doubt that you take this matter seriously. You must go through each of the stages suggested above, satisfying the requirements of each.

The implication of the advice given is that because you have been forced to take hold of yourself without the distraction of forward momentum, you now have the time to develop your inner strength. The effect of being checked in your progress at such a timely moment is to allow you to do some work on yourself. Paradoxically, it is the work on yourself which will ultimately be the means by which you will overcome the overpowering sense of restriction which you now experience.

8 What Do I Most Want From Life?

If you can resist the temptation to blame others for your present predicament, or to indulge in self pity or any wayward emotion of a negative character, you will perceive that this is a golden opportunity for you to look within and learn self-mastery. As you do this, your heart's desire will come into view.

THE LINES

One

You have just encountered an obstruction or check point. Your first emotional reaction is frustration. Part of you is tempted into direct assault on the problem, but before you do this look again and withdraw. The time to overcome it has not arrived. Wait.

Two

The normal rule when confronting obstacles in your path is never to meet them head on, as this would be to disregard wilfully the inherent dangers. This situation is an exception to the rule. The welfare of others depends upon you, and this invites – as it were – the problem to come directly for you. You are fortified in the knowledge that circumstances have compelled you to such action, and you have not brought this predicament upon yourself.

Three

You are confronted with the choice of either going out and facing the problem alone or staying at home with those who need you. Those you would leave behind are dependent on you. What would happen to them if anything untoward befell you? Choose to stay and take care of those who need you. In this case, only a lesser good would be achieved if you were to go.

Four

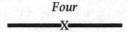

Do not take a risk on the strength of the support which you might have expected in overcoming the impediments before you. Instead, make sure of that support so you know you can rely upon it at the crucial moment.

Five

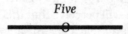

Out of a spirit of altruism, you are moved to shoulder the responsibilities of a friend in difficulty. You have the necessary qualities to take on the challenge. Others volunteer to help when they see what you are trying to do, and with their help you master the problems.

Six

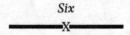

Here, you are moved by the highest moral responsibility to place yourself and your gifts of perception and qualities of character at the disposal and service of mankind. Up until now, your attitude in response to the call for help has been, 'They've made their bed, now they can lie in it.' Now somehow you cannot turn your back on them in their hour of need and so, in this way, you return to the trials and tribulations of the world, bringing with you the power to attract others to an excellent cause which will be the salvation of others.

This is the most difficult and noblest option for you to take, but your reappearance creates such a boost of morale that finally the obstacles are successfully overcome.

HEXAGRAM 40

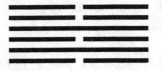

Convalescence (Deliverance)

1 Is This Person a Compatible Partner?

Relations with other people have been very difficult lately, and you have been hoping for some clear signs in order to make the right decisions about your life.

An old relationship which has caused much heartache has now run its course. A new relationship looks very promising, but you must not try to avoid the various stages a relationship must go through in order to allow it to blossom.

The intricacy of your present feelings cannot be communicated clearly, but you already know that your heart is growing lighter.

2 Does My Partner Love Me?

It is too early to tell whether or not love is waiting in the wings, but there is no promise of love at the present time, as this is a period of change from one situation to a completely new one. You will have to calmly wait and see.

3 Do We Have a Future Together?

After a period of strain and tension, there is a period of relaxation, and therefore of greater clarity. You will be in a better position to view the possibilities for the future in a more optimistic light. Since you have learned a great deal from the recent past, you will want to avoid making mistakes. A time of calm and forgiveness will place you in a position from which to view your future conduct in a new relationship with some optimism.

4 What is the Most Important Attitude to Adopt at This Time?

You must not attempt anything new after periods of sudden change or great tension. You should return as soon as possible to a normal style of life, doing things that you are familiar with and are happy doing. If there are still things left undone, you should not labour over them but do them quickly and efficiently, then return to normal life.

If you are overjoyed by events, do not indulge or boast.

5 Why Has Our Relationship Broken Down?

You and your partner have created a great deal of tension between you, and when this tension ceases and you bring your fears into the open it will be clear that you have exploited each other's weaknesses, taken advantage of confidences and dwelled upon those weaknesses until new and stronger tensions have built up between you. In doing this, you have been selfish and narrow-minded, and the relationship has become a burden. Mean-spirited people are difficult to live with and hard to trust, for there is little joy in them.

6 Will We Get Back Together?

A relationship which has broken down because of great tension cannot be repaired until the tension has been completely eased away. You and your partner should take a complete rest from each other, and only attempt a reconciliation when you are able to forgive each other for past mistakes. Until such a time the tension will remain, even though you may be apart. Of course, there is no room left for pretence. Forgiveness must be genuine and come from the heart. It should not come from a misguided obligation created by guilt.

7 What Can I Do to Put Things Right?

The essence of the advice here is, 'Let bygones be bygones'.

Forgiveness, they say, is divine, and you must forgive. Make a clean slate of it. Look to the future with renewed heart.

8 What Do I Most Want From Life?

Peace of mind. The cessation of tension. A clearly-perceived future. All these things are now well within your reach.

THE LINES

One

You are fortunate in having escaped from a bad situation. Now is the time to consolidate this position by resting.

Two

Between you and your aim there are several people who can only be described as 'yes men'. You must overcome them in order to achieve your aims, and the *way* in which you overcome them is important. You must not have recourse to the same behaviour as these people, and you must maintain your inner integrity without compromise. This is where your position becomes strongest, and even poses a threat to those who behave without integrity.

Three

The warning here is addressed to one who has experienced good fortune. If your response to good fortune is arrogance and conceit, you will attract the resentment of other people, and you may lose your good fortune through their resentment. The proper attitude is one of humility.

Four

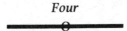

When you are stuck, you tend to become attached to people who are not necessarily your kind. When things are moving, it is important for you to find those people with whom your inner nature really accords, so that you can make trustworthy friends.

Five

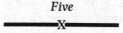

You are trying to detach yourself from unworthy people by an outward show. When this fails, the only way to achieve complete detachment from these people is by an act of will. When you are independent of them in your own mind, they will eventually come to realise that their attachment to you is based upon false grounds. You thus attract the respect of people who are of your kind. By relying upon your own inner resolve, you will attract good fortune.

Six

Someone, or something, is still hindering your advance. This person, or this idea, seems to be immune to your desire for release. Try to free yourself. It really is in your power to do so, by focussing your concentration in such a resolute way that you refuse to be beaten.

HEXAGRAM 41

External Poverty

1 Is This Person a Compatible Partner?

Possibly you are one who wishes to make grandiose prostestations of love to your partner. Perhaps you are accustomed to a slightly better material standard of living than you have now. However, you must accept that at the present time neither of these things is possible.

Despite your lack of wealth and resources, it is still possible for you to make a good account of yourself by the way in which you behave. What you lack in outward appearance may have the effect of fortifying your inner value and your inner riches. The simple development of these inner resources is where the treasure lies, and you should have faith in this.

Your partner should be more concerned with the condition of your feelings and the condition of your heart in relation to them than with material values.

There is no suggestion in this hexagram that your partner is not concerned with these things, but it is one way of determining the exact basis of your relationship.

2 Does My Partner Love Me?

Your partner would find you easier to love if you were less angry, if you were less stubborn and if you managed to control your passions a little more, so that they did not inflict harm on others.

3 Do We Have a Future Together?

If you disregard wealth as your principal aim in life, and instead focus your energies on developing your spiritual side, the future will have much to offer you. Providing the feelings of your heart show through in everything that you do, without shame and without self pity, you will be in a position to attract all that is good in life.

4 What is the Most Important Attitude to Adopt at This Time?

If you are agitated by your sense of poverty and lack of material fortune, then you should above all be calm. Cultivate inner strength by an attitude of gratitude. The most precious things in life are above all the simplest. Keep these things in mind and your agitation will dispel itself, and a lighter-hearted mood will replace it, enabling you to share what you have in good spirit.

5 Why Has Our Relationship Broken Down?

If your relationship with your partner has broken down, then you must look to yourself for the cause.

Have you been excessively angry, impolite or unkind? Have you refused to listen to, or give in to wisely and well meant suggestions from other people? Have you failed to accept your present situation with a joyful heart, and then inflicted this failure on other people? If the relationship has broken down at all, it is due to a lack of discipline on your part in slamming all the possible doors through which others could contact you and reach you in a more amicable manner.

6 Will We Get Back Together?

There is no explicit promise of reconciliation. Things will change in time and when this time has passed, there will be a different atmosphere. You must then do whatever seems best, appropriate and honest. You must above all be content with your present situation, and live in it in the present rather than for the future.

7 What Can I Do to Put Things Right?

The most valuable thing you can do at the present time is to exercise the greatest self-discipline. Do not impose your anger on other people, or yourself. Understand that your current position is likely to be displaced by better times, at least in regard to external circumstances, and therefore accept your present situation.

Have a little more faith in the deeper resources of human nature. By this means your inner truth will have a chance to shine.

8 What Do I Most Want From Life?

Your heart's desire at the present time is to attain a state of inner peace with your heart at ease, both in times of action and in times of rest. You already fully realise that peace with yourself is your greatest treasure. Seek to achieve this peace above all else.

THE LINES

One

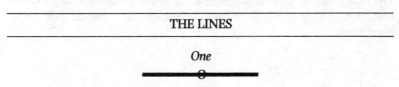

Here there are two people. One person wishes to offer both services and help, quite unselfishly, to another person, and the other person is the recipient of such help.

Where the relationship between these two people is a good one, and based on understanding, the help which is offered will be sufficient. Sufficient help in these circumstances is help that does not compromise the energies of the person who gives it. The person receiving the help must not allow the friend to be harmed by that generosity.

Civilisation finds its true roots in such a dialogue.

Two

If you really desire to be of assistance to others, you must not sacrifice your personal dignity. This sacrifice ultimately helps nobody. More importantly, it does not help you.

Three

Here the expression 'Two's company, three's a crowd' applies.

213

Intimate relationships are only possible between two people. If you find yourself alone, you will soon find the right person for you.

Four

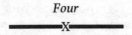

If you want to keep your friends, you must improve yourself. Part of the problem may lie in pressures from your environment. If you have the necessary self-awareness you will see the need either to move away from your present environment, or give up the people with whom you presently associate, in order that those people who truly are your friends can join once again with you. It will be to your mutual advantage to attend to this immediately.

Five

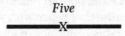

The time is highly propitious for you. Someone up there likes you. Fate has decreed that you will be lucky. Nothing can change this. Great good fortune.

Six

There are some people in the world who are of such excellent disposition that no matter how fortunate they become they share their fortune with everybody, and work hard for the general good of all.

Such people will never have any problem in finding others to assist them in their work, if and when these people are needed.

Spiritual Wealth

1 Is This Person a Compatible Partner?

This is a good relationship. Your primary responsibility is to be of help to others, to both the lowliest people and to the leaders of society. Between you and your partner you have a tremendous capacity to help and assist others who are not so well endowed with good qualities as yourselves. This displays a fine use of abilities. If you are willing to help and develop the potential of people who need such help, what you do will have excellent results. All your talents revolve around an ability for this kind of work.

2 Does My Partner Love Me?

As you are a person of vocation, the kind of work you do is very important to you. The kind of person you are most likely to attract will be similar to you in this respect at least. The sharing of ideas is of great value to the quality of your life. Through this, love manifests itself between you and your partner.

3 Do We Have a Future Together?

Due to the peculiar nature of the time, the future of your relationship

215

depends on whether or not you can sustain a life based on high principles of moral conduct. At this level, your relationship will definitely flourish. Even if others fail where you succeed, no blame can attach to you.

4 What is the Most Important Attitude to Adopt at This Time?

As your talents can have an important bearing upon the lives and welfare and fortune of others, it is fortunate that deep down you are a person of serious disposition, for a fickle attitude would be dangerous.

5 Why Has Our Relationship Broken Down?

This hexagram reveals an excellent time for personal development and growth. If there is an element of erosion in your relationship, then it is due to something extremely fundamental, namely that you are failing to live up to those high moral principles which must govern your attitude.

You are far too aware to ignore failings that you perceive in other people, in systems and in yourself. Persistently turning your head away or burying your head in the sand does not improve matters, neither does it make what is so obviously wrong go away. Allowing less noble tendencies in your nature to gain hold will eventually take its toll on the relationship.

6 Will We Get Back Together?

If you devote your energy to putting things right, then there is every chance of a satisfactory development. You will feel that in some mysterious way you are receiving help.

7 What Can I Do to Put Things Right?

The very short answer to this is 'clean up your life'. You do not need anybody to point out where the defects in your own character lie. Knowing about them should be enough to spur you on to put things right. This is your present task, especially if you are going to create any improvement in the relationship. This is a time of great energy for you.

8 What Do I Most Want From Life?

Your heart's desire can best be understood in terms of the idea of self-sacrifice. Through self-sacrifice you are able to do two things, help others and develop yourself. If you devote yourself to this ideal, your value to society will be boundless.

THE LINES

One

Due to an uplifting influence, you are able to generate tremendous energy to act. Applying yourself with the purest motives, you are able to achieve staggering results. In so doing, you honour the very special assistance which is at your disposal.

Two

You care very deeply about other people – this is the meaning of love – and in this way you are in agreement with the forces of the universe. You are graced with the feeling of being, in a cosmic sense, meaningful. You are thus able to inspire a sense of meaning in other people. This is a very special and rare gift.

Three

This is a time of magical power. Actions once disjointed acquire harmony and strength, and have the power to transform, quite literally, chaos into order in the world and in the hearts of others.

Four

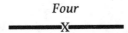

You are a person in whom a great deal of communicative power is entrusted for the benefit and use of other people. You are required here to exercise your power to the fullest for the benefit of others, in order to honour those who have placed the trust in you. It is an important position, and you are capable of transforming the future for the good.

Five

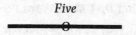

You are justly recognised by your partner and others as being a genuinely kind person. Your kindness exerts a positive influence on other people.

Six

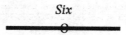

If you have the power to exert a powerful influence for the benefit of others, then it is your duty to do so. If you do not do so, then you invite severe criticism from those who would be the objects of your help, for they are aware of your position and your duties. This is a time which requires the sacrifice of your own needs for the benefit of others. Failing to fulfil your duty at this time will bring misfortune to you and to others alike.

HEXAGRAM 43

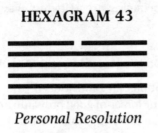

Personal Resolution

1 Is This Person a Compatible Partner?

You must cultivate strength in yourself and the other person, because during the course of this relationship you will encounter many difficulties. Pressures from outside will cause tensions within. You will be confronted by situations in which it will be easy to be dishonest in order to escape pressure, when it will be easy to give in, in the face of too great a pressure. There are two possibilities for your situation which you should note. You can either use your innate strength to break through the tensions which will otherwise divide you, or else the pressure from outside will break into your relationship and divide it from the outside.

The suitability or unsuitability of your partner is not really in question. It is a matter of whether your relationship has sufficient strength to withstand the forces of life.

2 Does My Partner Love Me?

Love is flexible and compliant. You will only know if your partner loves you by recognising the absence of violence in action and emotion in your partner. If your partner behaves towards you and towards others in an intolerant, angry, hateful way, then he or she is in no position to love you or anybody else. You must judge for yourself if your partner is behaving in a loving way by exercising your intuition.

3 Do We Have a Future Together?

The future of a relationship (and indeed, the future of the world) depends entirely on the forces of good prevailing over the forces of evil. That is to say that the forces of violence within a relationship must have no power over the relationship. If the forces of violence control the way the relationship develops, then it is doomed to collapse. So with the world: if the forces of violence in the world gain dominion over the forces of good, then the world is doomed to collapse.

You can only contemplate a bright, happy future where violence of emotion is controlled by the forces of reason. Although you have no power over what is happening outside you, you do have power over what is happening within you. Only by looking at the forces within you and bringing them under the control of your reason can you open up the possibility for a bright future. There is good reason here to be optimistic, because the power to change lies within yourself.

You are not at the mercy of outside forces. No matter how misunderstood you may feel, you still have the power to change things for yourself. The future of your relationship depends upon overcoming the evil within yourself and your partner. If you fail, there is no future. If you succeed, then the future is bright.

4 What is the Most Important Attitude to Adopt at This Time?

Above all, you must be aware of the danger of your situation, and that the forces which act upon you are real and not illusory. Where you lose control over yourself, you lose control over the relationship and over the future.

You must guard against any kind of selfishness. You must try not to hang on or be inflexible. This will only cause a complete collapse in the end. As you benefit in life, so you must give benefit to others. If you merely take the good from others and give nothing back, you will eventually lose all.

You must recognise that you are a part of nature and that as such, you must act in accordance with the rule of nature, which is to give and take according to the time. In order to do this, you must be flexible in your values and recognise the importance of giving. The value of love can only be understood in the world by the process of giving. As you receive love, so you must allow it to flow from you. Any hitch in this process is harmful to the spirit, and causes a hardening of values. If you become brittle and immovable, you are easy to break. If you are soft and compliant (like love), then you will be able to adjust and to change with the times. If you fully understand the nature of love, then you will find your attitude will adjust in relation to your own life and in relation to your partner.

5 Why Has Our Relationship Broken Down?

It is likely that when you are placed under pressure, you respond violently, and this is not the correct attitude. If you meet violence with violence, you are already defeated; for the forces which control violence are the forces which oppose both you and everything good about your relationship with your partner. If necessary, you must enlist the help of other, stronger people who better understand this principle.

Violence may also express itself through passion; the reason for any breakdown in your relationship may be due to explosive passions expressed violently. Such turbulent emotion drives away clarity of thought. You must understand that reason is the higher force, and passion the lower. In order to control passion, we must bring reason to bear with vigour and energy. Only the implacable application of reason can oppose the unruly powers which have caused this breakdown.

6 Will We Get Back Together?

You have been driven apart by the pressure of powerful and destructive forces, outside as well as within the relationship. You can only be reconciled when this pressure ceases.

The internal pressures which have brought about the problems can be controlled by the application of quiet but strong reason. The forces outside the relationship and outside you can only be repelled by an attitude of quiet reason. You cannot control these forces, however violent they may be, but if you respond to them with violence, then you will unseat your own reason.

There is nothing in this oracle to suggest that you cannot be reconciled, but many warnings are offered. You must cease from any violent response and cultivate a position of clear logical thought. Bring reason to bear. Understand that because violence is a represent-ation of the power of evil, you can only fight it by non-violent means.

However difficult it may be, you must act towards your partner and everyone else with deep and profound honesty. If your honesty is expressed in terms of friendliness, you will attract others who can help.

7 What Can I Do to Put Things Right?

You must stop feeling hatred, for while you do you automatically attract violence. When you stop hating, violence is automatically repelled. The longer you maintain a position of good-heartedness, the weaker the opposition to your relationship will be.

It is essential for you to root out any bad feelings in your own heart in order to perceive what good there is around you. You must understand that in pure terms, this is a fight between good and evil, but do not underestimate the subtlety of the situation. If you oppose evil directly, you will quickly fall into evil's own way of doing things. Its secret method is to try to lure you into open battle, but you must not even be tempted to fight, for how can you win?

The future of your relationships with your partner and with anyone else depends entirely on your recognising what is good in yourself and others and simply persisting in being good. In this way, you will win.

8 What Do I Most Want From Life?

Your heart's desire is to be free to give. If you show a willingness to give, you will find that others will be willing to give to you, but if you hold on to what you have to give, you will find that your gifts become useless and unwanted by others. You must simply give of your time, your thoughts and of your feelings without counting the cost.

THE LINES

One

You feel the energy to go forward in the world, but you encounter

222

opposing pressures. You are ignorant of your own strength. You must cautiously test your powers against the opposing force – without breaking your powers – in order to gain knowledge of yourself. If you encounter an early setback through your ignorance, then you may be stopped completely in your progress. You can only be successful in the light of certain knowledge of your real strength and not your imagined power.

Two

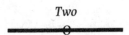

The chief requirement is caution. You must open your eyes. Danger is not far off and you must be suitably prepared to meet it. By being firm, you can develop your nature to a high point and this will be recognised by others, who will respond favourably towards you. You must be clear sighted, resolute and cautious. Without caution, you are blind to danger and therefore prey to forces which could bear you down, damaging your position and undermining your security.

Three

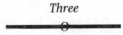

Because of your association with people who are less developed than yourself, you have a fear of being misunderstood. You feel alone in your struggle because others do not perceive or accord with your higher nature. Here, you are more wronged than wronging, and by insisting on a proper attitude, and refusing to be a part of anything which is devious and dark, you retain your freedom from errors. You must have belief and faith in your truth, and sustain yourself, because you are not motivated by selfish desires. To continue as you are will bring good fortune.

Four

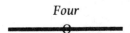

Are you being stupid in failing to heed the wise counsel of others? Have you ignored requests to be more flexible and less obstinate? If you persist in pushing against forces which will not yield, and thus set up inner conflicts which create profound discomfort in yourself, you must expect to attract bad fortune. You will lose the good will of others if you persist.

223

Five

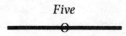

You are placed in a position of opposition to a person who is more powerful than yourself. It is apparent to you and to others that the person is not suitable to this position, and misuses the power. You are tempted to give up the fight because of the inequality of your position, but the oracle is clear that you must not. It is a just fight.

Six

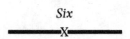

If you have been fighting less evolved people and powers for a long time now, you may believe that the battle has been won. You are warned that it has not been won. The power which has opposed you for so long is small, but cleverly hidden. It is so small that you cannot see it, and are thus tempted to believe that it is not there. This gives it the advantage. If you ignore its presence now, it will certainly grow into a powerful force again, and fresh damages will oppose you. Later you will realise that all the work you have done will once again be undone.

You must be thorough and seek out the remaining evil power. Only then can you safely claim victory. Remember, evil is a living force – it must be completely eradicated. Any lesser victory is no victory.

HEXAGRAM 44

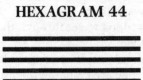

Seduction

1 Is This Person a Compatible Partner?

Your new suitor will not make a compatible partner for you.

This person's intentions definitely cannot be trusted. If a woman, she is a temptress, if a man, a tempter. He or she is full of guile, ulterior motives and dishonest affections. For this kind of manipulator, affections have a price. The smile may indeed be disarming, but it is what is beneath the smile that you should worry about. This person is out for what they can get. Your influence and power are preferred to your love, and your wealth preferred to your affection. This person does not want a companion, but a social passport, and beneath all the naive protestations is sheer deceit.

If you have anything to do with this person, you are likely to be enslaved by false passion. You will find your emotions coolly manipulated for selfish ends.

2 Does My Partner Love Me?

The right person for you is honest, without guile, has no need to pretend affection and asks nothing of you but yourself. Your real partner will love you for yourself and for no other reason.

Your suitor on the other hand, only pretends to love you for yourself for ulterior motives. One of the tricks often used by such people is to pretend to weakness, in order to attract your sympathy and care. Have the perception to see through the facade. Do not allow yourself to be so easily fooled.

The more these kinds of people are withstood, the more they will realise that ultimately they are cheating themselves of true affection, and that the things on which they place such a great value are worthless. They will learn that it does not pay to trifle with the truth.

3 Do We Have a Future Together?

You must be sure that you make the right distinction between your true partner and the suitor described in this oracle. If you do so, you need have no fear of the future.

If you have allowed yourself to become obsessed, or to be beguiled by the seductions of a suitor, you will have cause for regret. Such people are so fickle, that no matter how convincing they may seem to you, they can never be depended upon to be straightforward and honest: they always have some hidden motive. Ultimately, of course, they are only deceiving themselves and robbing themselves of what is of true value in life.

Such people have no future and are utterly dependent on chance to give them what they want. Therefore you must not let them rob you of your future.

4 What is the Most Important Attitude to Adopt at This Time?

Be wary, be suspicious. Although you may not be an easy person to fool, nobody is infallible.

You will be safe if you make the assumption that your new suitor has dishonourable and dishonest motives in cultivating a relationship with you. You do not need to confront this person with your suspicions, you have only to withdraw politely, but leaving no doubt of your intentions.

5 Why Has Our Relationship Broken Down?

If you have not already done so, you would be well advised to cut this relationship dead immediately.

Your suitor has nothing to offer you, and has no intention of offering anything to you that you really want, being interested only in gaining from you those superficial advantages that you may care to offer. You may rely upon the fact that this person's interest in you is not based upon affection, and therefore has no substance.

You may feel that your suitor is quite harmless, that is because you have not seen the hidden talons – yet.

If you do not bring this relationship to an immediate halt, you will certainly regret it later.

6 Will We Get Back Together?

You may be sure that the person really destined to be your partner will make themselves known to you, will meet you half way. When the time comes you will have no doubt. You will sense the mutual affection.

In the case of your new suitor, the question does not apply as the relationship should not have been allowed to develop in the first place.

7 What Can I Do to Put Things Right?

If you give this person an inch, they will take a yard. Do not be put off your guard by the easy smile, the warm handshake, the sudden look in the eye, or any other disarming trick designed to win your confidence.

Do not let this person grow close to you or take advantage of anything you have to offer. Do not trust this person with anything of value, especially not your heart or your secrets. If you take this advice, nothing will go wrong.

8 What Do I Most Want From Life?

What you most wish – if you have not already done so – is to meet someone who is willing to respond to your affections, and to care about you as much as you care about them. Provided you are prepared to go and meet this person halfway, and do not expect them to come to you, you will meet the right person. You will know in your heart that it is a good relationship if it is based upon an open, honest affection.

THE LINES

One

An unsavoury influence is making itself felt in your life. There is no indication in this line that a person is involved, though this may be so. The important thing is to put an immediate stop to this influence. If it is allowed to grow and take root in your life, it will cause you a great deal of trouble.

Two

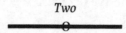

Here the way to stop an unsavoury influence from creeping in is not by use of a dramatic show of force or by any violent means, but by precisely the opposite. Treat the influence like a disease. Do not let it spread and come into contact with other people, lest it contaminate them, thereby strengthening itself.

Three

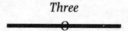

This line reflects the general tone of the hexagram. *You* must resist falling under the spell of an unsavoury influence. However, while you may be quite willing to subject yourself to such an influence, you are prevented from doing so by forces beyond your control.

The whole situation has caused you to lose clarity of mind. Take this opportunity to look more deeply into the situation, the better to understand it.

Four

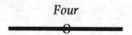

Even people of undeveloped character have a place in life. Although you may not wish, as it were, to give them the time of day, a reasonable level of tolerance is advised for your own sake as well as theirs. If you entirely dismiss such people, displaying an attitude of complete intolerance, your loss will be as great as theirs, if not greater.

Five

Here the spirit of toleration reigns supreme. The person described here is of an excellent disposition, but is modest. Thus the person does not stand upon a pedestal, but works through personal charisma. The response of those over whom this person has influence is to co-operate with a cheerful spirit.

Six

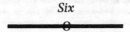

The person described here regards the world and the trials and tribulations of everyday life as tiresome drudgery, with which he or she will have nothing more to do. Whenever this person encounters the menial, slavish attitude of those who place too high a value on the superficial, this person's response is disparaging. Others will regard him or her as haughty and conceited, but since what others think is of no concern, it does not really affect the person, who ignores them and continues with life, disdainfully keeping the menial, humdrum world at a distance which is bearable. While this attitude is complicated, and not entirely without justification, it remains negative.

HEXAGRAM 45

The Group

1 Is This Person a Compatible Partner?

You and your partner are attracted to each other within the context of a larger social group, and are bound by some common interest or activity. The bond between you developed through an identity with some objective idea, cause, group or situation. This bodes well for you both, as your relationship will thrive because of your common interest.

2 Does My Partner Love Me?

You and your partner respect the group which provides the context for your relationship. In the atmosphere of this group, your love for each other flourishes. There is no doubt of a mutual bond.

3 Do We Have a Future Together?

You share common interests and common pursuits and a common identity with a larger group. It is reasonable for you, therefore, to optimistically expect a future together. The oracle does not offer any specific advice in respect of a personal relationship between you and your partner outside the larger social group framework.

4 What is the Most Important Attitude to Adopt at This Time?

If you look at the group which is the context of your relationship, you will find at its centre a person of principle and character around whom the social group is formed. If you and your partner both acknowledge this same centre, it is likely to have a fortifying effect on your respective attitudes towards one another and to the social group. This is perfectly correct in the circumstances. There is no need to force any adjustment in your attitude to yourself, your partner or to the group.

5 Why Has Our Relationship Broken Down?

If there has been a breakdown in your relationship, the cause can be identified with the same forces which are attacking the group as a whole. These forces come from outside, and their effect is unexpected. You must understand that wherever a large group of people live or work together with a common identity, negative forces are naturally attracted to the group. How destructive these forces are to your personal relationship and the group as a whole depends, of course, on their magnitude. Implied in this oracle is the idea that the forces which caused the breakdown can be brought under control once again.

6 Will We Get Back Together?

Where your relationship forms part of a greater whole, and you have heeded the advice already given by this oracle, then you have every reason to expect a reconciliation. It is likely, however, that the leader of the group will recommend some kind of protective measures in order to safeguard the group from future malevolent influences.

7 What Can I Do to Put Things Right?

The proper course of action at the present time would be to refer the problem of the relationship to the person who represents the centre of the group. The result of this person's counsel, advice and assistance is likely to mend the relationship.

You should reinforce your affiliations and feelings for your partner and your social group. Be a willing participant.

8 What Do I Most Want From Life?

You are aware that your social group does not exist simply to perpetuate its own existence, but to serve the ends of mankind as a whole in some way. You know that your own group is merely a microcosm of the macrocosm, and you are motivated by the realisation that the fortunes of mankind depend upon a growing awareness of itself as one family in one world.

Your desire is to play your part, however small or however large, in bringing about this beautiful aim. The potential exists for great deeds.

THE LINES

One

It is right and proper and justified for everyone within your large social group to have confidence in the person who heads it. Anything which inhibits your confidence in the leader necessarily acts against the best interests of everyone concerned. If you entertain any doubts about the quality of the leader, you should not take them to anyone but the leader. You will be gratified in the end because your doubts will be dispelled.

Two

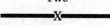

You are mysteriously and magnetically attracted to a certain group of people and to certain relationships. This is unquestionably right for you, and you should allow yourself to be drawn to these people. Do not question reasons or motives, but trust that on whatever level they exist, they are for your mutual benefit. There is an ambience of empathy and affinity among these people which requires no ceremony.

Three

You feel a sense of identity with a group of people who have formed themselves into a tight circle which you feel unable to penetrate. You recognise your affections for this group and you also realise that it is imperative for you to make your feelings known, even though this causes you embarrassment.

Four

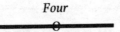

You are a valuable member of any group because you work for its continuation and in the spirit of those who form a part of it, without hope of reward or personal gain. Altruism quite properly illuminates your work and you receive your just recognition.

Five

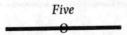

Worthwhile work will always come out of spontaneous attraction between people. However, not everyone is drawn to a group, or a particular leader spontaneously or naturally. Some people seek to cultivate the relationship through some private design of their own. Obviously, this is undesirable, and the only way in which the leader and members of a group can overcome such poorly-formed attitudes is to sustain their own positions and integrity and continue the work with a heightened vigour. Dedication to work inspires tremendous confidence in your companions, and in this way those people whose attitude is tainted by selfish or improper design are gradually won over, and align themselves with the work of the people around them.

Six

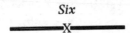

Your sincerity comes from the heart. Those people to whom you communicate your sincerity must comprehend that you bring no harm. It is false, therefore, for you to feel disappointed and upset, since you know that any misgivings are entirely misplaced. Since your sincerity runs through all your moods and is not affected or feigned in any way, people will recognise this and understand your real intentions. In this way you are finally welcomed.

233

HEXAGRAM 46

The Beginning of Ascent (Co-operation)

1 Is This Person a Compatible Partner?

This is a time for constructive action. There is little or nothing standing in your way. Yet nothing can be achieved without really trying. The oracle suggests that you know what you want from life, and from a relationship with your partner. Your objectives are clear. It may well be that in the past you felt thwarted and hampered in your efforts to make progress, but now those times are gone and any efforts made to go forward will find little resistance in events and circumstances beyond your control. You should therefore feel confident that this is a time for achieving what you want without fear or hindrance, and that if your effort is sincere and you act with consideration to others at all times, you will meet with unusual and friendly co-operation from your partner and others. Have no doubt, however, that the initiative lies with you. Nevertheless, the oracle points favourably to the fact that this relationship is right for you at this time.

2 Does My Partner Love Me?

There are times when your partner sees you as too strong headed for your own good. He or she admires you for being strong willed and decisive, and thinks of you as a person who likes to get things done, but at the same time recognises that you often need encouragement. There is a mixture of the positive and the negative in your partner's attitude towards you, but it definitely tends to the positive side.

You are a person of great possibilities, if only you would try harder. However, the implication of the oracle is that your relationship with your partner is based upon something profoundly spiritual.

3 Do We Have a Future Together?

Nothing can be accomplished at one attempt. You will achieve what you hope to achieve with your partner, but by way of a collection of small achievements which add up to something greater than themselves. For the time being, take each day as it comes, making the best of each opportunity.

Your purpose must be to make the most of the time. Maintain a positive attitude without giving way to small fears, and you can anticipate the future with every expectation of success. If you do not become overbearing in your desire to push forward with your aims, your attitude will not be oppressive to your partner. Will-power will strengthen the basis of the relationship, adding greatly to the general security of your future together.

When all's said and done, the future of the relationship rests with your desire and capacity to work hard to develop it. You both feel that achievement comes slowly. Take confidence in the fact that you have a strong basis for continuing.

4 What is the Most Important Attitude to Adopt at This Time?

Hard work will bring its rewards. This is the time to settle down with consistent effort to a long stretch of hard work. The old expression 'actions speak louder than words' applies now more than ever. Nothing will come of nothing. The basis of truly effective work arises from an attitude of humble devotion.

5 Why Has Our Relationship Broken Down?

This oracle is primarily concerned with effort, and suggests that this is a good time to make headway in any plans and ambitions, and in your relationship with your partner.

The admonition in the *I Ching*, is that you should conduct yourself properly. Nothing favourable can be achieved at the expense of other people's feelings. If you have ridden roughshod over them in order to attain what you wanted, you will inevitably have met resistance from above.

The relationship may also have broken down because you have tried to achieve too much too soon. Though you must apply a consistent effort of the will in all your undertakings, you must also act without rashness and without violence, and be prepared at all times for any slight change of plan which might be necessary. Failure to bear in mind any of these contingencies will have created discord between you and your partner.

Another possible reason for failure – and perhaps the most obvious one – arises directly from a lack of effort on your part. If you thought that results could be obtained without any effort from you, you will by now have realised your mistake, despite the fact that this is a very favourable time.

6 Will We Get Back Together?

First you must consult your feelings. Do you really want a reconciliation with this person? If so, you cannot expect to achieve it unless you make the effort. The initiative lies with you. On the one hand, if you are too wilful, you will be an unattractive proposition for your partner: on the other hand, if you are not wilful enough, you will appear insignificant. You have to strike the right balance. Your watchword is adaptability. However, this is a good time for you and you should feel confident. Above all, you must not allow yourself to be sidetracked or deterred.

Any positive efforts you make to bring about a reconciliation will be well rewarded. Indeed, you may find that with a distinct lack of resistance from outside forces, you will achieve more than you once expected.

7 What Can I Do to Put Things Right?

If obstacles stand in your way you must not force your way through them, but you must adapt to the situation. Go around an obstacle rather than through it. That is to say, qualities of flexibility and adaptability are paramount if you are to put things right. By being strong headed and forceful, you will only encounter opposition. If you are malleable and humble, you will find there is nothing to stop you going round the obstacle and pressing on. This is a time when much can be achieved if you bear these qualities in mind and adopt them fully. Strength of character and a hard-working disposition promise a favourable journey in your ascent to achieve your goals.

8 What Do I Most Want From Life?

Without any setbacks to detain you from your primary objectives, you possess all the necessary qualities to achieve considerable results. Acceptance by those who share your spiritual abilities will be the mark of a new era in your life, one which you will have justly deserved.

THE LINES

One

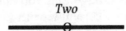

The time favours you with a natural advantage as you begin your rise from a position of relative obscurity to a position in which your abilities and achievements are recognised. Because those higher than you share an important common feeling with the work, you receive help from them, and from this you gain the confidence and the impetus to complete the work you have begun.

Two

The essence of your good fortune here lies in the fact that you are possessed of fundamentally good intentions, and although you appear to those whose approval you seek as a little rough around the edges, this is forgivable and you can still claim their support in your efforts to make something worthwhile of yourself.

If you recognise your inexperience, and your dependence on others for guidance, then you will not harm your fortunes.

Three

This is an excellent time for you. You are able to make tremendous progress without halt or hindrance. You already sense this and so you pursue your activities with a renewed will and zeal. One important thing to recognise here is that there is no time to entertain personal doubts.

Curiously enough, this line indicates a risk situation, and therefore the outcome for good or for bad is not determined. Nevertheless, you must ignore this possibility and hold fast to the inspiration which impels you along.

Four

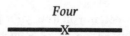

This line refers you back to the judgement under the eighth question, 'What do I really want from life?' Here, you have attained your desire, and the recognition and approval you have most coveted. This is an extremely fortuitous situation which has come about through all the qualities of hard work, endurance and will power which you have cultivated for so long. The effect of your achievements will honour you in time to come.

Five

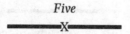

Up till now all that you have achieved in the way of good fortune has been richly deserved. Yet the pinnacle of success has not yet been reached, although you can see it in your sights. This is the point where you are going to make a mistake if you are going to make it at all. To avoid a mistake at such an auspicious moment, you must not cut any corners. It is imperative that you continue in precisely the way in which you began – carefully, with great attention to detail, with efficiency, and with a steady heart. If you continue in this spirit you will attain the pinnacle of success, which will justly be yours. If you allow yourself to be carried away at this point, you will fall short of the mark and disappointment will inevitably result. The final admonition then is to take good care in every single particular of the work.

Six

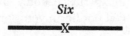

Even when things appear to be going well, it is still possible to lose sight of your main objectives. When you do this you can lose your path, and find yourself working in fits and starts to no significant end. The warning implied in this line is that without a clear goal, you cannot make your efforts count. Once your goal has been clarified, you must pursue it relentlessly, without giving way to the slightest distraction, and without yielding to the temptation to follow up wayward ideas which lie outside the scheme of the work. Here, the harm that you can do to yourself and your situation is only in potential. It is still possible for you to take off the blindfold.

HEXAGRAM 47

Depression

1 Is This Person a Compatible Partner?

At the moment, your partner is not finding you much fun to be with. You are depressed, down in the dumps, perhaps even at the end of your tether, or perhaps your desires weigh so heavily upon your shoulders that your head is filled with despondency. Perhaps you feel neglected or drained, perhaps in some measure all of these things. Although this makes life dismal for you, it also makes life fairly dismal for anyone who happens to be with you.

You already know that this is a passing mood. You have been in this mood before, and you will probably be in this mood again unless you make a conscious effort to keep yourself out of it. It is at times like these, however, that you can really tell the men from the boys. The boys indulge in such feelings, men hold them off and keep smiling even in adversity. They do something to change their feelings.

2 Does My Partner Love Me?

Love that can be measured is no love at all. Do not take the spontaneity out of your lover's life by weighing it down with heavy expectations. Love is free. Do not place weights and measures upon it. Love that is not given freely is not love. Love that is not offered from a

240

free heart is tyranny. The result will be jaded feelings, exhaustion, tired oppression. Give what you have, do not try to give what you do not have. You will just wear out yourself and your partner if you try.

All your partner wants is for you to be your usual cheerful self, nothing more. Take a risk on the heart. Let it grow lighter and let it grow.

3 Do We Have a Future Together?

The future is going to be all the bright for you if you learn how to overcome your negative emotions. Make an effort to learn how to change your feelings, especially in times of adversity. You attract good fortune best when you are cheerful. Bad moods usually arise from emotional greed. Emotional greed can only give you a heavy heart.

4 What is the Most Important Attitude to Adopt at This Time?

Whatever the cause of your feeling downcast, fight it. Adopt a spirit of challenge. Don't let it get you down. Refuse to give in to the temptation to sit around idly. At times like this you must practice self mastery.

Take advantage of this time to learn how to change your feelings.

5 Why Has Our Relationship Broken Down?

The reason for any breakdown in your relationship can only be that you persist in being depressed and despondent. Your emotional ups and downs can be most tiresome for your partner. Even if times are hard, you should still make the best of them. It may be that you have pushed your partner to the limits of endurance until they cannot take anymore.

6 Will We Get Back Together?

Success comes most easily to cheerful people. Happy people keep their friends. Friendly people have more fun. Forgiveness comes more easily with a smile.

The doors of reconciliation between you and your partner open when you are light-hearted. It is hard to carry the dead weight of someone's depression. Do not persist in feeling neglected. Do not feel

241

sorry for yourself. Do not indulge in self pity. If you have lost the interest of your partner, you will find that you can reclaim it if you put on a smiling face, and make an effort to change negative feelings to positive feelings.

First help yourself, then others will help you. This will have the effect of deepening your character and making you independent. Let your present situation suffice. Take life as it comes, one day at a time. In times of adversity, specialise in having fun, in this way you will find that the attractive side of your character will grow.

7 What Can I Do to Put Things Right?

Adopt a cheerful mood. Try to avoid sitting down and letting the feelings of gloom and despondency take a grip on you.

Get up and do something. It hardly matters what it is. The important thing is to change your feelings. Do the washing up, wash the floor, redecorate the house, write a book, play a musical instrument, go for a walk, talk to an old friend on the telephone, go for a work out in the gym – it doesn't matter, as long as you change your feelings, as long as you do something. New acts create new reflections.

8 What Do I Most Want From Life?

Perhaps, in the end, all we can do is trade the love we need for the love we need to receive. Sometimes life is hard through no fault of our own. Make yourself laugh and let God do the rest.

THE LINES

One

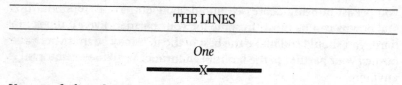

You are feeling downcast. You are allowing your depressed mood to get a grip on you. It is sapping your energy, dissipating your will power. The matter is in your own hands. Sometimes this is called the downward spiral, sometimes the slippery slope. Put the brakes on. Tomorrow is just another day. Today is all you have.

Two

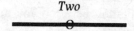

You have everything you need, but somehow it is not enough. You feel under pressure, but the pressure is self created. A new light is about to come into your life. It offers hope for self-improvement, the hope for release from inner tension. Be inwardly thankful. Try not to be in such a hurry. Take each day as it comes.

Three

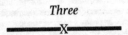

You are in too much of a hurry to get somewhere, for your own good. You are being too pushy. This is not the time for progress. You are banging your head against a brick wall, which will only wear yourself out and give yourself a headache. You are grasping at straws, putting your faith in flimsy hopes. You are walking on thin ice. People are losing their faith in you. If you are not careful all this will end in tears.

Four

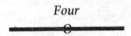

You wish to place your material and spiritual resources at the service of others, in order to help them to improve their lot. You feel frustrated at the lack of co-operation in such a noble aim from others who are also in a position to help. Do not allow yourself to be put off. Certainly do not entertain the idea that you might have been wrong after all. An improvement in circumstances is on its way.

Five

You want to help others, but you are rendered helpless by a frustrating predicament created by people less spiritually developed than yourself. Men help the man who is devoted, heaven helps the man who is true. Remain true to yourself. Gifts given in a spirit of faith are priceless.

Six

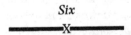

Here you are inhibited by your own sense of caution. Therefore you are reluctant to make an impression. Up till now you have not fully understood your predicament, but soon you will gain an insight which will dispel all doubts in your mind, and in this way you will overcome the restraining force of your caution. An act of self-mastery always results in firm decisions.

HEXAGRAM 48

The Well

In this hexagram the I Ching uses the image of The Well to symbolise something profound, immutable and fundamental in human nature – the primal essence of our beings which never changes – the binding force of life itself. This quality is common to all sentient beings and may be described as The Well of Wisdom, The Cup of Love and Inspiration, The Abundance of Life, Light in the Sun, The Fertile Waters. All these images refer to a simple idea with which we all have a common affinity, LOVE, and to the fact that we all need to give it and to receive it. Love forms the basis of our natures and this cannot be changed.

No matter how complex and sophisticated our political and social structures might become, no matter how subtle or refined our explanation of the universe becomes over millenia, the one underlying idea which remains forever constant is love.

Love is the assumption of life not its conclusion, just as the well exists to contain water, life exists as an expression of love.

Love is pictured in this hexagram as the very water of life – the water in the well. It is love that gives life its richness and meaning. Without this crucial nourishment we would spiritually dry up and cease to exist. The absence of love in our lives is the absence of meaning, without love there would be no purpose behind what we thought, indeed, would we think anything?

Life and love are in abundance, this is the significance of this hexagram;

the Well is inexhaustible, eternal. Everyone may draw from the well and become enriched by it.

The oracle describes the well as the foundation of all social and political structures. Without such a foundation, as the I Ching precisely describes, then everything we build in life, now and in the future, will have absolutely no value, and no meaning. It will be as if it were never there at all. It will be just illusion, maya, nothingness. In the same way this foundation forms the basis of all human relations.

1 Is This Person a Compatible Partner?

If the governing principles of your relationship with your partner are simply founded on tradition and a strict and uncritical adherence to what has always gone on, then such love is indiscriminate and unthinking. Alternatively, the love that you and your partner bear each other may be the very wellspring of life. If this is true then you are already aware that love is the source of all your happiness. You already perceive that every living thing contains the divine spark, and that love is the driving force behind the flower.

The *I Ching* also uses the image of *The Well* to describe our own hearts from which our love for others radiates.

2 Does My Partner Love Me?

The significance of the oracle lies in the fact that if we search our hearts deeply enough we will find that we truly love everything and everybody all of the time. The difficulty in life is realising this fact and then tuning our actions in accordance with this knowledge.

Your partner loves you.

3 Do We Have a Future Together?

The future of every relationship and indeed the future of the world depends upon comprehending the previous answer. This is the only knowledge of which we may be certain. Everywhere else is open to opinion. If we attempt to build the future upon any other foundation we may be certain that it will not last. On the other hand, if culture and civilisation are built upon this single understanding life will endure into time immemorial. If we fail to realise and apply this single truth, then as individuals – and as the human race – we will continue to make the mistakes of the past, learning the lesson painfully and by means of bloodshed, heartbreak, loss, destruction and fear – all of which are completely *unnecessary*.

The oracle is clear about one more thing, it is entirely without value to pay lip service to such a truth. *Real understanding must take place in the heart.* Nothing less is acceptable.

Put succinctly, you have a future with your partner, and the world has a future, if you comprehend that only love can unlock the door of your personal prison and only universal love – acknowledged by all in the heart, without exception – can set the world free. You may, without any reservation depend upon it.

4 What is the Most Important Attitude to Adopt at This Time?

The most important thing you can do at this time is to apply your mind to basic ideas by asking fundamental questions: What is the point of having all these laws? What is the point of erecting massive national defences? What is the meaning of trust? What is the purpose of trust? Why do I bother to eat each day? Why do I bother to feed others? Why do I bother to breathe? Why do I bother to do anything at all? Why do I bother to have children? What is my interest in survival? What, if anything, is the idea which gives validity to my life? Why do I exist? Why do I carry on living?

Initially you must be willing to go through a thorough self-purification of the heart. You must be willing to search beyond the intricate self-justifications which may, up until now, have sustained your actions. You have to be moved and impelled by what is fundamental in human nature.

If you cannot answer these questions now they will recur and keep on recurring until you can.

5 Why Has Our Relationship Broken Down?

The answer is very simple. Beneath the skin everybody is the same. Everybody needs love, everybody needs to give love. If you have placed more importance upon adherence to stereotypes, sticking to old ways, preserving social form for the sake of social form, keeping up with tradition for the sake of keeping up with tradition, maintaining outmoded values of the heart, then your relationship was based on sand from the very outset.

6 Will We Get Back Together?

If, in the past, you have not fulfilled your partner's deepest needs, and in this the oracle distinguishes from material desires (and the fulfilment of vain, superficial hopes) you will have made of *The Well* a hollow, dry, cask which echoes loneliness.

If you have not cared enough you will have broken your partner's heart.

If you have not trusted enough and you have built walls around yourself too thick and too strong (in the same way that military defences are built up between nations as final bastions of fear) then you will have invited wars, arguments and disagreements such as are required to break down those walls. The human condition cries out for freedom from fear.

All of this will have generated frustration, paranoia and fear, and the reason for it all is nothing more than the failure to give and the failure to trust. That is all.

Where love is thirsting to be set free in the human heart, no wall, no defence is strong enough to prevail against it in the end.

The advice of the oracle then is to set your heart free. Let your love abound. Where you are fearful and mistrustful, paranoid and disillusioned, you can take a risk on the heart, for the love in *The Well* is the source of everything and ultimately the healing balm of the world.

7 What Can I Do to Put Things Right?

Since we are all the same at heart and at heart all of Mankind's needs are the same, then it is to these we must turn first. We must fulfil each other's needs in their most fundamental sense.

You are required to give of your affection without pretence and to recognise that a properly educated person is one who understands and lives by the values of the heart. These can never be supplanted by any social or political system however deeply revered in tradition. In this respect we must complete our education. To do less would be to be a danger to ourselves and a potential threat to the well-being of others.

8 What Do I Most Want From Life?

True Love. This is the meaning of freedom.

THE LINES

One

You are a 'down and out' in the true sense of that expression. You offer mankind nothing and in return mankind offers you nothing. Your complete lack of interest in others reflects back in their lack of interest in you. This is a pitiable state of affairs.

Two

This describes a person who is not exploiting his or her gifts to their fullest potential.

You have a great deal to give – why do you not give it? Why do you debase your gifts so? If you do not use your talents you will lose them. There is a clear need to take stock of yourself and put matters into perspective.

Three

You have many fine qualities of mind and you are ready and willing to put your abilities in the service of others. It is a lamentable fact no opportunity presents itself at this time for you, even though your qualities are apparent to others.

If only someone would notice.

Four

This line concerns itself with personal development. Here, a fundamentally good person is taking time to sort themselves out. This process may be described as acts of self-purification. This is, in itself, a good and worthwhile work.

If this time is well spent, this person will later be able to make a very valuable contribution to others.

Five

The highest value in being possessed of wisdom is that it may be placed in the service of others. It must be at least as accessible to the people in the same way that a library is accessible to the public.

This line refers to a person who is symbolised as a well filled with the waters of life. As long as people can drink from this well, it will be of great benefit to them.

People should draw wisdom from a reliable source. Wisdom is the nourishment of the spirit. Drink of it and grow rich.

Six

This describes one of the world's special people whose capacity to provide what people need in the way of knowledge, wisdom, love and guidance is without limit.

Everybody can take what they need. Nobody is turned away. The more people partake of *The Well* the more they are enriched, the more *The Well* is enriched. In this is the embodiment of the legend of the well that never runs dry.

In such a person humanity is blessed.

NOTE: Love is also represented and symbolised in other hexagrams by the elements of fire, air and earth in their various dynamic contexts.

Dynamism

1 Is This Person a Compatible Partner?

When two forces act upon each other in a contrary way, they both revolve. You and your partner are not opposites by nature, but you act as if you were, often refusing to see eye to eye and therefore generating very powerful emotion out of the conflicts. Such a process of revolution produces changes which can run very deep in your respective natures, and the consequences are not to be dismissed lightly.

The apparent upset and turbulence which your respective natures generate are seasonal. The times of turbulence have the characteristics of chaos, but in fact, seen from a distance, occur regularly at intervals like the seasons. Your partner, like you, changes with the seasons. What is crucial in making a relationship of this kind work is self control in both of you, and the awareness that the seasonal quality of the turbulence means that it will pass. In times like this you penetrate through this motion more deeply into the true self of the other.

The deeper we perceive ourselves, the greater the requirement for self-control, since the deeper the perception, so the greater the responsibility needed to control the knowledge we perceive in each other. Indeed, this is knowledge.

Understanding the seasonal quality of this power to penetrate into each other will assist you in this formidable feat of self-control when the time comes. There is no judgement, therefore, as to your suitability for one another. There is only a requirement for awareness of the process and the effects of revolution.

2 Does My Partner Love Me?

The person who draws this hexagram is not prone to dwell on such questions for too long. You are the kind of person who does everything to deserve love, but you often fail to win affection through being inconsiderate. You must ask yourself truthfully if you deserve the love of your partner. Providing you do not deceive yourself, you should understand the truth immediately.

3 Do We Have a Future Together?

According to the seasons, this is a time of personal growth. You are in a position to make positive advances. Not everyone in your circle of friends will agree with you and your ideas on what you want to do, but you must consult first with *yourself*, satisfying *yourself* of the demands of the time which you must now fully understand. Your future will depend upon the attitudes which you carefully think through now.

After you have experienced a period of rapid and brilliant change, you require a period of time to take stock of your new situation in a calm and considered way, without at the same time halting the change.

There are no indications that the future bodes ill, but in matters of the heart you cannot afford to be complacent if you are to take advantage of the great possibility for self-fulfilment which now presents itself. This is a time to test your inner resources.

4 What is the Most Important Attitude to Adopt at This Time?

If you act in an unconsidered way during a time of rapid change, the effect will always be bad. If you cannot act with a high degree of self-control, self-discipline and personal restraint, you should not act at all. The purpose of self-control now is to prevent attracting bad forces to yourself. Otherwise the situation augurs well.

5 Why Has Our Relationship Broken Down?

Think of two intermeshed revolving bodies spinning too fast, without the necessary control. If you harnessed the energy being generated, the result would be to burn out the relationship. Perhaps you have both overdone it.

Another possibility is that, in a similar situation to the above, the interlocking elements in your natures are incapable of withstanding the speed and friction of your conflict, and disintegrate at speed, just as physical bodies do. Thus the relationship falls apart through too much power and speed.

Yet the universe has an infinite capacity for renewal and so the human heart has also an infinite capacity for renewal. Therefore, even if the relationship has burned out or decomposed, there is still a possibility that in another season it may generate life again.

6 Will We Get Back Together?

It is likely that the seasonal changes which created the dispersion of your energies will, in another season, create also the circumstances for driving you together again. However, there is no guarantee that your respective energies will necessarily focus on each other. All that can be said is that the natural dynamism of your natures makes transcendence of the past a perennial possibility.

Once again, self-control is the rudder which can steer you from your past to a point of intersection and therefore of reconciliation. The ideal state would be one in which this is a mutual desire, and not one which you impose upon the other person.

7 What Can I Do to Put Things Right?

It is a quirk of human nature that people do not, as a rule, welcome change. They get used to old patterns and old ways, and they are reluctant to respond to changes when they arrive. It is in your nature, however, to accept changes as they come. You are usually prepared for them, and so you are rarely taken off your guard.

In this case, sudden change *has* taken you off your guard, and in order to correct things, you must show a willingness to accept the alterations in your personal relationships, even though you might at first dislike them. Acceptance is an attitude which affects revolution in its profoundest sense. Through acceptance, you change the cycle of the time from high to low speed, from apparent chaos to a real ordering of your life.

This is not to say that you should do nothing. You must make every effort to meet with able people. At this stage, careful preparations of your inner attitude must be made, so that you are in a position where you not only accept the new conditions imposed upon you, but are also prepared to bring about further changes yourself. The only difference is that now you are in a position to acquire the *control* necessary to slow down the relationship.

8 What Do I Most Want From Life?

You most want a complete reform of your present relationship, in order to take it to higher levels of tolerance, control and love. This desire is one of the most difficult to satisfy, however, for it implies the need for sweeping changes in all areas of your life. At the same time, you feel compelled to act with utmost caution, which presents a problem. You cannot go too fast, but you must not go too slowly. Only from a position of resolute self-control can you hope to avoid serious mistakes. In this way, clarity will come, and important changes will attract the favour of the season.

You cannot rely on fate during times of decision. You must make your own decisions and act upon them. The emphasis now is on the manner in which you act upon them.

THE LINES

One

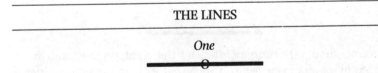

You must seek change only when change is necessary, and not for its own sake. You must be careful, therefore, to exercise calmness and patience in order to avoid excess of any kind.

Two

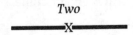

If you see a need to radically alter your circumstances now, you must prepare your ground thoroughly. If necessary, seek the assistance of an able person, a friend, whose reputation is based on integrity and good work. The help of such a person bodes well for you, but you must not expect such a person to come to you. Rather, you must seek this person out. By taking such steps, large changes may be successfully undertaken.

Three

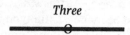

In order to bring about changes on a large scale, especially in the field of relationships, you must walk firmly in the middle of the road, avoiding the extremes of impatience and unfairness on the one hand, and undue hesitation and small-mindedness on the other. To lean in either direction will cause a disaster. You should also bear in mind that the call for change might not apply to all areas of your life. Some things can be left as they are, but those areas which have been a repeated cause for complaint do merit your serious attention, and should therefore be changed.

Take heed of good advice.

Four

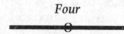

You are placed in the position of bringing about important changes, but you must ask yourself seriously if you are driven by altruistic or by selfish and petty motives. If changes are not based on inner truth, they will not gain the support of others. People will only react favourably to innovations that they feel instinctively to be just. Just changes will succeed, unjust changes will fail, and may result in loss.

Five

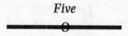

Profound change is contemplated by the right person, and this is noticed by others even before the system is made manifest. Such a person is in the favourable position of being able to claim the immediate and unequivocal support of those around without even consulting them. The quality of the changes themselves are of great moment. The situation brings good fortune.

Six

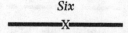

Once the major changes have been effected, and are deeply felt and understood, smaller ones begin to occur. These are not so deeply felt, but everything must be in balance. To push small changes too far is not well advised, as this would be to expect too much of the time. You must be content with what has been achieved, and leave smaller matters to evolve in the course of time. The most important changes, you should understand, have already been achieved, and you must be satisfied with them. Smaller alterations are a matter of evolution from great innovations.

HEXAGRAM 50

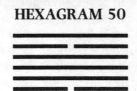

The Cauldron (Valuable Work)

1 Is This Person a Compatible Partner?

The context in which this hexagram has meaning is work which fosters spiritual fulfilment. The oracle concerns itself with a cultural environment and is very favourable. The person concerned here receives direction in life through the manifestation of mankind's highest values. It is for this reason that the oracle views you with such favour and augurs well for future success.

It is highly likely that you are a person who feels a strong sense of purpose and destiny running through your life. As your work helps to bring illumination to yourself and others, it is highly likely that your relationship with your partner exists in an atmosphere of enlightenment also. This is auspicious for personal happiness.

As far as material things are concerned, you are likely to be blessed, but since material things are not the main object of your life and are not your principal concern, you and your partner are able to keep your lives in a proper spiritual perspective. In this way, you are able to sustain a pleasing atmosphere of contentment in your busy lives.

Underlying your relationship is a basic honesty. Being undemanding of each other enables you to give to each other more freely across the whole spectrum of your physical and spiritual lives. With such qualities as love and honesty governing your daily lives, there is an unusual and tremendous potential for joy and fulfilment. Others think of you as gentle and sensitive, and this inspires a still greater trust in a couple so compatible.

2 Does My Partner Love Me?

Your love is mutual, of this there can be no doubt. You are able to express your spiritual love for each other through your daily work. Your enlightenment shines through your humility. The seeds of your love have grown strong, and will continue to flower. Because there is such strength in your unity, you are possessed of a great gift for others.

3 Do We Have a Future Together?

You need have no fear of the future. There is a promise of good fortune. You are already aware that the greatest joy lies not in the future, but in the present. Of the many stages through which one passes in the journey of life, the most important is the awareness that life consciously enjoyed in the present yields the greater fruit of the future. This is wisdom of which you have a keen understanding.

4 What is the Most Important Attitude to Adopt at This Time?

You are already endowed with the qualities of humility and reverence, and you already place spiritual insights far above any material gain. There is nothing further to add other than to encourage you to sustain so nourishing a basis for living. Wherever you depart from these qualities, you should seek to reacquire them, and reintegrate them into the fabric of your life.

5 Why Has Our Relationship Broken Down?

Even in the most blessed and fortunate of lives there are difficulties. The spirit of the oracle suggests that a rift between you is unlikely. If there have been problems in the work, minor discrepancies might be generated, but nothing to warrant a major breakdown in the relationship.

As long as you sustain an attitude of humility, a true objective understanding of your situation will yield a suitable resolution to the problem.

6 Will We Get Back Together?

For the person who draws this oracle, it is most unlikely that you and your partner will have allowed a difference between you to have separated you. You are both likely to be clear-minded and mature in your approach to problems of the heart, and this enables you to see each other in a proper perspective. You are not likely to be suffering from delusions as to each other's basic inner nature. The most satisfactory recommendation that can be made is to follow the dictates of your heart for, in your case, these will be the same as the dictates of fate.

7 What Can I Do to Put Things Right?

It is not necessary for you to plan any objective strategy for putting things right where they may have gone wrong. The answer lies in your inherent attitude to your work and to your partner in general.

No specific act is recommended, and therefore you should avoid making any uncharacteristically rash move, or taking any uncalled for emergency measure. There is a profound balance in your affairs, and any untoward action would only create an imbalance. You are warned to maintain your clarity rather than cloud it by these means.

8 What Do I Most Want From Life?

One of your deepest concerns is the development of the culture in which you live. You are aware that a materially-centred culture with no accompanying spiritual perspective cannot survive for very long. The way in which you live your life, and the work you do lends power to the creation of a more spiritually enlightened society. This idea is at the centre of your fate. Your most significant contributions to society will be on these terms. Be unrelenting in your pursuit of the highest aims.

THE LINES

One

The implications of this line are several. Firstly, it indicates a period of time in which you will undergo self-purification and the clearing away of unnecessary debris in preparation for future action. Secondly, the line is favourable for a woman who is unmarried, but possesses a child. She will be honoured in some way.

Thirdly, the fundamental meaning of the line is that anybody who has a will to improve their spiritual standing in life will be looked on with favour by others. This is inevitable.

Two

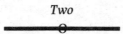

Within the context of developing the spiritual side of a culture, this line indicates that a great effort must be made to complete important work. Such work will be successful, and bring prosperity, but with it the enmity of others. Providing you sustain your attitude of humility towards your work and to others, you will come to no harm from them.

Three

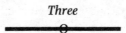

Take heart. Your lack of opportunity and favourable response up until now is absolutely no reflection on your gifts and abilities. Without question, your time will come. Things will go well.

Four

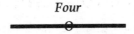

This line describes an unfortunate, though at present prevalent, situation in the societies of mankind. The words of Confucius describe people who hold powers and responsibilities beyond their abilities, and also those who have inadequate personal qualities for such important positions

'Weak character coupled with honoured place, meagre knowledge with large plans, limited powers with heavy responsibility, will seldom escape disaster.'

Five

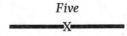

You have worked hard and suffered much to reach your present position in life. There is an admonition that you must not allow yourself to be distracted now.

Six

This line describes a person who is wise in the giving of advice. Those who receive this person's advice should allow themselves to be influenced by it, for the advice is gentle but firm, honest, and given in good spirit. There is a promise of good fortune.

The Jolt of Fate

1 Is This Person a Compatible Partner?

That which has happened to your relationship with your partner can be described as an act of fate, or an act of God. If you have been suddenly and unexpectedly forced apart, or if your house has fallen down or been consumed in flames, or if you have suddenly lost all your money, or met with an accident, or if there has been a sudden death, you can be sure that it was meant to happen.

Whatever has happened, in terms of your own life it amounts to a disaster, a catastrophe, and it was fated to happen. There was nothing you could have done to prevent it.

This hexagram concerns itself with how to cope with such a situation. During times like this, people tend to lose their heads, and panic. This is an inappropriate reaction and will only serve to create confusion. If you are to overcome the situation which, make no mistake, will have deep and far-reaching effects on your whole life, you must take stock of yourself now, take a few deep breaths, and allow the significance of the event to sink in.

Since what has happened is a matter of fate, you cannot answer ultimate questions of suitability or unsuitability in the light of the above. Even if the breakdown of the relationship actually *is* the catastrophe which has hit you, this should not be seen as a judgement that you and your partner are necessarily incompatible. The scale of events implied in this hexagram takes in your *whole* life.

2 Does My Partner Love Me?

At times like this, love finds a higher manifestation. In the light of your present situation, you and your partner will realise that you both have a great deal to learn about love. This knowledge will almost certainly surprise you, but as the full significance of the event which has touched you begins to sink in, you will realise that this is true.

3 Do We Have a Future Together?

This is a period of momentous change which will lead to greater self-realisation in both of you as individuals. Do not rely on any promise of reconciliation. Certainly, there is no possibility of recreating what you had before. In the light of all that has gone before, you will become aware that this is a time of tremendous personal transformation. You are being compelled to evolve by the construction of new and more solid assumptions about reality.

4 What is the Most Important Attitude to Adopt at This Time?

Firstly, do not panic. Secondly, do not be tempted to make light of the situation. Thirdly, be *humble*. The forces behind these events are more powerful than you could possibly imagine, therefore there is no point in allowing yourself to become needlessly anxious.

Look within with steady eyes. Do not look around for scapegoats.

5 Why Has Our Relationship Broken Down?

This hexagram does not concern itself with the intricate details of why the relationship has broken down, but merely says that for the time being you must only accept the fact that what has happened was inevitable. First cope with this idea, for its far-reaching effects cause you to explore regions of your heart that you have never visited before.

6 Will We Get Back Together?

You and your partner will be engaged in individual self-renewal.

There is no promise of a reconciliation, though there is no doubt that this event will mark a momentous period in both your lives. With a proper attitude of humility, a tremendous amount can be learned from this event, which can only have the effect of enriching your future lives, though there is absolutely no promise that this will be together. The memory of the event, however, will touch your future relationships with others in a very constructive way.

7 What Can I Do to Put Things Right?

The effect of such a monumental event in your life will ripple down into the deepest regions of your consciousness. It will cause a gradual expansion of awareness. It will bring about many internal revelations and set you on the path of rigorous self-examination.

You will be involved in much soul-searching, which will be a basis for profound insights into the human heart. The things about which you were certain in the past will now seem uncertain. You will begin to question the assumptions you have made about yourself and other people. All this promises greater understanding.

8 What Do I Most Want From Life?

You may feel that all you want is what you had before, but already you know that this can never be. There is no going back.

When you have ceased to want the past, your mind will begin to turn to higher things, namely the fulfilment of a greater potential.

THE LINES

One

The events you are currently experiencing are so momentous that you are forced into an ordeal of conscience. This does not necessarily imply a whiplash of guilt, or a karmic summing-up, but rather that the shock of events has caused illuminating light to fall upon even the most well-concealed shadows in your heart. All this has the effect of making you feel even more humble. This is a good thing, and bodes well for the future.

263

Two

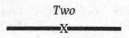

In such an extraordinary time of personal upheaval, you are dispossessed of many of your material goods and acquisitions, and this causes you sorrow.

You must rise above such a deprivation. Under the present circumstances it is impossible to reclaim them, but at some later point you will be able to reduce your losses without too much trouble.

Three

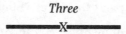

What has happened to you could not have been avoided. In a special sense it was meant to happen. The impact of fate can often threaten personal stability of mind. Do not go to pieces. Keep your wits about you. Such events have a way of propelling you forward into action. Where you can act, act.

Four

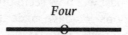

Even with the best will in the world, you still need some freedom of movement in order to make an impact on the situation. This line suggests that circumstances beyond your control hamper your ability to act, just as if your thumbs had been lashed together.

Five

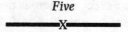

Fate is dealing you blow after blow, but nevertheless, you do not lose your centre of gravity. Therefore you are able to withstand the knocks without being badly harmed. Others, however, do not come off so well.

Six

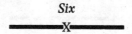

Events have shaken you up rather badly. The full impact of what has happened has just struck you. The tendency now is to panic, to lose all self-control. Panic is as contagious as laughter. All you can do is calm down, cool off, take hold of yourself and beat a hasty retreat. No one will thank you for taking such a course of action, but that is their business.

HEXAGRAM 52

Learning to Relax (Stillness)

1 Is This Person a Compatible Partner?

The oracle offers no direct advice on the question of the compatibility of your partner. It is likely that if you have drawn this oracle, these are not the issues with which you are primarily concerned.

What is of the greatest importance at this time is that you learn to achieve peace of mind.

Your thoughts are whirling; you are confused; you are going around in circles; your heart is troubled; you are aware of the need to become quiet again.

It is almost certain that while you were shaking the coins in order to find this oracle, your concentration wavered, thoughts popped into your mind as if out of nowhere; it is unlikely that you were able to focus your mind on one topic for very long. All this points to a requirement to quieten your heart and mind; to be at rest, to be easy, to relax, to release the tensions. If you are not already in the practice of yoga or a physical discipline of some kind, involving the control of breathing and the precision and control of muscle movement, then you are well advised to seek instructors in these disciplines.

The focus of attention here is in the back. Only through proper guidance and exercise can you release these tensions, which in turn will help you to quiet your mind and control your thoughts, so that you can focus your concentration in one place. The *I Ching*'s view is that peace of mind is essential if you are ever going to be in a position to comprehend the deeper symmetry of life. However, it does not state that you have to be in a state of peace with yourself all the time, for peace implies stillness and there are times when we must be in a state of activity, which is generated through the deliberate creation of tensions. For example, in order to walk we must create a tense relationship not only in our muscles, but in the relationship between ourselves and the ground. Forces and pressures acting upon each other enable us to gain volition and momentum.

Now is the time when movement must come to a stop in order to take stock. The necessity for this in personal relationships is obvious. Spending time with your partner in a state of perfect stillness can open the doors to greater intimacy. Through learning to quiet your mind, and bring ease to your heart, you can find a way for you and your partner to grow still closer. This requires practice.

2 Does My Partner Love Me?

We often find after strenuous physical exertion that we are able to sink into deeper states of relaxation. If you feel that your partner does not love you, then it is because you do not keep your heart still enough to be receptive to your partner's affections. If your partner does love you, it is in spite of yourself.

You might do your partner the courtesy of showing him or her the real you more often, and giving them the benefit of the doubt whenever a discrepancy arises in your mind. It is extremely difficult to love someone who is wound up like a spring. You are not entitled to love – you have to deserve it.

3 Do We Have a Future Together?

You are both going to enjoy the future together much more. It will be enhanced if you make a point of learning to relax. This is the imperative of this hexagram. You would do well to consider that, from your partner's point of view, you are a very difficult person to live with; and because of your temperament, your reactions are un-certain. Through learning how to relax, you will not only be able to enjoy more your everyday life with your partner, but you will also make yourself accessible to those qualities in the relationship that you have been missing all along.

4 What is the Most Important Attitude to Adopt at This Time?

First of all you must recognise that much of your mental confusion, tension, and inability to relax arises from tensions in your body. You cannot think relaxed thoughts with a tense body. If you accept the advice of the oracle, and learn an art which releases the tensions from your back, you will notice an almost miraculous change in your attitude towards those you live with. You will discover, perhaps to your astonishment, that ego is merely an artifice of the mind, arising from a tension in the back. Rarely does the *I Ching* focus upon a physical solution to a moral question, but in this case such a solution applies.

5 Why Has Our Relationship Broken Down?

If your mind has been in a frenzy, how can you possibly make important decisions? If your heart is constantly troubled, how can you hear what your partner is saying? If you are filled with tension, how can you be gentle? If you are constantly preoccupied with thoughts, how can you renew yourself? The primary reason for the breakdown in this relationship is that you have become so tense that you cannot even communicate with yourself, let alone your partner. Like an over-wound clock or an overstretched elastic band, you have lost the ability to be flexible.

6 Will We Get Back Together?

The crucial issue here is whether or not you can get yourself together first. You are no good to your partner unless you can find peace of mind, or greater self control. This, of course, will be reflected in your ability to respond to positive stimuli. This is an *if*, and only *if* situation. There is no promise that a reconciliation will take place. The reason why you allow yourself to be wound up like this is because you are filled with too much self importance. What is difficult for you to understand, however, is that you do not see it this way, while other people do. Try to see yourself as others see you.

7 What Can I Do to Put Things Right?

If you have not already overdone it, and caused yourself serious damage which could also be physical, it is still possible to put things right. But this does not mean talking things over with your partner or making any special arrangements. The fault lies in the tension that you have allowed to build up in yourself.

The first step is to release the tension in your body, which will then release the tension in your mind. You have to develop the power to focus your concentration in one place so that you think about what you are doing, and do not think about one thing while doing another, or attempt to do more than one thing at a time.

8 What Do I Most Want From Life?

Peace of mind and quietness of heart. Once you have managed this you will find your mind will expand beyond its normal fixed and narrow tracks. It will be as if somebody has just polished your glasses. You will be able to see much more clearly, and enjoy life a hundred fold.

THE LINES

One

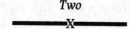

This line describes a situation where – at the outset – you intuitively knew in which direction to set your course. The important thing here is not to allow the profusion of ideas coming at you from all directions to distract you from your original purposes, even though you may be forced off your path. If you need to go round an obstacle, never take your eyes off that final destination which you perceived at the outset.

Two

This line describes the process of inertia. The situation is this, when you realise that you are travelling in the wrong direction, you may be able to stop yourself in order to change to the right direction. However, others are carried along by their momentum in the wrong direction, and although you would like to help them, their momentum is too strong and there is nothing you can do to stop it. Accept the situation for what is is. Hard though it seems, you can do nothing but go your own way.

Three

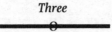

It is not possible for you to relax in your present state of mind. The principle is this; you cannot force a state of peace and calm. It must come naturally.

There is no value in simply going through the motions of meditation and relaxation if what you really want to do is burn off your excess energy through vigorous exercise. Go for a five mile run or a long walk, or swim a few lengths, and then sit down and quiet your thoughts. You will find that you will meet with less resistance in your efforts.

Four

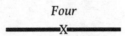

You are doing everything in your power to achieve peace of mind by way of learning to relax, meditation and easing the pressures in your back. This is all to the good. However, before you can advance further in your efforts to achieve a complete state of rest, you must recognise the final stumbling block for what it is. This is the little knot of self-importance. Learn humility.

Five

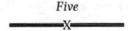

At some time in the near future you may wish to say to yourself, 'I wish I hadn't said that.' You have not yet said it. People are inclined to say things which they do not mean, and you are no exception when you find yourself in an uncomfortable position which makes you nervous. The advice of the oracle then is to think before you speak, 'Don't put your foot in it.'

Six

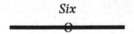

You have achieved a supreme state of peace. You are without burning ambition. Your peace of mind has brought you contentment. A tranquil heart and a tranquil mind bodes well for the future. Good fortune.

HEXAGRAM 53

Development (Gradual Progress)

1 Is This Person a Compatible Partner?

Here, the relationship has the prospect of being long-lasting, rich, beneficial and rewarding. But you must not rush into it headlong. The advice given is that you must act slowly and cautiously, and above all perseveringly, to bring this relationship to its full potential. It takes time and effort to build the necessary foundations for a long-standing relationship. Allow each stage to develop naturally, without anxiety or worry about the future, which will come of its own accord. You must have faith in this process.

Your own inner development can progress unhindered in this environment, and this is, of course, crucial. Go slowly and with gentleness, but guard against sluggishness, for progress must still continue at this time. In this way your circumstances are invested with a strength and momentum of their own, which allows for adaptability.

The hallmark of this relationship is that you are faithful to each other.

2 Does My Partner Love Me?

You are the kind of person for whom love is not an immediate reaction to a person or situation. For you, love grows gradually and slowly. Only after you have known someone for a long time will you be sure that your love is true, and so you cannot know, until a sufficient period of time has elapsed, if your partner loves you. What is certain, however, is that through steady progress, the potential for a strong and lasting love relationship is present.

3 Do We Have a Future Together?

In order for you to contemplate the future with this person seriously and in a good light, you must bear two things in mind. The first is that your relationship will deepen with time, provided that you are not hasty. The second is that you are not only cultivating your relationship, but you are also cultivating yourself.

In order for you to have a strong and binding influence on each other, you must proceed with gentleness and, above all, you must be adaptable. You have all the necessary qualities to sustain you, and you have the necessary emotional stamina to see things through to the end. By maintaining an attitude of dignity and virtue, you will foster and encourage the same attitude in your partner. This is the way to a future together.

4 What is the Most Important Attitude to Adopt at This Time?

If you are delicate in your approach to your loved one, then tenderness has firm roots for the future. These roots can be trusted to grow and blossom at the appointed time. If you over-nurture your affections, you may cause sudden and immediate results in such a fertile heart, but the comforts arising from this will be short-lived. You may also damage your own reputation for the future, as you will appear to lack weight and integrity.

If you recognise that a gradual approach is recommended as appropriate in this case, you will bring about the desired results while taking nothing away from the higher development of you or your partner. Your relationship will be fortified.

If a relationship is to last, influences on it must be gentle and based upon a clear sense of dignity and devotion. If these qualities have already been lost, it is unlikely that they will be rediscovered with the same person.

If the relationship was new, and the breakdown followed soon after it began, then the chances are that there was not enough of lasting value between you. If the relationship was a long standing one, and you have both cultivated your personalities through profound co-operation, then there may be hope for the future.

It is, of course, possible that the breakdown between you was caused by a loss of interest on both sides, and that your relationship came to a natural end. If progress or development was too slow, then it may well simply have ground to a halt. In order to reconcile you now, a quickening of interest would be necessary. You must be genuinely affectionate towards each other, and persevere in this affection.

5 Why Has Our Relationship Broken Down?

The primary reasons are a loss of faith in each other, and too much haste. Where a relationship has the possibility of being long lasting, the most dangerous thing you can do is to rush into it and make hasty decisions. By doing this, you grow out of time with each other, and so any understanding which might have grown is forestalled.

It is likely that you now falsely assume that you will find your happiness outside the relationship, but the seeds of the breakdown lie within you and with your respective attitudes. You would probably be caught up in exactly the same dynamic with someone new and find yourself repeating the same mistakes over and over again.

The failure of the relationship may be understood as the failure to co-operate.

7 What Can I Do to Put Things Right?

Your hopes are based on sound principles of conduct. Do not lose faith with yourself, lest you undo all that you have achieved. You are bent on real achievement.

8 What Do I Most Want From Life?

You are a person who likes to feel that the seeds of the present will bear fruit for life. If your love is true, and you sincerely want the best for your partner, then you will satisfy yourself that the relationship will last for life. This is your true desire.

272

THE LINES

One

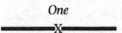

Your relationship has the stamina to last for life. Faith and natural affinities are inbred into your respective natures, but you feel isolated from the beginning.

At present, you are not being encouraged by the positive responses of other people, and you feel that there is no help to be had. This has the effect of making you hesitant and unwilling to take any risks on human nature, particularly on its finer qualities. However, through caution and watchfulness in the early days, you are wise. As you are not by nature a demanding person, and as your view of love is basically quite simple, you can expect good fortune in the end.

Two

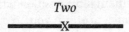

Lately, the situation has been very difficult, but you have progressed a little, and this puts you in a position of greater independence. Although you are unwilling to proceed you are cautiously confident of the circumstances, and of your aims and of your ability to cope with the new demands placed upon you. Having now seen opportunities to act, you are happy at the chance to create a future for yourself and your companions.

Three

There are two possibilities here for your consideration, both of which are based upon a single principle, namely that of natural development. The first is that you have transgressed this natural principle, and have overplayed your hand. This has placed you in a situation for which you are not suited, and so you cannot cope. You have strong-headedly challenged the world to an unequal struggle, and you have brought a calamity upon yourself and your family.

The second possibility is that you are in danger of rushing wildly into a situation which is contrary to the law of natural development, and you are warned to stop now before you cause a serious disaster. You must not provoke an avoidable conflict which will end badly for you and your family, although you would of course be justified in defending yourself against unavoidable assaults.

273

Four

You are in a position which is not altogether suitable for you. This is not your fault. Sometimes in the course of natural development, people are placed in awkward or inappropriate situations which, though dangerous, cannot be avoided. In order to cope, you must not take the offensive, but you must instead rely on common sense and give ground in the face of events. By following this path, you are able to continue in your personal development in the midst of difficulties, and another path will suggest itself to you in time.

Five

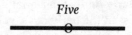

This is not a happy situation for you. You find yourself, through no fault of your own, in an unenviable position which is generated by the lies and deceits of people around you. You are misjudged and misunderstood by the very people upon whom you are dependent – perhaps your employer, or your partner. This situation will persist for a while, and then in the course of your development these misunderstandings will be cleared up and you will once again be reconciled with those you love and need.

Six

This is the end of your life. You have achieved your work in the world of deeds and also in the world of the heart. You have achieved that spiritual grace which is the true purpose of life.

Your life now represents a perfectly formed pattern, and the things you leave behind you are beacons of light to guide others on their path to spiritual purity. Your own life stands as a bright light to show others on the earth an example of what it means to perfect the self.

HEXAGRAM 54

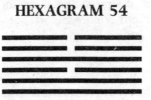

The Marrying Maiden

Affection is the most important quality in any relationship in the world. Spontaneous affection is the basis of true unity.

1 Is This Person a Compatible Partner?

Your partner is not your equal. Here an older man marries a much younger woman. The difference not only lies in your respective ages – indeed this may be slight – but in your relative maturity and experience of the world. Here the woman is the younger. However, it is your profound love and affection for each other which makes you compatible with one another above any other differences.

The hexagram pictures a young woman who is delighted to enter marriage with the older man. Such an eventuality brings her security and happiness. Beyond the obligations expressed in the vows of marriage it is really the affection you have for each other which binds you.

2 Does My Partner Love Me?

The relationship has yet to be tested against time and experience. No shadow is cast over your initial love for each other.

When two people freely and independently (without coercion and guilt) choose each other as partners in marriage, as distinguished from 'arranged marriages' of tradition and custom as is common in several cultures, the couple's affections for each other are the backbone of loyalty. It is therefore important for the couple not only to love each other as man and woman but also to bear each other a special respect.

3 Do We Have a Future Together?

You must be prepared as a couple to work for the relationship. The formality of marriage is no guarantee that the relationship will prosper. You must be mindful of your marriage vows; the words have *meaning*. Therefore you should be careful that you intend to keep the promises you make in the spirit that you make them.

There is a suggestion that the future will be a brighter prospect for you both if you reinforce the bond between you through some common responsibility, by co-operating in a shared task. This shared experience may imply the having of children. Provided that you both retain a special respect for each other as free people this relationship is capable of maintaining a happy balance throughout its life.

4 What is the Most Important Attitude to Adopt at This Time?

You should both show your feelings for each other, openly and spontaneously; do not condition your behaviour towards one another according to the expectations of others. Your best affections should not be hidden.

5 Why Has Our Relationship Broken Down?

If problems and misunderstandings arise between you in the early stages of the relationship – especially after a mutual commitment has been made – their roots will be a lack of tact on one or both your parts. An ostentatious display of disloyalty or the loss of a sense of propriety will not be met with a sympathetic response.

You have only yourselves to blame for problems of this kind; the consequences may be humiliating.

6 Will We Get Back Together?

If you and your partner separated under humiliating circumstances a reconciliation can only come from a genuine attitude of forgiveness. Reconciliation will not appear as a matter of duty because you both entered the relationship freely, therefore the desire to forget your differences will be inspired by an inclination of the heart.

The oracle makes no promise of a rejoining, it merely describes the conditions in which one can take place.

7 What Can I Do to Put Things Right?

The focus of the oracle is upon a new relationship containing all the potential for a blossoming. The essence of your attraction is a strong affection for each other. It is this affection which makes everything else between you worth working for. If, by your conduct you have harmed that spontaneous affection in your partner, it must be awakened or reawakened. There is nothing else to be done. You must find a way of being attractive towards your partner.

There is no possibility in succeeding through a pretence of any description. Only fearless, honest love really communicates the vital information.

There is no promise that it will be returned. There is no promise that it will not be returned.

8 What Do I Most Want From Life?

The love you and your partner feel for each other is perfectly real. You both want the relationship to last. You seek an even more perfect union. You both know that.

THE LINES

One

You are not in the ideal position, that is to say you would not have chosen it for yourself. Indeed you may have wished for something better, something closer perhaps? Despite this, you do your best and you earn the confidence and security of your partner who learns to appreciate your finer qualities.

Two

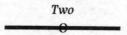

A young woman's expectations of her husband are impossible to fulfil, but her loyalty to him is not harmed despite the lamentable circumstances.

Three

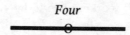

A woman expects far too much of you but this is not a licence to compromise yourself. You cannot escape the consequences of the mistakes you make now. The outcome is uncertain. You are warned not to take unnecessary risks with your credibility.

Four

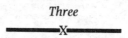

You will marry when the right person comes along. You are right not to have thrown yourself away at the first available opportunity. Your patience and integrity are their own reward.

Five

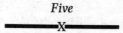

The woman pictured here accepts a man in marriage knowing that she will not be able to enjoy the comforts to which she has been accustomed. However, in this case the woman possesses a deeper insight into the meaning of marriage and is unconcerned with the superficial compensations of material wealth. She is aware that balanced against honest affection and love, material possessions are a poor substitute. This woman adjusts very easily to her new life, obviously displaying a preference for a life of greater quality.

Six

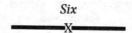

This is a situation where a man and a woman go through the motions of marriage, paying lip service to the vows they have taken. Neither feel emotionally or spiritually committed. The value of the ceremony therefore is rendered pointless. Why marry a person you do not love? Why show contempt for your partner and for the idea of marriage by denying the heart?

Clearly this is not a promising beginning.

HEXAGRAM 55

The Brimming Cup

This oracle is important because it concerns the high point in spiritual, emotional and material affairs, symbolised by the idea of the midday sun. However, despite the fact that you sit at the zenith of achievement in life, you do not feel joyful or happy. A soft melancholy, a gentle sadness pervades your feelings, because you are aware that while everything you have, everything you have done and the respect accorded to you by others means a good deal in worldly terms, in spiritual terms it could so easily mean nothing at all.

The panoramic view that you have of your life at this moment is poignant indeed. Your reflections have a sharpness and clarity which only come to a person who has tried to do their best in life, and who has to a large extent succeeded. The oracle implies that you are aware of the need for higher spiritual attainment and fulfilment, but thinking about the idea does not fill you with the same expectancy of joy that others might feel.

In an undramatic way, your life is filled with the ambiguous feelings of loss accompanied by abundance, joy without happiness. Most of all, you are aware of the fleeting and transient nature of life. Something in all this makes you pause and wonder for a while.

Be reassured. Shine on and be glad. Now is the time to drink from the cup that you have filled to brimming. Put aside your cares and misgivings and set your mind to enjoying the life that you imagined a long time ago, for you have earned and deserved it.

279

1 Is This Person a Compatible Partner?

Your partner, in a quiet way, reaches out to you with tender feelings which fulfil your best ideals of love. Now is the time to honour it, to recognise that what you have most desired you now possess. It is not something over there, it is something here. While there is wisdom in your perception of life and love, you must now acquire that extra dimension of wisdom which makes it all make sense in the here and now.

Share what you have, give what you can without counting the cost and without heaviness of thought. Accept now, in all your wisdom, that the joy you want to feel only requires your permission to come to the surface of your life.

2 Does My Partner Love Me?

Your partner is free from pretentions, and for a while now has been transmitting to you all the care and love you could possibly want from life. The only censure offered to you is that perhaps you have not appreciated it as much as you should have done, or perhaps you have not expressed your appreciation. By now there should be no room in your heart for doubt about your partner's true feelings for you.

3 Do We Have a Future Together?

For both you and your partner, the future promises to be brighter and better than the past. If you have any fears, they will be dispelled.

4 What is the Most Important Attitude to Adopt at This Time?

Generally, you are a very positive person. If you can only be aware that it is still within your power to bring happiness and joy to other people. You will make good use of such an excellent time.

5 Why Has Our Relationship Broken Down?

For you, the expression 'broken down' should be replaced by the words 'slowed down'. If there has been a falling off in affection, it may have arisen through overfamiliarity with your partner. Taken to its extreme, one of the causes of disenchantment might well be an overburdening sense of futility. It is unlikely that you will have allowed such feelings entirely to cloud the relationship, but be cautious that such a decline of interest does not become a habit.

6 Will We Get Back Together?

There is no indication in the oracle that you have actually parted. If you and your partner have been suffering some kind of estrangement in your life together, then you should take comfort in the fact that, as yet, things have not gone beyond repair. Indeed, this is a very good time to make amends.

7 What Can I Do to Put Things Right?

You should express great happiness and joy without restraint. Give energy to your wisdom, be just in your appraisal of events and people. Shine a stronger light through the polished windows of your mind. If there is anything unpleasant to do, you should do it with speed and thoroughness and the minimum of fuss.

8 What Do I Most Want From Life?

You desire that any residue of sadness that clings to your feelings may be supplanted by the real joy symbolised by the midday sun shining in the heavens.

THE LINES

One

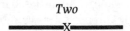

This line signifies the coming together of two people in a time of plenty. Both people possess different qualities which, when combined, amount to a considerable power for doing good work. One of you possesses the attribute of clarity of mind, the other possesses tremendous energy. Time spent together is well spent, and together you will meet with favour and honour.

Two

Two people make an excellent team, one person acting on the

instigation of the other to produce excellent work, but a dark force comes between you and inhibits your power and therefore impedes the progress of the work. Neither of you should fight this dark force, for your opposition would only augment its power at this time. Instead, you should bring to bear, through profound thought and meditation, a greater strength which aligns with the good forces in the universe. This will enable you to overcome the obstruction so that the excellent work may continue.

Three

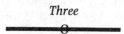

The situation here is the same as in the second line, except that here the dark force is represented by a total eclipse of the sun. This has such an overpoweringly inhibiting effect that neither party is able to do anything about it. Such a situation is extraordinary, and therefore cannot persist.

The dominant area in which these forces will be most keenly felt is in your social lives. Do not allow people with no credibility to ingratiate themselves with you.

Four

The eclipse of the sun gives way to the light of day. This is the symbol of joy, and with elevated feelings you can continue your association for the creation of great benefit.

Five

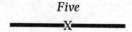

Because you are of a mild disposition, you never consider yourself above taking advice from others who may have something significant and valuable to offer. Through this, you receive good ideas which will lead to an incredible rise in good fortune and personal acclaim which will also bring with it considerable benefit to others.

Six

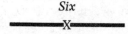

This line depicts a wealthy person who is narrow minded, stubborn, unwilling to listen to new ideas and isolated from others by their own self-opinionated conceit. This person stays at home and does not share what they have. Even those who were once close draw apart. The situation persists and offers only loneliness.

HEXAGRAM 56

The Traveller

The subject of this hexagram is a person who travels from town to town, city to city. Such a person, constantly on the move, touches the lives of others only lightly. The questions and answers therefore address themselves in a special way to The Traveller.

1 Is This Person a Compatible Partner?

The answer to this question, as to all the others, very much depends on what you expect from the relationship. It also depends very much for its interpretation on whether you are the traveller or whether you are contemplating or are involved in a relationship with such an individual.

The traveller's relationships with other people, especially in matters of the heart, are usually short-lived, by virtue of the style of this person's life.

The partner here could well be a temporary, fleeting stranger who came into your life suddenly and will probably leave it suddenly. You have nothing to fear from this person if his or her manner towards you is courteous, polite and kind. This person has nothing to fear from you if you display the same virtues. It is unlikely, however, that this person will gratify any need for a long-standing, stable relationship. The traveller must not pretend to offer this, and anyone in receipt of the traveller's affections should not be under any illusions as to this person's intentions.

2 Does My Partner Love Me?

In a fleeting and temporal way, the answer may well be yes, but on the same terms it might equally be no. Such a person is unlikely to be indifferent, however.

3 Do We Have a Future Together?

This is unlikely, if you have considered carefully what has gone before.

4 What is the Most Important Attitude to Adopt at This Time?

As a traveller, you experience a myriad of impressions of the trials and vicissitudes of life, together with its joys. Yet at all times, you must maintain a keen sense of your own integrity. If you maintain a humble disposition towards those you meet along the way, you will be well received and well treated.

5 Why Has Our Relationship Broken Down?

The traveller who expects a deeply fulfilling relationship must also expect to give to it time, energy and commitment.

If you are the recipient of the traveller's affections, you have been foolish to expect such fulfilment and such commitment from one who is not accustomed to such a way of life.

6 Will We Get Back Together?

Who knows? If the traveller passes your way again, then it may be fated that you make a bond with each other. If you are the traveller, then you have the power to make such a possibility concrete.

The oracle suggests, however, that a reunion between you is unlikely, unless of course the fates intervene; there is no indication that this will or will not happen.

7 What Can I Do to Put Things Right?

This is a situation which was always supposed to be of a fleeting nature. You can best help yourself by understanding this, and accepting the limitations imposed upon the relationship from the beginning. There is no cause for regret.

8 What Do I Most Want From Life?

You are one who, like fire, is always in search of new food at the inner feast.

THE LINES

One

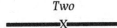

As a traveller, your experience of other people's lives is fleeting and transient, and so your perception of their problems is correspondingly lacking in depth. You should not make light of what other people view with gravity. You must blend humility with integrity.

Do not deceive yourself that people do not see you for what you are – a traveller passing through.

Two

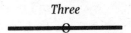

You are a person of a certain inner composure. This is a quality which is transmitted to those you meet along the way, and for whom it is an attractive quality. You win a valuable friend through it.

Three

It is unwise for a traveller to become deeply involved in local affairs, without having the corresponding commitment to see them through. You do not have the necessary commitment and therefore the situation generates danger for you, as there is very little sympathy for a person who can rely on nobody as a friend.

Four

Asking little, but in a controlled way desiring much more, you find a place to settle, but you cannot find your ease or feel at home there. The feeling of being a traveller persists, and for once, this feeling is perhaps a discomfort to you.

Five

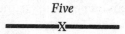

You have been compelled to seek a home in a place or a land that is foreign to you. By your actions you commend yourself to those who are in a position to help you settle. You are commended and offered work.

Six

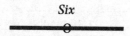

One of the most precious qualities of the travelling person is unpretentious adaptability. It is this quality which enables the traveller to make himself or herself welcome at any place he or she encounters, and enables the traveller to rest. If this quality is lost or forgotten then the traveller might live to regret it. The camaraderie of the road is coveted by fellow travellers. You should not abuse it.

HEXAGRAM 57

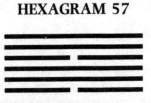

The Impressionable

1 Is This Person a Compatible Partner?

There are some people in the world we either take to immediately, or we don't take to them at all. Here you have taken a shine for someone, but there is some ambiguity in your mind as to why. You do not know whether behind those eyes lie dark designs and intrigues (should you trust or not?) or, is this person as they seem, a clear open and light individual with nothing darkly cryptic behind the smile?

First impressions are often misleading. The question is do you want to find out if you have been misled? If so, there is only one way to do so, you must give this person the benefit of the doubt.

Until you are sure what kind of person this is, do not make a total commitment. The oracle advises which attributes you should watch for.

2 Does My Partner Love Me?

Yes – it certainly seems that your partner is surrounded by an opaque screen through which you cannot see. This is very frustrating. You cannot be sure that your partner's intentions are entirely honourable but, on the other hand, you cannot really be sure that they are entirely dishonourable. It may well be that the dishonourable intentions are not directed at you specifically, but at somebody else – a wife or husband, for example. *Perhaps* this person is committed to somebody else already, and they are not being entirely open and frank with you.

Perhaps your partner has a secret. If you are not committed to each other, you may feel that this is none of your business. If a commitment has been made then perhaps you ought to probe a little deeper, to find out where your partner's heart really lies, if not with you.

It may be that your partner is confused and needs your help to unravel the problem. For the time being you can safely stay with the problem. It is certainly too early to draw any definite conclusions, therefore you are advised not to jump to any without good reason. (Nothing penetrates the heart better than kindness.)

3 Do We Have a Future Together?

Any future your may have with this person is certainly a contentious issue in your own mind, though you may not publicise this fact to friends and family.

However, if there is to be a future you will have to work hard for it without any promise that it will be worth your while.

You must exercise your intuition, play it by ear, as they say. If, in the pursuance of this relationship, you do not compromise your integrity or indulge in any underhand practices – for whatever reason – you can ensure your own personal good fortune. In these matters you must be unswervingly self-disciplined. Do not give in to easy temptations which weaken your own position. All this applies in meeting with difficulties which have not been of your own creation.

4 What is the Most Important Attitude to Adopt at This Time?

Since you are not dependent upon the present situation, you have no axe to grind. Therefore you can bring your personality to bear in a subtle way: in this way you can be a force of light where others are confused. Because you have it within you to assume responsibilities impartially and yet lovingly you can help without being imposing.

These qualities are attractive to your partner and others, and this invites their confidences. You will therefore be able to encourage open honesty and true communication. On this basis reliable decisions can be made.

5 Why Has Our Relationship Broken Down?

Relationships grow through the penetrating power of real kindness. If the relationship has collapsed it is due to meanness, sudden outbursts of emotional anger, frustration, violence, intolerance and impatience with one another.

If the relationship has broken down for any of these reasons, it is a great pity. It may well be that the strength and decisiveness of one partner, balanced against the extreme gentleness and indecisiveness of the other, place an unnatural and unfair burden on you both.

Neither of you have been sufficiently resolved to make the relationship work and this is why it has not so much broken down as eroded – dwindled into nothing.

6 Will We Get Back Together?

Before attempting a reconciliation you are advised to talk to people who may be able to help, like personal friends, counsellors, members of the family, people whom you recognise as spiritually aware.

You must make up your own mind about your partner; you must be sure you really want a reconciliation. If you do, then you must be prepared to be determined, to cultivate and focus your will in this direction. You can achieve this best by infusing the spirit of kindness into every exchange with your partner and by being kind with yourself. You will gain an insight into where your own heart truly lies at the moment.

If your intentions are not completely honourable you will attract bad fortune.

7 What Can I Do to Put Things Right?

When dealing with complicated emotional situations, we are very often at a complete loss. Clearly you want things to turn out well for all concerned. Do not expect to hit upon a simple solution, there is no short answer which makes everything fall miraculously into place.

The answer will evolve as the situation becomes better understood.

Anything you decide to do must be carefully thought out well in advance. Consider the consequences of your actions before committing yourself to any particular plan. If you want to be a beneficial influence then you must not do anything 'out of the blue' as it were. So your actions must be tempered with caution and kindness.

You must be gentle but you must not be indecisive and above all you must be discriminating.

8 What Do I Most Want From Life?

At present you want reliable information. You want to do the right thing by others and you want the present situation to turn out happily with no losers. But beyond all this you want others to be honest with themselves.

THE LINES

One

Guard against being too impressionable. Give your character the cutting edge that comes from being decisive. Do not allow circumstances to dictate to you, take the initiative. Although you are not usually of a forceful disposition you must apply more dynamic energy to the affairs at hand.

Two

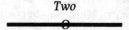

The people who mean you harm operate under cover. You neither know who they are or where they hide. They are thus able to do their worst without hindrance. In order to recognise such people you require spiritual insight. If necessary take the appropriate advice. It is of primary importance to make evil visible, to bring it out into the open, into the light of day, which is the first step on the way to destroying its influence, and lessening its malignance.

Three

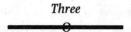

You have done enough thinking, now it is time to act. Do not procrastinate, or go over the same ground yet again. Unless you act soon you will lose your chance. You have enough experience to do what you plan to great effect.

Four

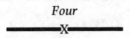

You have the necessary qualities in abundance to carry off a resounding success.

Five

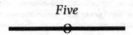

The recent history of your current activities have been characterised by many difficulties which, unfortunately, are not yet over. You have now encountered an important new development, or several, which augur well. Providing you avoid unnecessary taints to your character you will be in the best possible position to carry out the next step without mistakes. Be sure to give the matter some serious thought, however, before making your first moves. Do not rush; good beginnings promise good outcomes. Take care in *how* you proceed. All other things being equal matters should turn out happily.

Six

You have done well up to now, but you seem to be running out of steam. You do not have the necessary resources, energy or influence to go any further, even though you can see the need to. Do not overdo things at this stage lest you harm yourself. Take a break from this important work until an appropriate time to continue suggests itself.

HEXAGRAM 58

Friendship (Enjoyment)

1 Is This Person a Compatible Partner?

The relationship you have with your partner is a very pleasing one. You are not only compatible emotionally, but also mentally. If the relationship is allowed to develop this could be a marriage of the minds. You both have an enjoyable propensity to share ideas, and you derive a great deal of satisfaction from talking to each other about all manner of things. You both have the capacity to discuss even deep and intimate ideas, and this can only serve to develop the bond between you.

Your basic affection for each other serves as an excellent foundation for learning. In general, compatibility between two people, founded on mutual affinity and natural attraction, enhances the exploration of new ideas and phenomena as such pursuits acquire a sense of mutual enjoyment. Taking such a positive and simple pleasure in each other's company removes a lot of the tedium from some areas of life.

2 Does My Partner Love Me?

What is so valuable about your relationship with your partner is your ability to communicate freely with one another, unhindered by any competitive spirit. Through the exchange of ideas and a shared sense of humour, many of life's greatest pleasures are already available to you, or are waiting to be explored.

There is no need to doubt mutual affection, and no need to doubt the empathy that you so obviously feel with one another. Your love for each other is based upon mutual respect and the integrity of character, and all this adds the dimension of friendship to your love.

3 Do We Have a Future Together?

The rules which govern friendship are generally more expansive than the rules which govern two lovers. It is not necessary for you to co-exist or co-habit in the same dwelling for your friendship to flourish and to grow. Indeed, you may spend a great deal of time apart without communicating. This does not harm the relationship in the slightest, or even weaken it.

Your love for each other in friendship is deep and honest. You will be able to derive a great deal of enjoyment from each other's company throughout the rest of your lives. Knowing this will be a great source of joy to you both. Added complications of being a lover as well as a friend present great challenges, which can be overcome providing your mutual respect and nobility of heart are never allowed to deteriorate. Intimacy grows through the sharing of intimacies.

Knowledge is more readily acquired by joint inquiry. Learning about the world is more fun in an atmosphere of friendship and companionship, than if acquired in a solitary way.

4 What is the Most Important Attitude to Adopt at This Time?

The opposite to joy, as it is understood in this hexagram, is sadness or melancholy. If you have lost your friend, then this is how you will be feeling. The only way to overcome such a feeling of sadness is to re-evaluate what it is you most loved about your friendship with your partner and instil these qualities in yourself.

If, on the other hand, you have not lost your friend, you can enhance such enjoyment by making your character stronger. Even the best of friends need time to renew and rejuvenate themselves.

5 Why Has Our Relationship Broken Down?

The distinction is crucial between enjoying each other's company and indulging in frivolity to the point of excess. If you do not understand the difference then you must realise that the true expression of joy and pleasure is always tender, moderate, unextreme.

The reason for the breakdown in the relationship is that the source of joy between you has deteriorated. Your friendship has become a licence for indulgence in insubstantial, meaningless frivolities. There is no doubt that if things have come to this stage it is a great pity.

6 Will We Get Back Together?

If the circumstances described in the last question apply, then you may have already damaged the possibility of reconciliation between you. If your excesses and indulgences have undermined your mutual respect, an open avowal of friendship may bring you back together. Provided that the basis of such a proclamation is genuine and comes from the heart, and providing you express yourself with due decorum, it is possible to re-instil mutual trust.

7 What Can I Do to Put Things Right?

We should never depart from the principle that real enjoyment and real pleasure spring from genuine friendship. Once lost, friendship is very hard to recapture. As individuals you must elevate your minds once again in order to rediscover the true nature of your compatibility.

8 What Do I Most Want From Life?

Joy is contagious. Be willing to share it. If you have not already discovered the fact, you will find that many of life's obstacles can be very easily overcome through unaffected friendship with others.

THE LINES

One

Your sense of personal joy is not dependent on other people, and neither is it interfered with by the external allurements of the material world. You are a free-hearted individual who enjoys being alive. Herein lies your attraction to others, and since your personal security demands nothing of wealth or even friendship itself, so your heart is strong and your mind is clear. You are free.

Two

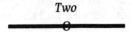

If you show an unwillingness to be attracted to questionable pastimes and leisure pursuits, you will automatically repel those who offer them. Do you feel tempted into indulging in the pleasures of certain iniquities? If you succumb, you might regret it.

Three

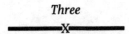

If you feel hollow with despair and life appears meaningless, or if you feel meaningless to yourself, then you are vulnerable and susceptible to any enticing temptation which offers relief. You may want to drown your sorrows in an alcoholic stupor, or abandon yourself to some alluring delight. Take care that you do not lose your centre of gravity, or your mind.

Four

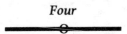

Two courses of action are open to you, and you are trying to evaluate which of the two you would most enjoy. Ask yourself, 'Which of the two would I most physically enjoy?' and, 'Which of the two would I most spiritually enjoy?' And, 'Having chosen, which of the two can I live with?' Choose the one that will bring you peace.

Five

We cannot escape the consequences of any decision we make in life. We must therefore choose cautiously and carefully. Even the most stalwart of people are confronted with dangerous options. Nevertheless, there is always the wise solution. You should consider the consequences of the decisions you make – before you make them.

Six

This is the line of the out and out hedonist who has abandoned himself or herself completely to the indiscriminate pursuit of pleasure for its own sake. As a result, you have lost your inner sense and sensibility,

your centre of gravity, your willpower and the ability to direct your
life by the operation of conscious choice.

You have long since passed the danger point.

You are at the mercy of the wind and the wind is not a good master.

HEXAGRAM 59

Dispersion/Dissolution

1 Is This Person a Compatible Partner?

You have drawn this oracle because you are emotionally frustrated and you have come to spiritual deadlock, but the cool refreshing wind of change is beginning to blow in your heart.

Here, you are not so much in the process of fortifying your strength by gathering it into one point of focus, as unravelling the knots you feel in your stomach. This hexagram describes the process by which you may achieve this.

The myriad of circumstances which brought you to this head are principally of your own making. You cannot escape the realisation of your own complicity in the shattering break-up of a relationship, the failure of a major ambition or the sudden collapse of an old order. Perhaps these things amount to a karmic summing-up. They all now conspire to attack you where it most hurts, in the place where precious self-importance resides within you.

In the past, when faced with challenges when trying to achieve your ambitions, you have ultimately fallen back on the strength of belief in your own self-importance. In the face of conflict, it is always this knot that tightens in your stomach. Now you must untie the knot, and in so doing you will come to understand those things about yourself you could not face before.

Nobody can do this work for you, but if it proves difficult and you make every effort then you will naturally be drawn to the people or the individual who is best qualified to assist you in the process.

Among the things you will learn in the process of driving out bad habits, rooting out deeply planted evils and sweeping your life clean, is that in the past you have only paid lip service to the ideas which you pretended to serve. It is one thing to speak of a newer and better order, and quite another to imagine what this really means. It is one thing to speak of the driving force of love, and quite another to be really moved by it. It is one thing to speak of the highest integrity and truth in your dealings, but quite another to act according to those principles. It is one thing to describe the elevated aims of mankind, but it is quite another to set a personal example.

As you untie the knot, you forego that sense of self-importance which prevents you from achieving an open heart and an expanded mind. Even now you may be enlisted in the work of generating a higher system of values for Mankind. But ask yourself if even now you possess any secret ulterior motives of your own. Are you exploiting others for your own ends and calling it by another name?

Make no mistake that the work you are doing on yourself must be done thoroughly. Leave no corner of your heart unswept.

Even a relationship with the most highly compatible of people cannot last unless you do this work well. Everybody and anybody who accepts your invitation to love you will eventually come up against the hard granite wall of your conceit, and against that wall the relationship will shatter every time.

The meaning of this hexagram, then, is that now is the time to dissolve that wall, to soften the hardness of your heart, to untie the knot of self-importance and to invest your intuition with real understanding.

2 Does My Partner Love Me?

If you were to ask your partner this question directly, the reply would probably be in the affirmative. However, the love your partner offers you is not the love of a free person or of an equal. It is the love of someone who has been harassed into submission. You have turned your lover into a slave of your desires. If your partner's heart has not already rebelled against such tyranny, and broken free of the relationship altogether, then through the operation of your own blind conceit – which you falsely call wisdom – you will have systematically broken your lover's heart. What you called love was really emotional slavery, not even service.

3 Do We Have a Future Together?

It is highly unlikely that you will be reconciled with your partner until the work on yourself is completed. You must understand that the only love worth having is love freely given. A tortured and suffocated heart will admit anything in the hope of being set free one day.

You must realise that the bars you put around your partner's love are the bars you put around yourself. It is your own heart that grows harder, your own knot of self-importance that grows tighter. Your only path to freedom is to develop higher consciousness and to concentrate on your vocation. You must learn that love is the binding force of the Universe, and not the walls of its prison. *Love between people expresses itself in the spaces between them.* In the end, love will break down the walls that divide people and will overcome the architects who designed such walls and caused them to be built.

For yourself the future depends upon a choice. You will either choose to be a force of love in the world, or you will choose to be one of its jailers. What you must be careful to do, however, is to recognise what is being locked out and who is being locked in.

4 What is the Most Important Attitude to Adopt at This Time?

The process of mental expansion requires that you break through the tunnel of your own vision. A genuine flexibility of mind and a genuine insistence on understanding the wider implications of your moral aspirations are called for.

5 Why Has Our Relationship Broken Down?

All of the foregoing answers should have given you a very good idea of why the relationship has broken down. From your partner's point of view you will appear to be egocentric, conceited, selfish, incapable of taking good advice, incapable of letting others take the initiative. You will have appeared morally insensitive and you will often have walked roughshod over your partner's feelings without knowing it and without feeling the hurt that you caused. You will, in fact, have behaved very much like the hard-hearted Scrooge in Dickens' *A*

Christmas Carol. Yet all along, you will have regarded yourself as reasonable, rational, helpful, practical, wise and even gentle and forgiving. These are the qualities you must now display towards yourself in the face of the harsh truth.

6 Will We Get Back Together?

Your thoughts should not be turning towards the possibility of a reconciliation at this time, as this will only serve to distract you from the work you have to do on yourself and the attention you must give to your vocation.

If you have actually nailed your partner to the cross of your ego, do you not feel that thoughts of reconciliation at this time are highly presumptuous?

7 What Can I Do to Put Things Right?

While all these internal realisations are taking place, you may be called upon to act in the service of morally superior aims in the external world. Throw yourself into this work with unabashed honesty and uncompromising tenacity and integrity, and in your dealings with others treat them with the utmost forbearance and gentleness, keeping yourself at all times free from all selfish motives.

8 What Do I Most Want From Life?

The winds of change have come to blow through your heart and set it free. By a rigorous perseverence in the service of the higher aims of Mankind, you can untie the knot of self-importance that keeps your heart from being free.

THE LINES

One

━━━━━X━━━━━

Conflicts, arguments and mutual misunderstandings are on the horizon. If you wish to avoid mutual estrangement, quarrels over differences of opinion and tunnel vision, you must immediately and amicably set about gently reinforcing that essential trust upon which the future of the relationship so completely depends. *There is no time to be lost.*

Two

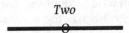

Your vision of others is now beginning to be clouded by the feelings of resentment welling up in your heart. This feeling is divisive. It separates you from others and separates you from yourself. It is no good getting into a bad mood or losing your temper. You already know the harm that this causes. Make a conscious effort to change your feelings. Conjure up positive feelings and positive influences in your mind and turn to these to give you strength.

Three

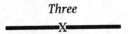

This is a time when your work must become more important than anything else in your life. If you wish to focus matchless energy on the task before you in order to overcome its inherent difficulties, you must for a time put aside all distracting influences, including personal desires and preoccupations.

Four

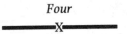

This is the line of the visionary, a far-sighted individual bent upon achieving long-term aims for the benefit of others. In order to achieve such noble aims, you must be above loyalty to partisan factions, unlimited by the private demands of friendship and you must be willing to make short-term sacrifices for the sake of long-term achievements.

Five

It sometimes happens during times of pain that a great and redeeming idea bubbles to the surface. At such times there is nothing more powerful than a brilliant idea for reconciling the heart and bringing people together in an otherwise impossible situation. In the light of such an elevating idea, misconceptions give way to real understanding.

Six

━━━━━━━○━━━━━━━

This is the line of a person who recognises a danger which threatens to consume others, but who also sees the way out with the minimum of pain and hardship. Being personally free of the danger this person is also in a position to assist others in achieving freedom.

HEXAGRAM 60

Limitation (Discrimination)

1 Is This Person a Compatible Partner?

You are a person of very wide sympathies. Past experience will have taught you that you can get on with any number of people very well. Being an adaptable and fluid person, you no doubt view yourself as being suitable to any number of different kinds of partner. The truth is that you are not really sure what sort of person is best suited to you, and this makes it doubly difficult for the partner you choose. You have a propensity for making yourself attractive to a range of people, at varying levels of superficiality. Look deeper into yourself and ask yourself what are your real needs, and examine closely those qualities you possess which will enable you to fulfil the needs of your partner.

If you are constantly wanting to fulfil your potential in many different directions at the same time, you will discover that your personality and character lose their definitive edge, and this will have the effect of eroding your personal centre of gravity. This is not, of course, a desirable state.

You must recognise the need to impose certain limits upon yourself in the sphere of human relationships; not so restrictive as to inhibit your actions, but rather to enable you to make the most of your potential.

You must not be content to flit about on the surface of relationships for fear of the deep waters. It is often true that while the deeper waters

303

present a greater challenge and are more dangerous, they also present the possibility of a far more enriching relationship than you have hitherto experienced. You will also find that by clearly defining what you want most from a relationship, you will be more effective in directing your energy towards achieving it.

It is highly likely that you are afraid of making a commitment for fear of being tied to any one particular person – a sort of Casanova tendency – but remember that you are free to determine the conditions according to what you believe is right. Deciding on the rightness or wrongness of a particular partner, therefore, depends on just how much commitment you yourself are prepared to offer.

The degree of commitment that we are able to make, and indeed choose to make, depends upon a combination of personal inclination and emotional maturity.

2 Does My Partner Love Me?

Your partner loves you when you are sincere, when you are discreet when you are genuine and when you are sensitive to his or her feelings. Your partner loves you when you are clear headed, and most of all when your actions are governed by a strong sense of purpose. When you do not display these characteristics, then your other charms appear shallow.

3 Do We Have a Future Together?

Since you are a person of wide abilities and potential, and since it would be fruitless for the oracle to give advice, offer assistance or make conditions which you would be incapable of fulfilling, it is clear that your future together will depend upon following the *advice* of the oracle. By imposing restraints and limitations on your actions for the purpose of giving focus and poignancy to your life, you will also find that in the process you will gain a sense of real satisfaction derived from real achievements, some of which will be very special to you in times to come.

4 What is the Most Important Attitude to Adopt at This Time?

Many of your problems in life arise from the fact that you are not discriminating enough in love. It is important for you to see the wisdom of organising your time properly, organising better the values by which you live, placing them in orders of priority and though, of course, you perceive that all values converge upon a central idea of the sincere heart. In general you should therefore adopt a more serious and responsible attitude, particularly where other people's feelings are concerned.

At the same time, you must remember that fluidity and adaptability are your most attractive qualities. There is no need for you to place unnecessary or unusual restraints upon yourself, but merely to infuse your life with a clearer sense of direction and a clearer sense of priority. If you are naturally inclined to go around loving everybody, then remember that you have to love those closest to home the best, since they are the people from whom you expect the most.

5 Why Has Our Relationship Broken Down?

You are the last person in the world to put all your eggs in one basket, but that may be one of the reasons why the relationship has broken down. If you have not felt sufficiently committed to your partner, then he or she will have been aware of this at one level or another.

The higher your commitment in a relationship, the more your actions will sparkle with the energy and devotion of love (assuming, of course, that your interest is not suffocating or inhibiting for your partner). The lower your commitment, the less directed your activities for building the relationship. This does not mean that you have not been doing enough. It is more likely that you have been doing too much.

It comes down to a question of how you focus your energies. Sometimes, in order to communicate your positive feelings you have to consciously aim them at your partner.

If you have been trying to do too much, in too many different areas of your life at the same time, you will not succeed in any of them. In so far as this affects emotional matters, the result will be a confusion of feelings.

6 Will We Get Back Together?

The answer to this question depends on you, rather than on fate. The answer is not dependent upon any extraneous influences, or upon the dictates of other people's reason.

Perhaps by this time your partner will quite correctly take a lot of convincing that you are sincere and that you are going to work for the relationship in the proper way, and your partner should not be criticised for such doubts. Only by a voluntary acceptance of the situation can you hope to come to terms with its seriousness.

In general, you are not a person who likes to be confronted with the serious responsibilities of life – those which involve a sense of moral duty and imply commitments – but if you really want your partner back, then you will have to think very much in these terms and be prepared to prove it – though you probably won't adopt overly demonstrative ways of going about it.

7 What Can I Do to Put Things Right?

Give yourself time to think about what your partner thinks is important in life. It is likely that your partner is not a very demanding person and is not asking too much from you. If you make an effort to give what you are not giving, in time, patience, tolerance and loyalty, and cultivate in yourself a higher sense of care, then you will be doing the right thing to improve relations between you.

8 What Do I Most Want From Life?

You have a strong desire to fulfil your potential in life, but due to a lack of self-discipline you cannot do nearly as much as you would like to do. You already know that life is too rich and too varied for you to absorb it all or experience it all, therefore you must choose, select and be discriminating if you are to fulfil any of your cherished dreams. To fulfil at least one of these to your own satisfaction is more important to you than you let yourself believe.

THE LINES

One

This is not the time to act. The potential for considerable achievement lies in the future. You should not waste your energy at the present time in trying to overcome the difficulties which stand in your way. Things are in their beginning. Save your energy and wait patiently for your time to act. You are also cautioned to keep your thoughts to yourself at this time.

Two

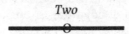

Now is the time to act. He who hesitates is lost, as the saying goes. This is the time to grasp the opportunity presented to you. Nothing stands in your way.

Three

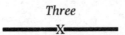

You are indulging in a selfish excess of pleasure. You are losing all sense of propriety. If things go wrong, there is nobody to blame but yourself. You would do well to appreciate that you are the architect of your own fortunes and misfortunes.

Four

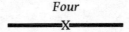

You obviously feel the need to restrict your energies to a given field of activity. Only exercise upon yourself such restraint as feels comfortable. Too much restraint is as bad as too little. In this way you will be able to focus and direct your energies in just the right proportion to achieve your desired ends. The middle way is the best way in this case.

Five

Here, a high degree of respect is accorded to the person who, in a position of responsibility over others, imposes the appropriate limitation upon his or her own actions before demanding that others impose restraints upon themselves. This is a fine example of the principle that actions speak louder than words.

Six

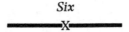

The principle is this: there is a minimum amount of freedom which people require in order to live their lives in reasonably happy moderation. If people are forced to restrain themselves below this minimum level, they will only be able to withstand such pressure for a short time. First they will experience distress, and then they will rebel. Such a response is proper and justified.

Only when the spirit is in dire jeopardy is it necessary and justified to impose severe personal restraints and limitations.

The overall wisdom of the oracle suggests that the idea of limitation has its advantages and disadvantages, but in order for the idea to serve us properly, we must judge carefully what is appropriate in circumstances where the quality of life is at stake. We pay for misunderstanding.

HEXAGRAM 61

Inner Truth

1 Is This Person a Compatible Partner?

The love referred to in this oracle is not the love restricted to your partner, although your partner certainly feels your love very strongly. It is the love of the world, the love of mankind. It is a higher love, far reaching and profound, springing from the depths of your being, a sublime awareness of your true nature in relation to the rest of mankind.

True love comes straight from the heart, and is expressed in thought, word and deed. Such a deeply felt love for humanity cannot be restrained, though its effects are felt from an invisible plane. The implications of this oracle, therefore, penetrate into the heart of the meaning of truth.

Although love expresses itself in human action through the way we make our moral choices in life, the love that you bear your partner is similar to the love you bear for humanity. It is a special, all pervading love, genuine and precious, but in a sense indiscriminating in so far as you do not single out any particular characteristics in your partner that you love more than others. You love the whole person, complete with faults and misgivings, as well as excellence and virtues. Only a high and special kind of love is able to be indiscriminating. It is the higher love of one whose 'truth to self' is strengthened and supported by a powerful spiritual insight. It is this combination of qualities which lends the power of influence to words and actions.

The oracle intimates that there is a connection between the power of inner truth and the meaning of love, which is beyond words. The oracle hints at a mysterious event which occurs in the human heart – and at the same time in the universe at large – where the quickening light of inner truth in Man's heart seeks to connect, as it were, to the light of the intelligent universe as it tries to penetrate the skin. The oracle itself acknowledges that it is of little importance to be able to explain this process, but it is of paramount importance to perceive and feel its occurrence.

Here then, communication can be achieved through gentleness, delicacy and refinement of understanding. Since you are without any preconceptions, and unjustified habits of thought, you have the power to communicate with the least receptive of people and the least willing to learn. Such is the power of inner truth.

The all embracing quality of the time presumes that your relationship with your partner has a very sound basis. Where your love arises from true understanding, you are able to focus it at will. The strength and force of such love transcends the limits of space.

2 Does My Partner Love Me?

Where you have no hidden secrets between you, the answer is definitely yes. However, the situation is not as simple as it at first may seem since, if there are terms and conditions attached to the relationship which are not based on the utmost integrity, then what started out as an amicable and friendly union could turn into its opposite. What is important here is for you to look at exactly what forms the basis of the relationship. It is the strength of this bond which holds everything else together.

3 Do We Have a Future Together?

The oracle reaffirms that open honesty is the only basis upon which you can reliably consider the future together. Without a doubt, the oracle is generally favourable since the qualities which you bring to bear on your own life, and on the life of your partner find their roots in inner truth and the love of wisdom.

As far as your ability to communicate and empathise with people on different levels of awareness and enlightenment goes, there is no challenge in life that you cannot successfully overcome. However, there is one warning which you are advised to heed. Take care that the people who wish to form strong ties with you are prepared to do so openly, with integrity and without secrecy or hidden motives.

The *I Ching* affirms elsewhere that the basis of all relationships is affection. This forms the cornerstone of all ties between people. If you form relationships with people who lack these qualities in whole or in part, then such relationships are not made for weathering storms. Therefore you are advised to distinguish between friends and associates. You can best do this by looking at motives.

4 What is the Most Important Attitude to Adopt at This Time?

You are a seeker after the truth. The ideas which most interest and inspire you are those which lead to a greater understanding of yourself and others. You are constantly looking for the connecting principles which can make mankind whole. You already know that everyone is the same at heart.

In a sense, you are fascinated by the idea of an elixir of love. You cannot help but be devoted to wisdom, and you already know that wisdom, the stone of destiny, the all-pervading truth, cosmic reality, the inter-dependencies of mankind (social, political and economic), feeling, belief and imagination, hope and despair, are all intimately connected by the one idea of love.

If you can find a new way to put all the pieces together then you will be a creative genius, and you already know that every human being is a manifestation of this very potential. Thus you purge yourself of arrogance and conceit, and thus you keep open the door to inner truth.

5 Why Has Our Relationship Broken Down?

The essence of real influence lies in the truth of the heart, and not in the power of persuasion. The ability to focus influence arises from an inward state of balance. The essence of intimacy is natural empathy. If you can claim to be without prejudice and without partisan motives, and if you can act impartially while at the same time sustaining a high degree of care, then the cause of any estrangement will not lie with you. If, on the other hand, you have not acted in accordance with these principles, then this will be the reason for an estrangement in the relationship.

311

6 Will We Get Back Together?

Providing you do not make any secret of your real feelings towards your partner and to others, and providing you do not withhold information which you feel your partner should possess, there is no reason why a straightforward reconciliation should not be proposed immediately. In the light of all the foregoing, it is absolutely imperative that you make no compromise on your best attitude.

7 What Can I Do to Put Things Right?

If in all conscience you are aware that you have pre-judged somebody's motives unfairly, or that you have suffered from misconceptions about yourself and your partner, then you must put these ideas out of your mind immediately. In so doing, you will find that your clarity of perception and accessibility to the truth will grow. Once you have the right assumption on which to base your evaluations, you will be in a position to act confidently in the knowledge that you are capable of overcoming the greatest of difficulties by the decisions you make.

8 What Do I Most Want From Life?

Be true to yourself and you cannot be false to anyone else. It is through your experience and understanding of this that you are able to look into men's hearts. All the clarity of your perception arises from your own personal honesty.

THE LINES

One

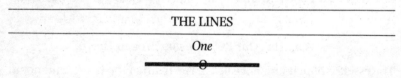

If you have given the responsibility for moral choice to others, then you will lose the impetus and the initiative to act independently of them, whether they are right or wrong. This is an unwholesome situation, for you should rely upon your own feelings and your own integrity in making evaluations about life. The ultimate responsibility for right and wrong must be centred within you, otherwise you risk losing a sense of yourself. The imperative of this line is that you should not give away your inner freedom.

Two

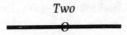

There is a natural attraction between people who are alike. Such an inner affinity is expressed most clearly in times of happiness. Celebration in all its forms brings together people who are in accord. Those who know the truth in themselves recognise it immediately in others, no matter how far away it is. The good has a mysterious power of linking hands all over the world. Nothing can stop it, since the truth resides in the heart. Bear in mind however, that no special conditions can be attached to this feeling – its strength lies in its purity. It cannot be consciously manipulated, and it prevails because it is immune to this kind of interference.

Three

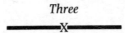

It is a fact of life that if you are constantly dependent upon other people for your happiness, you are automatically enslaved by their will. The source of happiness lies within your own heart. You must tune your mind to your heart or you will find yourself swinging between the poles of joy and sorrow, not according to your own experience of life but according to the experience of others. This form of slavery is a kind of spiritual non-being. You must ask yourself, 'Am I being true to myself?'

Four

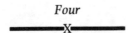

This line concerns itself with your personal, spiritual inner growth. Since you are already on the path to enlightenment, you can only augment your power through the guidance and assistance of those who precede you. Progress can be made through humility. Keep your heart open and free, keep your eyes on the road.

Five

The oracle constantly affirms and reaffirms that the real source of strength and influence arises from inner truth. Here is described a person who is able to be a guide to those around him through the force of honesty emanating from powerful charisma.

If a person placed in this position is deliberately and consciously deluding those people who look up to him, this strength will crumble at precisely the moment when it should hold together in the face of a challenge.

Six

Despite your timely eloquence, actions speak louder than words. If the meaning of your words is of great importance, then you must follow them with your actions to give them support and weight, for they cannot stand on their own, and neither for that matter can you.

HEXAGRAM 62

Over Enthusiasm (Distortion)

1 Is This Person a Compatible Partner?

The question of compatibility or incompatibility does not arise in either a general or specific sense in this hexagram. The tenor of the oracle points towards your being aware of where your greatest strengths and weaknesses lie. If you maintain a cautious, humble reserve in the rather dignified work in which you are engaged, you will not acquire an inflated sense of your very real gifts and abilities.

There is no doubt that the situation in which you find yourself is extraordinary in every respect. Not only have you arrived at your position by extraordinary means, but the situation itself is almost unprecedented.

Your gifts and abilities radiate through you, making you a natural medium through which higher forces can express themselves.

While from the outside you do not appear to possess the necessary strength to take full responsibility for your great talents, nevertheless your partner recognises your true worth, and so long as you are able to truthfully respond as the person *your partner sees*, you will find the necessary compatibility to see things through without illusions or mistakes. You will also be less likely to create tensions in yourself and in the circle of people with whom you work.

The oracle specifically advises that you cultivate a strong conscientiousness regarding your work, in order to offset any tendency to waste your abilities. You have a natural gift for enlightenment in the same way that a bird has a natural gift for flight, but you must keep your feet firmly on the ground when circumstances require you to do so. As long as you do your best then the strength you really possess will manifest itself in everything you do.

2 Does My Partner Love Me?

Your partner is aware of your true self and responds only to your true self. Where there is a discrepancy between the way you see yourself and the way your partner sees you, it is your partner's view that can be relied upon as being the more accurate perception. This perception can be a rudder to guide you through these times. The proper response is to trust it. Although such love as your partner bears you may seem restraining, it is only there to prevent you misjudging yourself. Be clear that your partner's role at this time is profoundly supportive. The oracle advises that you respond with due respect, with due dignity and love.

3 Do We Have a Future Together?

If you do not try to give what you do not have, but only give what you can, then at least you may be sure that the future with your partner will be based on honesty. This is perfectly acceptable to your partner, even though he or she is more devoted to you than your responses seem to indicate. You are warned not to pretend affections you do not feel, or to express them out of character.

Do not feel inclined to turn up the volume of your emotional expressions simply because you feel obliged to do so in response to your partner's increased urgency of expression. The result would only be disorientation for your partner and a gradual erosion of sympathies between you. To prevent resentment developing as the relationship develops, great self-honesty is demanded.

4 What is the Most Important Attitude to Adopt at This Time?

The first thing to notice is that you are not living in a vacuum, and that you are required by circumstances to make some contact with the outside world. Here you encounter problems, and here you must have exactly the right attitude towards your work and towards your partner. If you expect too much from yourself and from others, particularly your partner, this will have the effect of distracting your attention from the work in hand.

Although other people may not understand your motives, the proper way to behave at the present is to be without pretentions, to be extraordinarily self-contained, and to cultivate a high sense of awareness in all you do.

No matter what happens, be it good or bad, you must not waver from this way of behaving, even though such imperatives are unusual. In this way you will avoid making mistakes in what can only be described as extreme circumstances.

5 Why Has Our Relationship Broken Down?

The old expression, 'Pride goes before a fall' is appropriate.

The breakdown of your relationship is certainly not your partner's fault, but your own. Here the situation is simply that you have tried to do things which are beyond your strength and capabilities. You have flown too close to the sun, and your waxen wings have melted.

You have not been modest, you have not been cautious, you have neglected your real talents and pretended to strengths which you do not possess, and you have come unstuck at the seams. You have pretended affection towards your partner which you did not feel in order to make your partner feel secure, but fortunately your partner has, all along, been able to see your true worth. You have distorted that true worth by a misunderstanding of yourself. The general advice of the oracle is 'know yourself'.

In such an unusual predicament, this knowledge is of paramount importance for the completion of those activities which have been entrusted to you by fate.

In summary, the reason for the breakdown between you and your partner is a serious defect of character. You must rein in unjustified exuberance, since it creates a false impression of reality – not for others, but for yourself.

6 Will We Get Back Together?

Attempting to transcend the limits of your capabilities and strengths has brought you serious misfortune. Once you have hit the ground, assuming you are not damaged by such a fall, you will be in a position to seek pathways to reconciliation not only with your partner, but with your true self.

7 What Can I Do to Put Things Right?

Your relationship with your partner has not been under any unusual pressure and the implication is that mistakes have been made because of your own lack of personal awareness.

The situation can be put right if you modify your expectations of yourself and bring them into line with your actual potential and your actual achievements. You will then be able to reinstate integrity into the relationship by making an effort not to place yourself below your partner. In other words fortify your dignity without arrogance.

Guard against interpreting everyday affairs in an extreme way. Being self-contained does not mean being self-righteous. Someone who is morally aware need not be a prude. You should not equate having a sense of destiny with excessive fatalism, and if you see the possibility of developing ideas, you must not feel that you have yourself been granted the power to shoulder massive responsibilities in the world.

In extraordinary circumstances such as you find yourself, you must tune your perspective to the actual demands of your work, your life and your relationships. At the same time you must not go to the other extreme and belittle yourself, for this is certainly not called for. Nothing too much, but nothing too little is advised.

8 What Do I Most Want From Life?

You have a voice that should be heard by others. You have always sensed that you would one day be heard, and so you will. If your voice is to be clear and strong (for these are qualities you cherish), then allow yourself to be moved by a natural grace, and do not impose unseemly demands upon yourself, the roots of which can only lie in pride.

THE LINES

One

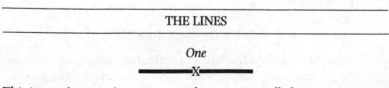

This is not the time for action, neither are you called upon to act; you

318

are not ready to do so. Wait until the time comes, lest your efforts prove to be a waste of energy.

Two

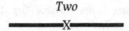

In unusual circumstances, unusual qualities are brought to bear. You find yourself placed in a situation where, without cause for regret, you are possessed of a special insight upon which you alone are required to act. Providing you do so conscientiously, fulfilling everything that is expected of the circumstances, modestly and without aggression, nothing will go wrong. Good fortune.

Three

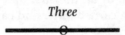

You are over-confident. From the outside it seems to you that things are safe and are going forward unhindered. You are therefore unprepared for unexpected contingencies. You are off your guard. The oracle warns you emphatically that the situation is not as safe as you think it is, and that you must take precautions against snares, loopholes and traps that are hidden in the details of events. Prepare for them now to avoid falling foul of them.

Look more closely at the details.

Four

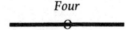

What you do does not make sense in terms of outward action in the world of events and men. You *appear* to be doing nothing, but in fact you are concentrating your will on the situation.

Here you must strike the exact balance between hard and soft. If you try to go forward now without consulting others, you will be leading with the hard edge of your character, untempered by the softer part. In this lies the danger. Be careful.

Five

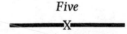

This is a line indicating significant energy and the power to do good for others. The person in question is rendered ineffectual due to the lack of exactly the right help. Such help is forthcoming if it is sought after in the right way – if those chosen are chosen not because of their renown, but because of the shining quality of their deeds. But remember, such helpers are not obliged to give their help. They must feel called upon to do so by seeing in you a quality they value and respect.

Despite all this, the line is favourable, for it suggests that the very special work which needs to be completed finds the right people to complete it.

Six

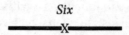

This line contains two principal ideas. Firstly, a very close attention to detail is of paramount importance and, secondly, the effect of such concentration on detail in an unusual time such as this will be to prevent you from being carried away and causing the work to fail.

HEXAGRAM 63

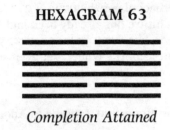

Completion Attained

1 Is This Person a Compatible Partner?

You and your partner have reached the point of perfect balance between you. You have individually achieved inner unity as well as the larger unity of your relationship. The cycle of time is complete and you experience the ideal moment between you and feel a moment of perfect accord between you. Disorder has given way to order and you experience your full potential compatibility.

Despite any warnings given in the lines, the oracle is generally very favourable. There is a sense that fate is working for you.

2 Does My Partner Love Me?

As things stand at the moment, you are both in tune with each other. Your love is mutual and the relationship works. Yet your love is entering into a new vista. You are about to compose, as it were, a new repertoire of songs which find new levels of harmony.

3 Do We Have a Future Together?

You must not expect to feel as good as you feel now *all the time*. Moods change, the demands placed upon you vary in intensity. Different challenges require different aptitudes. You must expect new changes as you enter a new wheel of possibility.

The pattern for the future has already been laid out. Providing you do not interfere with it, but carry on as you are, you will be carried along by the momentum of the wheel. Yet even so, you must never allow yourself to become complacent.

4 What is the Most Important Attitude to Adopt at This Time?

One of the main characteristics of a period of transition is the interplay between negative and positive, hot and cold. All this creates an invigorating tension by which things change. When these opposing forces become perfectly balanced, a new time emerges from the energy created.

If there is too much heat, the cold is destroyed, if there is too much cold, the heat is destroyed. Your main task is to maintain the balance between these two opposing forces in order to create the tension necessary to give the relationship forward motion.

The concept of tension here is something like that of the required tautness of a guitar or violin string. If the string is too loose, the quality of the note decays. The same applies if the string is drawn too tautly. Only the right tension in the string will produce the right note.

5 Why Has Our Relationship Broken Down?

When everything is in perfect balance, the slightest change brings about an imbalance. A feather is enough to tip finely-tuned scales. This possibility is inherent in your present situation. The whole pattern of your life is changing. All your routines are adapting themselves to a new pattern. When the general structure of a relationship such as yours is well formed, there only remains the need to attend to details. Insufficient attention in these areas will certainly cause trouble.

Although you have done well, avoid being pretentious, as this will be the root of any subsequent division between you.

6 Will We Get Back Together?

If a reconciliation between you and your partner is of paramount importance to you, and if the fires of the relationship have not already

322

been extinguished through excessive behaviour, such a possibility exists. Beware, however, of being presumptuous about your partner's feelings. Observe all the rules of tact and courtesy. Do not take affection for granted, and beware of sitting in judgement on the past in a time when completely new circumstances are emerging.

7 What Can I Do to Put Things Right?

When emotions and feelings are in equipoise, things seem all too easy to achieve. If you give in to an easy, accepting attitude towards such an ideal situation, then be sure that the tables will turn. You can best express your love at the moment by caring about the little things.

If you have won laurels, do not rest on them. You must continue to prove that you care by at least matching the excellence of the past. All this requires a consistent effort on your part. Keep up the good work.

8 What Do I Most Want From Life?

The sense of well-being which you are currently experiencing is indeed precious, as you well know. As you enter upon a new time – and this will involve new harmonies and discordances – you will eventually return to this place, and the general progression of life promises that if you have done your work well your present sense of well-being will be unimaginably enhanced. *This* time also changes.

NOTE: There is more than a hint of the *eternal progression*, the spiral of life in motion in this hexagram. If you have drawn this oracle the forces of fate are running powerfully through your life. It is an auspicious time.

THE LINES

One

Avoid becoming over-excited by the prospect of the wonderful new possibilities now opening up for you. Hold on to your energies. Pace yourself. Things have only just begun in this new direction, so relax and keep calm. Do not anticipate the starting gun – it is fine to be eager, but not too eager. Things are looking up.

Two

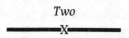

In the fields of both relationships and of work there is a general ambience of prosperity and high potential, and there you are with all your once hidden gems, shining and sparkling for all the world to see, except that nobody is looking in your direction. You must not think that this is your fault. It is the loss of those who fail to notice what great qualities you have to offer.

What you must *not* do now, although you may feel strongly tempted to do so, is to draw attention to yourself by artificial or deliberately calculated means. Do not cast your gems deliberately into the paths of others so that they will be noticed. This kind of activity has no integrity. If you can but understand the need for patience, for continued hard work, there is absolutely no doubt that what is right for you will come without your having to do anything about it. Continue as you are, but do not fret.

The sun is only just beginning to rise for you. Give it time.

Three

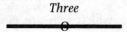

The natural corollary of the completion of one cycle in your life is the augmentation of the new power you have attained through the experience of the expansion of your possibilities. This is right, and to be expected. After all, at present you stand on your past efforts, only you can know what it has cost you in blood, sweat and tears. Now that you are in a position to reorganise your life in order to facilitate larger plans and grander schemes, there is the corresponding need to be absolutely impeccable if you are to be able to draw upon past experience to meet the almost certain challenges that lie ahead.

The oracle offers a warning. Do not look down your nose at the other people. Arrogance can never be justified, no matter how grand your schemes may be, or to what heights you may rise. Conceit is always ugly, and in the challenges ahead you cannot afford to carry any blame.

Four

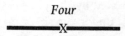

The boat is successfully launched amid celebrations, but you notice a hairline fracture on the rudder as it slips into the water. The miners digging for coal have just found a hitherto undiscovered new seam. This brings great joy as everybody sets out to exploit the new wealth, but you notice that one of the mine canaries has died.

The situation might not be serious at the moment. It might be possible to get away with the fault as it stands, because it looks so slight, but sooner or later you are bound to pay for your negligence.

These are only portents of the future, and you have done well to note them, but you must not now go to the opposite extreme and sniff around for mistakes in the machine or the odd unnoticed leak in the Ark. Here the oracle speaks of a watchful, thoughtful person who has the sagacity to take note of something he or she sees has gone wrong which might have consequences for the future.

Five

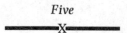

This line concerns itself with religious hypocrisy and false piety. We are reminded of the pharisee who had no charity in his heart. We are reminded of our churches glistening with gold while the congregation is cold with spiritual poverty, and of the humble old beggar who gives the only penny he has as a real gift and a real sacrifice and of the rich man who gives only a fraction of his wealth out of a sense of guilt.

The expression, 'Man only sees what is before his eyes, while God looks into the heart' applies.

These are pertinent considerations for the person who draws this line. It is the treasures in the heart which really amount to something. All the rest is dross.

Six

You have done well, but do not rest upon your laurels. Do not indulge in vainglory. Do not blow your own trumpet. Do not sit in front of the mirror paying yourself compliments.

While you are busy falling in love with your newly acquired image of yourself, unseen dangers lurk just above your head. Just keep going, and put aside all the deliciously tempting conceits.

HEXAGRAM 64

Final Preparations

If you have drawn this hexagram, you are advised to consider its meaning very carefully. While only parts of the oracle will be directly relevant to your particular situation, you should read the passages under all the questions in order to grasp the full import of what is being said.

1 Is This Person a Compatible Partner?

The meaning of this oracle is far-reaching. While no idea ultimately transcends love, the meaning behind this oracle transcends *personal* love. You are at a crucial and important stage of your own spiritual development. There are great difficulties to be overcome.

In order for you to evaluate the suitability or unsuitability of your partner, you must first overcome the next obstacles on your path in life, your journey. In general there is good justification for optimism. It is irrelevant to your path at this time to look outside yourself for assistance and help. You are in the situation of creating order in your own world.

There is nothing to impede you. There is nothing to prevent you achieving anything. Only the circumstances which prevail make the situation in itself difficult, and you must take heed of the warning to be cautious and careful and to guard against over-indulgence in any sphere of your life, if you are to achieve success.

A quiet, balanced watchfulness is recommended. At the same time, cultivate a sense of the deliberateness of your purpose. It could be said, in answer to your question, that the accent of the oracle is upon you yourself becoming a suitable partner. However, it is doubtful that your thoughts and feelings are directed specifically at another person at present. You are certainly aware that this is a momentous time in your life.

2 Does My Partner Love Me?

It is highly unlikely, if you have received this oracle, that the answer to this question is of any concern to you at the present. The only parallel that can be drawn here is that the search for love, or the truth of love, is exactly the same for you as the search for inner meaning.

3 Do We Have a Future Together?

The destiny of mankind depends upon unity in love for all. Every value ultimately leads to this. The answer to your question is that only through correct conduct will there be a future. However, the feeling of the hexagram tends towards great optimism, and you should keep a light heart.

4 What is the Most Important Attitude to Adopt at This Time?

If you are in a state of confusion, then this is because you have forgotten one very important thing: which is that everything already exists in a state of harmony, and that the value to be attached to everything in the world is ultimately equal. If you hone your activities in accordance with this principle, you will arrive at the correct view of the world.

You must not place too high a value on one aspect and too little a value on another aspect of your life. The act of walking depends on there being a consistent hardness in the ground. Even though there are different hardnesses in the ground, there is a minimum requirement in order for you to walk at all. Recognise the values of softness. Do not limit yourself to any specific conditions for action. We may walk as well on sand, for example, as upon the hard road. To extend the metaphor further, although you cannot walk on water, you can

THE I CHING ON LOVE

swim, if it is necessary for you to do so in order to reach your
goal.

5 Why Has Our Relationship Broken Down?

This is a crucial time in your own personal development, and as the
imperative is placed upon a deliberate and purposeful caution, any
breakdown in relationship between you, your partner and events in
the world are caused by rush, hurry and over-optimism or an
inappropriate facetiousness. You are out of tune with the demands of
the time.

As you have been warned that the circumstances are in themselves
dangerous, no specific aspect of your life is indicated. You will feel as if
the carpet has been pulled from under your feet, and that all your
recent actions have been without any value. While we are taught that
the method of acting is more important than the end, in this case the
achievement of the result justifies the process. If you have not
succeeded in bringing about the total completion of this cycle of action
in your destiny, then the preceding events come to nothing.

6 Will We Get Back Together?

By starting from the very beginning, and maintaining a true course,
everything is possible. There is no added promise of good fortune,
merely the desire to go through the process which will once again lead
you to the place you have just failed to reach. There is no doubt,
however, that the attainment of this goal is supremely worthwhile,
and you should set your mind on it.

7 What Can I Do to Put Things Right?

The challenge of the situation can be described, very simply, in terms
of transcending your past self and uniting with a larger order. If you
have this goal in mind, it will be clear to you that your actions will to
some extent be determined by the seasons themselves. It is right for
you to act at certain times in a certain way, when those actions would
be wrong at another time. Your sensibilities and your intuitions are
the chief tools for progress here.

By taking a great interest in your immediate circumstances, you
will see the need for order and for caution. You must be impeccable in

your feelings. This is not a time to indulge in fears and petty attitudes. If you act rashly, you will be acting incorrectly. The accent of the oracle is emphatically on the *way* in which you conduct yourself.

8 What Do I Most Want From Life?

Your journey so far has brought you almost to the end of the cycle. Your heart's desire has been to successfully complete this cycle before embarking on a new cycle, a higher cycle of spiritual attainment. It is to this end that all your actions and all your feelings have been tending. The consummation of this end is what you seek, and what you will always seek until it is attained.

THE LINES

One

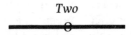

When the end is in sight, there is a great temptation to run towards it without due caution. If you do so you will fail. Correct action at this time is to hold back, stop, take stock and prepare to move forward with your eyes open.

Two

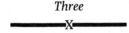

Wait, relax, be watchful. You must keep a strong interest in your objective but at the same time you must be patient and enduring. The coming acts must be the flower of all the impeccability you have learned so far.

Three

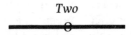

You perceive that the chance for action has come. If you do not act now, then you must forego this chance.

The only way to see a situation in its true light is to place yourself in a different situation. The importance of this is to avoid an obsessive state of mind. You can do this by acting in a different way. Engage your energies, with the assistance of others, in a completely different field of action. Do something positive, however trivial it may seem. View yourself, as it were, out of the corner of your own eye. In this way you will perceive elements of the situation you could not see from your earlier stance. These new elements are important in order to fulfil yourself.

Four

The positive forces are stronger than the negative forces in you, but the negative forces are nevertheless powerful and they must be fought resolutely. The time of struggle has arrived.

You must fight like a tiger if you are to restore order out of chaos.

A correct attitude is not one of confidence or over-confidence, but one of striving to control the whispering voices luring you towards failure. By disciplining your inner voice, you may effect this transition from lower to higher, thereby laying the foundations for the future.

Five

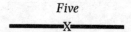

The way is clear for you to change yourself. Nothing impedes your path.

Six

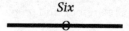

Hold your ground and overcome your doubts. Having attained the transition, you will experience a precious feeling of well-being. Your natural impulse is to share this feeling with others. This is right. By maintaining the good that you feel, you increase its strength. The future not only seems bright to you in comparison with the past, but actually is bright. Believe in your own feelings of well-being.

HEXAGRAM CHART

To use this hexagram chart, first find your bottom three lines (lower trigram) in the column on the left, then find your remaining three lines (upper trigram) in the row of trigrams along the top.

Trace right from your bottom trigram until you cross the line of numbers running down from the top trigram. The number to be found where these lines cross is the number of the hexagram that you have thrown.

TRIGRAMS

UPPER ▶

LOWER ▼

	1	1	2
	1	34	5
	25	51	3
	6	40	29
	33	62	39
	12	16	8
	44	32	48
	13	55	63
	10	54	60

HEXAGRAM CHART

3	1	1	2	3
26	11	9	14	43
27	24	42	21	17
4	7	59	64	47
52	15	53	56	31
23	2	20	35	45
18	46	57	50	28
22	36	37	30	49
41	19	61	38	58

INDEX OF HEXAGRAMS

Hexagram numbers are given in **bold**